TWO OLD FOOLS ON A CAMEL

NEW YORK TIMES BESTSELLER

VICTORIA TWEAD

Ant Press
Large Print
Edition

Ant Press
Large Print
Edition

Copyright © 2013 by Victoria Twead

Formatted and published by Ant Press - www.antpress.org

Paperback ISBN: 978-1-922476-09-8

Hardback ISBN: 978-1-922476-32-6

Paperback Large Print ISBN: 978-1-922476-19-7

Hardback Large Print ISBN: 978-1-922476-52-4

Also available in digital editions

All rights reserved.

No part of this book may be reproduced in any form or by any electronic or mechanical means, including information storage and retrieval systems, without written permission from the author, except for the use of brief quotations in a book review.

This memoir reflects my recollections of experiences over a period of time. In order to preserve the anonymity of the people I write about, some names have been changed. Certain individuals are composites and dialogue and events have been recreated from memory and, in some cases, compressed to facilitate a natural narrative. —VT

CONTENTS

The Old Fools Series	vi
FREE Photo Book	vii
1. FOOTPRINTS IN THE SAND	1
Tahini Sauce	12
2. A PARTY	13
Mussakhan	24
3. NOT A DROP TO DRINK	26
Foul (pronounced Fule) Medames	37
4. ASS	39
Shish Taouk	50
5. FRIENDS	52
Arabic Salad	62
6. THE WORM	64
True Falafels	75
7. GIVING UP	78
Mejeddarah	89
8. ADJUSTING	91
Spiced Lamb and Date Tagine	103
9. CRAZY TEACHERS	105
Beautiful Beetroot Dip	111
10. BENNIGANS	113
Sfeeha (Middle Eastern Lamb Mini-Pizzas)	124
11. CHILDREN AND CHICKENS	127

Lebanese Minted Liver	137
12. BRENT	139
Sheikh-al-Mahshi	151
13. A HORRIBLE DAY AND SHOPPING	154
Shawarma	167
14. BASKETBALL	169
Stuff Ya Potatoes!	179
15. PARENTS' CONFERENCE	182
The Gin Twins' Chuck-It-All-In Curry	193
16. THE TREE OF LIFE	195
Jake's Dad's Thanksgiving Sweet Potato Wonderful	207
17. WINTER BREAK	210
Sambousek	221
18. CONFRONTATIONS	224
Cousin Elias's Easy Peasy Carrot Cake	235
19. FIELD TRIPS AND TERRAPINS	237
Harissa	248
20. BIRTHDAYS AND VALENTINE'S DAY	250
Rosewater and Pistachio Ice-cream	262
21. FUNERALS AND AN ATTACK	264
22. UPHEAVALS	276
The FNJ (Figgy-Nutty-Jammy) Brioche	286
23. CRAZY TEACHERS AND A PARROT	287
24. GET OUT!	297

25. PICTURES	310
Lentil Dream	321
26. LETTERS	323
Parsley Tahini Dip	337
27. EXAMS AND CHEATING	339
Courgette Muttabal	350
28. BAD BEHAVIOUR	352
Baklava	362
29. BRENT AND CAMELS	365
Tepsi	377
30. HOME	380
Garlic Prawns with Smoked Paprika	394
31. EPILOGUE	396
A request…	400
So What Happened Next?	401
The Old Fools series	415
The Sixpenny Cross series	419
More books by Victoria Twead…	421
About the Author	423
Contacts and Links	424
More Ant Press Books	429
Publish with Ant Press	433

THE OLD FOOLS SERIES
ALSO AVAILABLE IN PAPERBACK, HARDBACK AND EBOOK EDITIONS

Two Old Fools on a Camel is the third book in the *Old Fools* series by New York Times and Wall Street Journal bestselling author, Victoria Twead.

Chickens, Mules and Two Old Fools

Two Old Fools ~ Olé!

Two Old Fools on a Camel

Two Old Fools in Spain Again

Two Old Fools in Turmoil

Two Old Fools Down Under

Two Old Fools Fair Dinkum

Prequels

One Young Fool in Dorset

One Young Fool in South Africa

Latest Release:

Dear Fran, Love Dulcie: Life and Death in the Hills and Hollows of Bygone Australia compiled by Victoria Twead

FREE PHOTO BOOK
TO BROWSE OR DOWNLOAD

For photographs and additional unpublished material to accompany this book, browse or download the

Free Photo Book

from

www.victoriatwead.com / free-stuff

For Jake and Colton
Thank you for sharing that year of your lives with us, and making us laugh every day of it.

And thanks to Nadia Sawalha for her wonderful Arabic recipes, and her mum, Bobbie Sawalha, for answering all my silly questions.

1

FOOTPRINTS IN THE SAND

"Do you think we'll see camels wandering the streets, like those elephants we saw when we went to Bangkok?" I asked.

"I don't know." Joe was lost in his own thoughts.

"Perhaps some of the kids will come to school on camels?"

"Maybe."

We were on the last leg of our journey from Spain to Bahrain. I peered out of the plane's porthole. Far below us, the sea stretched endlessly, the early morning sun transforming the blue into gold. The Persian Gulf. How exotic!

We were stopped at Madrid airport and nearly refused permission to board because without the correct visas, we couldn't enter Bahrain. Deep down I'd willed the authorities to send us home to our little Spanish village of El Hoyo. But the airport staff had phoned our Bahraini employers, the American Specialist School, or ASS, and, somehow, the problem melted away. Our journey to the Middle East continued.

"That's it!" I squeaked. "I think that's Bahrain!"

Joe leaned over me to share my view. As our plane descended, the map-like view of the island below sprang into detail. Skyscrapers, metallic and gleaming, multi-lane highways, snaking sand roads, flat-roofed buildings and houses, glimpses of tempting-looking swimming pools, all in miniature, but growing larger. The land was flat, dusty and yellow. Everything looked baked, even though it was barely 7 a.m. Then the runway opened up in front of us and we landed with a bump.

"That's it," I said again. "We're here."

We passed smoothly through Customs and purchased temporary visas. Reunited with our luggage, we made our way to the exit doors. Both of us were silent, drinking in the foreign sights and smells. I tried not to stare at the white-robed Arabs with their expensive leather luggage, trailed by wives in black, flowing *abayas*, only their eyes visible behind *burkas*. In stark contrast, Indian workers milled about, dressed in simple robes or tattered, Western clothes. I was pleased to see a few Europeans and Americans, and felt a little calmer.

Once through the doors, the heat hit us like a giant fist. My body instantly broke out into a most unladylike sweat. Droplets poured down my scalp, through my hair and ran down my neck. We had only just emerged from the air-conditioned coolness of the airport building and already my clothes stuck damply to me.

"My word," Joe breathed, "I've never felt heat like this before. Not in Spain, not in Thailand, not even Australia." Perspiration ran down his face unchecked.

"I agree. And it's still early morning! Daryna did warn us." Daryna was the new Principal of the High School, Joe's future boss, and we'd formed an online friendship. She'd arrived in Bahrain a week earlier and had frequently emailed us.

"So," said Joe, scratching his nethers irritably, "wasn't somebody supposed to meet us here?"

We searched the thinning crowds. Nobody appeared to be looking for us.

"Never mind," I said. "We've got the address. We'll just take a taxi." Secretly, I was quite relieved. I needed a shower and change of clothes before meeting anybody.

We approached the line of taxis and I couldn't resist searching for tethered camels. Sadly, I didn't see a single one. A white-robed Arab, with white headdress, detached himself from a group and ushered us into his taxi. The car was modern, clean and air-conditioned. Gratefully, we sank into the comfortable seats.

"Look," I whispered to Joe. "He's even got a feather duster to keep his cab clean." I didn't know then that the feather duster on the dashboard served another purpose.

The journey to our hotel took nearly an hour, which surprised me. Previously, I had located both hotel and airport on a map, and they hadn't seemed so far apart. Our driver never spoke as we drove along wide, well-maintained avenues lined with palm trees, and crossed modern bridges. Joe and I occasionally nudged each other, pointing out sights of interest.

As we approached the city of Manama, the buildings became skyscrapers, stretching up to the empty blue sky. Vast white-stone sculptures adorned the highway, including one that looked familiar from my Internet research. This one had massive curved legs and supported a huge stone ball. Beneath it, a water fountain played. It stood in the centre of a large roundabout, the intersection of many motorways.

The Pearl Monument

"Joe! Look! That's quite a famous statue, the Pearl monument! The ball on the top represents a pearl and reminds people of what Bahrain used to trade."

"Yes, I see it. Vicky, are you sure you gave the driver the right address? We seem to have been in this taxi for hours."

"Quite sure."

Daryna had already told me that the teachers would be accommodated in a hotel before being moved into brand-new apartments that the school was building for us.

"Daryna told me the new apartments will be ready in a week or so. This hotel is just a temporary measure."

Signposts were written in English and Arabic. Traffic was heavy and every car seemed to be more expensive, larger and cleaner than the last.

How do they keep their cars so clean in this dust? I wondered. *And what are those round, doughnut shapes burnt into the road?*

We passed shops and restaurants, all closed. We passed many shopping malls advertising familiar brands: Marks and Spencer, Virgin, Starbucks, Kentucky Fried Chicken. I wondered what time they opened.

At last the taxi stopped in front of a tall building with dark-tinted windows. The driver helped Joe pile up the luggage on the roadside. There was no pavement and sweat poured from Joe's brow, dripping down his nose and into the soft desert sand.

"How much is that?" Joe asked, opening his wallet.

"That'll be 17BD," said the driver, avoiding eye contact.

"That sounds very reasonable," said Joe, handing the driver one of our crisp new 20BD (Bahraini Dinar) notes, decorated with a smiling King Hamad on one side and a splendid mosque on the other. "Keep the change."

While Joe and the driver had been manhandling the luggage, I'd been reading the stickers inside the cab. One said something like, 'By law, all taxi fares depend on the meter reading. If the driver does not use the meter, you should not pay.' I looked for the meter and discovered it, obscured by the feather duster on the dashboard.

"That taxi was a bargain, wasn't it?" said Joe as the taxi roared away, throwing up clouds of sand. "I only paid him 20BD."

I wasn't so sure. I said nothing then, but checked later. My suspicions were correct. At the very most, the trip should have lasted 20 minutes. And 20BD translated to about £34 or $53. We had been taken for a ride. Literally. The fare should have been between 3 and 5BD.

The sun beat down without mercy. I stared at my feet as I stood in the sand, my shoes already covered in a layer of dust. Perhaps it was the long journey and tiredness, but I was transfixed by my footprints in the sand. First impressions.

I blamed Joe, of course. It was August 2010, and our lives had just been spun upside-down. It was Joe who wanted to work with children for one last time, before retiring for good. It was Joe who'd surfed the Internet and found us jobs in the Middle East. It was Joe who'd pointed out that, thanks to the 'credit crisis', our funds were low and unless we earned some serious money, we'd be unable to pay our bills.

Technology is a wonderful thing. Everything was arranged online. We'd applied for teaching jobs, been accepted, and our flight e-tickets had arrived in our email inbox. And everything we knew about Bahrain was what we'd gleaned from the Internet.

We knew that it was a fabulously wealthy country, with a Royal family, and were happy to read that it was peaceful. It was described as 'tolerant', unlike its closest neighbour, Saudi Arabia, connected to Bahrain by a causeway. There was no Ministry of Virtue (the infamous Religious Police) in Bahrain, and women were permitted to drive cars and work. Women were not forced to wear the all-covering abayas or burkas, although most did. Even alcohol was legal and available, for non-Muslims, if one knew where to look.

We knew that expats accounted for a large proportion of the population of Bahrain, attracted by the high earnings. Bahrain's fortunes had originally come from pearl fishing, then oil, but now it had become one of the major financial hubs of the world. Also, we knew that the USA Navy kept their Fifth Fleet in Bahrain.

We knew that we wouldn't have to pay taxes. That our accommodation, transport to school, health care and flights would all be paid for by our employers.

All this knowledge was comforting and we felt sure we'd made the right decision. Perhaps we'd enjoy our new life so much that we'd stay longer than the one year we'd agreed to?

How could we guess that we were catapulting

ourselves into events that would soon dominate world news?

But no words could describe the wrench of leaving our crazy little Spanish mountain village behind. Waving goodbye to our villager friends was excruciatingly painful. Turning our backs on our home, friends, chickens, animals and the rolling, ever-changing Spanish mountains was heartbreaking, but necessary if we were to survive financially. Perhaps it was a good thing that the whole process, from application to arrival in Bahrain, had taken just two weeks. Two short, frantic weeks hadn't allowed us enough time to brood over our decision, to get cold feet or change our minds.

So here we were, in August, the hottest month of the year, standing outside a strange hotel in Bahrain. A smiling Indian hotel porter burst from the reception area to claim our luggage. The receptionist took our details and consulted a computer. Joe and I stood waiting, more than a little shell-shocked and exhausted after our journey halfway around the world.

"Ah yes," said the male receptionist, looking up. "Miss Daryna asked for you to have the suite opposite her. Your room number is 748."

We whooshed up seven floors in the lift with the porter.

"American?" he asked, revealing a single, yellow tooth that pointed up like a tombstone.

"No, British."

He unlocked our door with a flourish and ushered us inside. The suite was nice, if a little old-fashioned. Two bedrooms, two bathrooms, a spacious living room and a decent kitchen. The furniture was bulky and dark, the curtains thick and heavy, doing a grand job of blocking the outside glare and heat.

Toothy fussed with the curtains, tested the lights, opened and shut every door, and finally stood still, hand outstretched, face frozen into what he may have thought an attractive smile.

"He wants a tip," I hissed to Joe.

Joe fumbled out 5BD and Toothy backed out of the suite, bowing at regular intervals. Joe had given him £8.50 ($14) and Toothy probably thought Christmas (or Diwali) had come early.

We were exhausted. Joe used the bathroom (he calls it 'marking his territory'), we washed, then collapsed into bed, despite it being just 10 a.m. We laid our heads on Egyptian cotton pillows and instantly fell asleep. But not for long.

I was roused by a knocking noise. Somebody was tapping urgently on our door. I forced my eyes open and wondered where I was. This bedroom, with its huge bed, many wardrobes, marble floors and en suite bathroom, looked nothing like our familiar cave bedroom in Spain. Of course! We were in Bahrain! I sat up and poked Joe.

"Joe! There's somebody at the door."

"Probably Toothy. Go back to sleep."

"Whoever it is, he's knocking again, I'll have to go."

TAHINI SAUCE

As this sauce seems to be a key ingredient for many of Nadia's recipes, it makes sense to include it early. It's extremely versatile, and can be served with fish, any grilled meat or, if thinned down a little more, as a salad dressing.

Ingredients (Serves 4-6)

4 tbsp tahini (from most big stores and online)

3 tbsp lemon juice

Salt

2-6 tbsp warm water

Method

Place the tahini, lemon juice and salt in a small bowl.

Gradually add the water whilst whisking. (You may need more water if it's sticky)

Ready when it has the consistency of double cream.

2

A PARTY

I pulled on a bathrobe and staggered to the door. The knocking had become more insistent. I tried peering through the peep-hole but saw nothing but a blur. I pulled the door open, and the visitor fell in with a startled squeak, landing in a crumpled heap at my feet.

It definitely wasn't Toothy.

"Vicky! It's me, Daryna!"

"Oh!"

I reached out a hand and helped her to her feet, not easy as she was wearing heels high enough to require a step-ladder. So this was the headmistress of the High School, Joe's new boss? As she dusted herself off, I had the chance to look at the lady I'd been communicating with for the past couple of weeks. We were the same age and I liked her immediately.

Daryna was an attractive lady, blonde and beautifully dressed. Her emails, arriving in quick succession, warm and unedited, had already given me a hint of her personality.

In real life, she was the same; full of energy, with a breathless way of speaking. I was to discover that Daryna was almost childlike, bubbling with enthusiasm, always cheerful, generous and thoughtful, but, unfortunately, a little inclined to make rash decisions. However, her giddiness hid a fine brain. Her dedication to her job was often misinterpreted and I was to find myself caught in the middle of awkward situations many times in the months to come.

We embraced. Joe and I had much for which to thank Daryna. She had helped us with our applications, insisting that our ages were an asset, not a hurdle. The school had agreed, but it was the Ministry of Education, the overriding authority, that needed convincing. Luckily, permission was granted.

"The staff at the desk told me you'd arrived. How was your journey? Have you explored yet? What do you think of your rooms? Where's Joe?"

I filled her in on all the details.

"Right!" she said. "It's Ramadan, so everything is closed at the moment, but the stores

A PARTY

will open at sundown. I'll show you our nearest supermarket, it's pretty good. It's just a shame that it's Ramadan. Then the school is taking all the newbies on a night-tour of Manama. I've done it already, so I won't go. Tomorrow, there's another tour of Bahrain, and, the next day, there's a big meeting at school. You'll be able to take a good look around."

Just listening to that agenda exhausted me. And, although I knew that we'd arrived during Ramadan, I hadn't understood how that would affect us. I was to find out later.

Daryna left and I was about to head for the bedroom and resume my nap when a note was pushed under our door. I picked it up and read it. Joe and I had been invited to a 'Meet and Greet' later, hosted by someone called Dr. Cecily, at her apartment across the sand lot. But for now, all I could think about was sleep.

Joe and I are not party-goers by choice, but we felt that we should make an appearance, and it would be a good opportunity to meet our fellow teachers. Reluctantly, we trudged across the sand lot and entered the apartment block.

We tapped on the door and a buzz of noise from the 'Meet and Greet' escaped as the door opened. We were shown into a spacious lounge which, by now, only had standing room. A table was laden with party food and, to my surprise, plenty of alcohol was on offer. Most people were drinking beer or wine.

"And your name is?" drawled our hostess, Dr. Cecily, her eyes firmly focused on a point somewhere on the ceiling. She was a stout, imposing figure. She had no neck, and her head and body moved as a single unit. I wasn't exactly sure who she was, but she possessed an air of authority.

"I'm Vicky, and this is Joe."

Dr. Cecily's head and body turned to face Joe, her eyes fixed on a different part of the ceiling.

"Joe's teaching Maths and Physics in the High School, and I'm in the Middle School teaching English."

"Well, I sure am pleased to meet you both," said Dr. Cecily, addressing the light fitting, and walked away before she'd even finished her sentence.

"I'm going to mingle," I whispered to Joe. "See you later."

I searched for Daryna, but she wasn't there.

"Come and sit with us," said a voice. "There's space here." The owner of the voice was a large lady, even larger than Dr. Cecily, and she was patting a tiny vacancy on the sofa between herself

A PARTY

and another plump lady. "I'm Dawn, and this is Rita."

Rita was even larger than Dawn. With difficulty, I squeezed myself into the hot gap and looked around. All these new teachers! Apart from Dr. Cecily, Dawn and Rita, I calculated their average age must have been about 24. I felt very old. These young things were on the brink of their careers, while Joe and I were finishing ours.

"I see that Daryna, the High School Principal, isn't here," I said to Dawn, after our introductions. "She's new, too, isn't she?"

Stony silence.

"It's her first year, too, isn't it?" I persisted, perhaps a little unwisely.

"Miss Daryna wasn't invited," said Rita. I saw her exchange glances, and raised eyebrows, with Dr. Cecily and Dawn. I sensed a grudge lurking somewhere but, as yet, was unable to fathom the cause.

It seemed that Dr. Cecily was responsible for hiring most of the new teachers as a result of a Job Fair in middle America. Every voice was American, apart from ours, and I remembered very few of the names or faces. There was, however, one exception: Brent.

I first noticed Brent when he was talking to Joe. Joe is six feet tall but Brent was taller. I guessed that he was about 30 years of age. He had a mane of unruly hair, growing untidily around a central bald patch, and instead of a can of beer or wine glass, he clutched a notebook and pencil. Perhaps he was a reporter? I excused myself from the Three Fat Ladies, extracting myself with difficulty from the suffocating depths of the sofa.

"Please, what is your name, please?" Brent was asking Joe.

"I'm Joe." Joe extended his hand, but Brent chose to ignore it.

"Please, how do you spell that, please?"

"Er, J.O.E…"

Brent scribbled in his notebook and looked up again. "And where do you come from, please?"

"I'm British, but actually we live in Spa…"

"And what will you be teaching, please?" Scribble, scribble.

"High School Maths and Physics."

"Hello, I'm Vicky," I said, joining them and smiling at Brent. "I'm Joe's better half."

Brent swung round to face me. I tried shaking hands but he ignored me, too. Joe rolled his eyes and shook his head.

"Please, what is your name, please?"

"I'm Vicky."

"Please, how do you spell that, please?"

"V.I.C.K.Y."

"And where do you come from, please?" Scribble, scribble.

"England. Via Spain."

"And what will you be teaching, please?"

"English."

Brent wrote, then turned away from us to face a young couple, cutting into their conversation.

"Please, what is your name, please?"

"Who was that?" I whispered to Joe. "A reporter?"

"No, that's Brent, teaching TOK in the High School. I think he's a bit of a weirdo."

"Oh. What's TOK?"

"Theory of Knowledge."

"Oh."

I was out of my depth, and felt a wave of homesickness for El Hoyo, for our house, for the chickens and neighbours, for the simple life. What were we doing in this alien place, with these strange people?

The front door opened again, and an attractive, veiled Arabic lady entered. The Three Fat Ladies welcomed her and introduced her to the room.

"This is Miss Naima, head of Human Resources," announced Dr. Cecily.

Miss Naima smiled, looked down at the wad of brown envelopes in her hand, and then started calling out names. Her English was accented but excellent. Our names were called, we stepped forward, and she handed us our envelopes.

Impatient as ever, Joe peeked into his envelope

and his eyes widened. "It's money!" he said. "Lots of it!"

"Okay, y'all!" called Dr. Cecily, officiously clapping her hands. "Miss Naima has just given you your settling-in allowance. Now let's get this show on the road! The school bus is waiting below to take y'all on your night-tour of the city."

Joe and I were first out of the door, but when we reached the waiting bus, Joe kept on walking.

"Make some excuse for me," he said over his shoulder. "I can't face any more polite smalltalk. Take some photos, tell me how you get on. I promise I'll come on the trip tomorrow."

I sighed. This wasn't unusual. Since his military days, Joe had developed an allergy to crowds. I watched him march away across the sand and boarded the bus alone, just as the evening prayer chants began. A wail floated from a minaret above a mosque, then another, then more, all from different directions of the city, filling the air. I looked at a large building opposite, decorated with a giant picture of the King, several floors high. The King smiled benevolently down upon his subjects and, more than ever, I felt like a fish out of water.

The others now boarded the bus. I was a little surprised at the condition of the interior. Some seats were slashed and graffiti scrawls were evident.

A PARTY

"The students," explained a Fat Lady who caught me staring. "They're spoilt, those kids. They just do whatever they want. They know somebody will clean up after them."

The driver started the engine and we set off across the sand lot, heading for the road. I'd noticed that the Bahrainis seemed to build their apartment blocks first, not concerning themselves with paving the roads until later, if ever.

I don't recall much of the tour. I know I saw brightly lit mosques, malls, the Pearl monument (again) and the famous Financial District with its modern towers. Most of the time I just watched neon signs flash past in a blur. I should have been excited, but I felt homesick and deeply lonely.

The Three Fat Ladies pointed chubby fingers at buildings and landmarks, rarely pausing in their running commentary. The youngsters on the bus chattered and squealed. For them it was a huge adventure. Newly qualified, most had never travelled, and I could hear Brent with his, "Please, what is your name, please?" repeated over and over.

Little did I know that not many seats away from me were two of the greatest friends Joe and I would ever make. Colton and Jake, younger than our own kids, would delight us and transform our days in the Middle East.

And there was somebody else on that bus

whom I instantly liked, and who would play a big part in our everyday lives. It was Jasim, the bus driver, and I was to discover that his mood would affect every one of our days at the school.

At last the tour was over and I rejoined Joe in our hotel suite. He was fiddling about with the TV, unable to find many English-speaking programmes.

"Did you see any camels?" he asked.

I shook my head and went to bed. Perhaps things would look brighter in the morning. Tomorrow was going to be another very busy day.

Next morning, we woke well-rested and ready to face the day. We had coffee and I was reading the hotel's rules and information when I made a discovery.

"Hey! The hotel has a swimming pool!"

Things were looking up. Joe and I had plenty of time before being picked up by the bus for our next sight-seeing tour. More than enough time for a swim. We grabbed our stuff and took the lift to the roof. We passed the gymnasium with averted eyes; this was not a place in which we intended spending much time. We pushed the door to the open-air pool and squealed as we touched the metal hand-rail. It was hot enough to grill a chorizo.

Somebody else was already in the small pool. A fit young man swam up and down, up and down. Brent.

Joe and I settled ourselves on sun-loungers, waiting for Brent to tire. But he didn't. Eventually we could stand the heat no longer and slipped into the shallow end, only to find that the water was hot. Far from being refreshing, it was more like swimming in soup.

"Hello, Brent," Joe said cheerfully, as Brent slowed to turn.

"Please, what is your name, please?"

"I'm Joe. We met last night."

"And where do you come from, please?"

Joe gave up and started swimming. We swam awhile, then departed, leaving Brent to continue with his lengths, up and down, up and down, up and down.

Jasim arrived more than half an hour late to pick us up for our next sight-seeing trip. Joe was annoyed but it was a taste of things to come.

MUSSAKHAN

Nadia describes this as, "Roasted Chicken on a Magical Carpet of Bread, Onions and Sumac". This delicious dish is perfect, especially if careful attention is paid to the slow cooking of the onions. Shrak bread (available from Middle Eastern shops or online) is preferable but may be replaced with tortilla wraps or even pita bread.

Top Tip

Prepare the onion mixture the day before and marinate the chicken pieces with it.

Ingredients (Serves 4)

8 chicken pieces, dried with paper towel

2 tbsp vegetable oil

Shrak bread (or tortilla wraps, or pita bread)

For the onion mixture:

6-8 good glugs of olive oil

8 large onions, sliced

125ml (4 fl oz) chicken stock

A pinch of caster sugar

8-10 tbsp sumac (berry-red, available from Middle Eastern shops)

Method

Heat the olive oil in a large frying pan.

Throw in the onions, with salt, and cook really slowly for 20-25 minutes, stirring frequently.

When soft and glistening, add the stock, stir, and allow to bubble a little.

Add the sugar and stir continuously.

Add the sumac and stir continuously.

Preheat the oven to 180ºC/Gas mark 4.

Brown the chicken pieces in the vegetable oil.

Line the tin, or *cazuela*, or baking dish, with a couple of layers of shrak bread and half the onion mixture.

Lay the chicken on this and cover with the rest of the onion mixture.

If you have time, leave to marinate again.

Place in the oven for 20-25 minutes or until the chicken is cooked through.

Serve with steamed rice, garnished with pine nuts and almonds, yoghurt and a green salad.

3

NOT A DROP TO DRINK

Arriving late did not bother our bus driver, Jasim, at all. Jasim came when Jasim was ready, not before.

And if Jasim was in a good mood, the journey was smooth. However, if Jasim was unhappy, we'd soon know about it. He'd rattle our bones as the bus lurched through the sand, wrenching the steering wheel from side to side, causing us to be thrown around like dried peas in a box. He'd ignore traffic lights and every corner became a fairground ride.

The itinerary of our sightseeing trip looked interesting. We were going to the museum, the Grand Mosque, the Formula 1 racetrack, and, best of all, to see the King's camels.

By now, many of the teachers had become

familiar to us, although new ones were arriving all the time. We avoided Brent as far as possible, but others we liked and chatted with.

Daryna didn't join us as she was spending her time at the school and had already seen the sights. I heard her name frequently mentioned by the Three Fat Ladies, Cecily, Dawn and Rita, our self-appointed sightseeing guides. And, judging by their frowns and whispered exchanges, Daryna was not the flavour of the month. This astonished me, as Daryna had not yet begun her job as Principal.

The heat was indescribable, and the air-conditioned interior of the bus was our sanctuary, but we all streamed out obediently to mill around the museum. Joe was fascinated but I couldn't find much enthusiasm for the few 6000 year old, unrecognisable artifacts. Everything looked dry and shrivelled. Joe tried to pique my interest by showing me a restored Buick, donated by the American government in 1932. He failed miserably.

At the beautiful Grand Mosque, or *Al-Fateh* which I recognised from the 20BD banknote, we all removed our shoes. The females of the party were ushered into an anteroom where we were issued with all-covering *abayas* and *hijabs*, without which we would not be granted access. The mosque was only 22 years old, sparsely furnished and decorated, unlike Christian places of worship. We all sat on the carpet under a vast fibre-glass dome, listening to an Imam's lecture. My concentration was thin. I was more interested in studying fellow members of our party, and two little girls, with only their faces visible, playing on a bench.

By the time we'd visited the museum and the Grand Mosque, Joe and I were parched. There was nowhere to buy a drink, everything was closed. And now we understood why. Ramadan. No food or drink, not even a sip of water, was permitted between sunrise and sunset. Not being Muslim, we could eat and drink, but only in private, for fear of offending the devout.

"Okay, y'all," said one of the Three Fat Ladies. "We're going to the Formula 1 racetrack now."

The news was greeted with damp enthusiasm by the passengers, who were hot and irritable. But not Joe.

"Crikey! The Bahrain F1 racetrack!" he yelled. "I can't believe I'm actually going to see it!"

Joe is a huge fan of the Grand Prix, and this was the highlight of his day. I noticed other teachers giving him sidelong glances, and I guessed Formula 1 was not high on their interest list. The sun hammered down as just a handful of us left the cool bus to explore the circuit. Apart from us, the grounds were deserted.

"Vicky, can you believe it? Look, there's the starting grid! And the pits! Wow! I can't wait for March when the Bahrain Grand Prix is on! Did you know that Bahrain is hosting the opening round of the season?" Joe's head was beetroot red, caused by a mixture of heat and excitement.

I like F1, but not enough to stand in the searing heat admiring the track's bends and grandstand. All I really wanted was a drink. Even my enthusiasm to see the King's camels was fast diminishing.

Back on the bus, Jasim made an announcement, gold teeth glinting through his broad grin.

"Today not go see King's camels."

"Why not?" asked Joe.

"Very hot, too much hot."

I was disappointed, but going home was attractive. I was hallucinating about our fridge's interior, and the glasses of cold water that I would soon be pouring down my throat. The camels would have to wait.

Tomorrow we'd visit the school for the first time. We'd meet the owners, check out the facilities, and see our classrooms. I was more than a little nervous.

"Vicky, I don't understand it. I'm getting no support at all from Dr. Cecily, Dawn or Rita. In fact, they block everything I suggest." Daryna was already a constant visitor to our suite, and she frequently reported back, providing us with juicy snippets of the school's preparation for the new term.

"The Three Fat Ladies?"

Daryna chuckled. "Is that what you call them? Good name!"

"Well, I don't know what's going on there, but I'll try to find out." I said. I remembered witnessing the Three Fat Ladies' hostility towards Daryna at the 'Meet and Greet' party. Perhaps our first school visit would shed some light on the mystery.

"And wait until you meet the owner, Mrs. Sherazi!"

"Why?"

"Wait and see. I have to give a speech, too, and you'll meet your Middle School Principal, Mr. Brewster."

"What's he like?"

"He seems okay. He's American, of course. A man of colour. He seems a bit on the defensive and I'm not sure why."

At 7 a.m. the next morning it was already hot. I'd hidden a bottle of water in my bag, knowing there would be no refreshments during the day. Ramadan was a harsh time.

Jasim, the bus driver, was late and we waited for him in the cool of the hotel foyer. Our favourites, Jake and Colton, kept us amused with tales of their home towns. Jake was from Chicago and Colton hailed from Boise, Idaho.

This was Jake's first teaching position and he had arrived in Bahrain with his lovely girlfriend, Emily, full of hopes and ambition. Fair-haired, polite, with a competitive streak, Jake was a born showman and teacher. His stories and his ability to mimic fellow teachers, including Brent and the Three Fat Ladies, often left us weak with laughter. Jake had presence. Everybody gravitated towards him and he was popular with Arabs and Westerners alike.

This was Colton's first year of teaching, too. Having completed his college education, he became a waiter in a Boise restaurant. He was hugely successful, earning money hand over fist, but decided serving was not enough. He trained to become a teacher and accepted the offer from the American Specialist School, or ASS.

Colton was impossibly good-looking, but never vain. He had the kind of face that could have originated from anywhere: Arabia, Spain, America, wherever. His brown eyes sparkled with fun but he never took himself very seriously. He attracted female attention wherever he went, but it was not only his looks that attracted. Colton was gentle, sensitive, generous and incredibly thoughtful. In spite of their age difference, Joe and Colton soon developed a special bond and later would spend hours together, watching movies, arguing, talking about nothing and roaring with laughter.

Later on, both Colton and Jake became popular with the students, although their classroom styles were poles apart. Jake was strict and ran a tight ship, although humour was an important part of his delivery. Colton, on the other hand, was relaxed and friendly with his students, and they adored him. Both were extremely effective teachers.

The other young teachers milled about, some leaning against walls, all chatting. Brent was there, notebook at the ready. I saw him closing in, pencil poised, but luckily the bus arrived. I steered Joe away before Brent had the chance to ask our names yet again.

Jasim was in a good mood, and that first drive to school was fascinating. Forty years ago, the area where our hotel was located, was under the sea. The land was reclaimed and modern skyscrapers sprouted up where once there had only been water.

The houses were large, expensive and hidden

behind walls with only their upper floors visible. We caught glimpses through ornate gates of Indian servants washing cars or watering flowerbeds. Between houses lay sand lots, no doubt earmarked for future construction.

Now and then we stopped to pick up teachers, already veterans at the school, who chose to live in preferred accommodation. Although the school was quite close to our hotel, the frequent stops and heavy traffic turned a ten-minute journey into one of half an hour.

We swung off the main road and left the tall, opulent buildings and gated compounds behind. Now the road was narrow and dusty. Here the houses were low, flat-roofed, cramped and crumbling, often festooned with black flags. Arabic graffiti adorned bare walls. In a few short weeks, we were to discover that the graffiti spelled out political messages, like 'Freedom!'

Our school lurked behind very high walls topped with wire fencing and we could see nothing, except huge metal gates guarded by uniformed security men. I don't really know what I'd been expecting, but the building looked more like a prison than a school.

We piled out and passed through the gates into a courtyard. The main classroom block was three floors high and, together with a few administration blocks, surrounded the large, partly shaded courtyard. I tried to imagine the place filled with Arabic kids, as it soon would be.

The Three Fat Ladies herded us into an administration block and introduced us to the square gadget fixed to a wall.

"Hey y'all, this is where you punch in every morning, and punch out at the end of the day."

Joe and I exchanged glances. So we were expected to clock in and out every day? I hadn't done that since I worked on a factory assembly-line, making fire-guards, when I was a student.

"And if you're late three times, y'all lose a day's pay."

"And if you're sick, you need to call in yourself and explain, or y'all lose a day's pay."

"And if you don't have a doctor's note, y'all lose a day's pay."

As we digested this, the Three Fat Ladies led the way across the courtyard to the main classroom block. Once through the entrance doors, we saw large portraits of the King and his uncle, the Prime Minister, prominently displayed on notice boards. Straight ahead, a flight of stairs led to the upper floors. To the left, and above a swing door, was written 'Middle School'. Opposite and above another swing door, 'High School'. The Kindergarten, Elementary School and Gymnasium were in separate buildings across the street, we were told. In total, the school accommodated more than one and a half thousand children. We were led up the stairs to the first floor and ushered into an auditorium large enough to seat about five hundred in neat rows.

And then the meetings began.

Whether in the UK, America or the Middle East, I'm sure school staff meetings are pretty similar. But the meetings we endured that day were lengthy, made twice as long because everything was announced in Arabic and then repeated in English. Brent sat in front of us, on his own, pen and notebook poised.

"Welcome to ASS, the American Specialist School," Dr. Cecily said into the microphone. "Where..."

"ALL STUDENTS SUCCEED!" chanted the veteran teachers, led by the Three Fat Ladies. Joe and I looked at each other. Was this an American thing? None of the staff meetings in England incorporated jingoistic chants. Further along from us, Jake and Colton appeared unconcerned. Must be an American thing I concluded.

Dr. Cecily spoke at length and then introduced us to Mr. Brewster, the Middle School Principal, who was my boss. My first impressions were favourable. An African American, middle-aged, short, stocky and bespectacled. All the new teachers now had to stand and introduce themselves and I saw Brent's scribblings go into overdrive. When it was my turn, everybody laughed.

"Why did they laugh?" I hissed to Joe, as I sat down.

"Because you said you're English. Your accent gave that away in your first sentence. We're the only British here, as far as I can see."

Dr. Cecily again claimed the microphone and her face stretched into an unnatural, showbiz-like grin, eyes focused somewhere over our heads.

"And now, I want y'all to welcome the school's wonderful, talented, glorious owner, Mrs. Sherazi!" She led the applause, quickly taken up by the other two Fat Ladies and obediently echoed by the rest of us. All eyes turned to the back of the auditorium.

FOUL (PRONOUNCED FULE) MEDAMES

A RICH DIP FOR THE POOR

Nadia says, "In the Middle East this is known as the dish of the poor, as the ingredients are very cheap, but rest assured there's nothing cheap about the flavour. It is absolutely delicious (everyone I have ever made it for has demanded the recipe) and an added bonus is that the fava beans, garlic, parsley and olive oil make it highly nutritious!"

Top Tip: Experiment! Throw some chopped chilies over the top.

Ingredients (Serves 2-3)

3 tbsp tahini

Juice of 1 lemon

Large pinch of salt

2 tbsp warm water

2 large garlic cloves, peeled and chopped

400g (14 fl oz) can cooked foul medames or fava beans (available from big stores, Middle Eastern/Turkish shops, online)

FOR THE GARNISH:

A little chopped garlic

Cayenne pepper

Fresh parsley, chopped

1 hard-boiled egg per person, peeled and quartered

Olive oil

Method

Gradually mix the lemon juice and salt in a small bowl of tahini. Stir until the mixture begins to go 'whitish'.

Add enough warm water to give the mixture a consistency of double cream.

Add the chopped garlic.

Gently heat the beans in their liquid.

Mash with a fork, leaving a few beans whole.

Place in a wide serving bowl and drizzle with the tahini sauce.

Sprinkle the chopped garlic, cayenne pepper, and parsley over the top.

Arrange the quartered eggs and finish with a drizzle of olive oil. Serve with hot pita bread.

4

ASS

Was this the school's owner? A hunched figure made her way slowly down the central aisle to the front, her eyes never lifting from the smooth parquet floor. I estimated that she was quite possibly an octogenarian, but the many face-lifts had rendered her face immobile, and her eyebrows were arched in permanent surprise. A wig made from impossibly thick, glossy black hair cascaded over her shoulders. When she reached the microphone, she straightened her wig and began to read from her notes. I confess, I was fascinated by her.

"Welcome to a new year at ASS," she said.

"Where ALL STUDENTS SUCCEED," chanted the auditorium.

Mrs. Sherazi paused but her expression didn't

change and she didn't look up. She carried on reading. These sentences were the longest I would ever hear her utter as she normally restricted herself to just a few words at a time.

"For ten years we were fortunate to have Mr. Denny as the High School Principal. As you know, Mr. Denny had to leave the school because of poor health. I will now introduce the new High School Principal, Miss Daryna, who is from Canada."

I watched the other two Fat Ladies nudge each other, directing looks of sympathy at Dr. Cecily. It suddenly dawned on me that Dr. Cecily had expected the appointment, and her hostility to Daryna stemmed from her disappointment in being overlooked. The Fat Ladies' resentment of Daryna now made sense to me.

Daryna stood to moderate applause and spoke a few breathless words of thanks into the microphone before returning it to Mrs. Sherazi. I noticed that the Three Fat Ladies did not join in the general applause that concluded Daryna's speech.

"Things are going to change here at ASS," said Mrs. Sherazi.

"Where ALL STUDENTS SUCCEED," chanted the auditorium.

"During the school day, no teacher is allowed outside the premises without a pass. The pass must be signed by either Miss Daryna or Mr.

Brewster. This is my school and all teachers will follow my rules."

Clearly this was a formidable lady, a fact that would be reinforced in the months to come. We found her to be an astute businesswoman who never agreed to anyone's request for a salary increase (which often occurred, especially amongst the veteran teachers), no matter what the circumstances. Western teachers at other schools, we were told, earned so much more than those at ASS. (Joe and I were quite satisfied with our conditions and we felt our salaries were fair.)

However, she could be very forgiving. She rarely terminated a teacher's contract, even when the teacher was guilty of the most shocking crimes.

I'll gloss over the dull parts of the meeting and will report only the parts that made me sit up straighter:

1) Mrs. Sherazi's extraordinary wig, which had a tendency to slip forward, requiring constant adjusting.
2) The fact that there were "a few last-minute problems" with our timetables, or 'schedules' as the Americans call them.
3) That we would *definitely* be moving to our new apartments in a week or so.

Eventually, Dr. Cecily wound up the meeting.

"We sure are looking forward to a productive new school year," she said, "here at ASS, where..."

"ALL STUDENTS SUCCEED!" chanted the teachers, Joe and I included.

Mrs. Sherazi bowed and departed to another round of celebrity applause, and we new teachers were taken to the library for an 'orientation' meeting. Chaired again by the daunting Dr. Cecily and assisted by Dawn and Rita, we were instructed on what to do, what never to do, and what to expect in Bahrain. Joe and I sat with our new friends, Colton and Jake, and as each nugget of information was delivered, our eyes met in either amusement or disbelief.

Ramadan was further explained. We were informed that during daylight hours, Muslims abstain from eating, drinking (including water), smoking and marital sex.

"So non-marital sex is okay, then?" said Joe.

I kicked him under the table and Colton and Jake sniggered. Dr. Cecily ignored Joe and continued.

"Muslims believe that every part of the body must be restrained during Ramadan," she said. "The tongue is not permitted idle gossip, eyes must not look on anything unseemly, the ears must avoid hearing unsuitable or obscene words and the feet must not lead one astray."

"Do all Muslims observe Ramadan?" asked Andrea, a dark-haired, dark-eyed young teacher from Texas.

"Sick people, travellers, the very young and very old, the mentally impaired and pregnant ladies are exempt," Dr. Cecily answered.

"What about our students?" I asked. "Will they be fasting?"

"Most will be fasting and observing Ramadan," she said. "Most won't even bother to come to school until it's over."

"So we teach half-classes to start with?"

"We sure do."

Joe leaned forward. "So what you are saying is that when school starts on Tuesday, hardly any of the kids will turn up?"

"That's right. And when Ramadan finishes, the *Eid Al-Fitr* holiday begins, so there won't be any school anyway."

"And when does Ramadan end?"

The Three Fat Ladies laughed.

"That depends on the moon," explained Rita.

"And whether you are Sunni or Shi'a." said Dawn.

"One percent of the crescent moon has to be visible to the naked eye before Ramadan can end. Or three percent, depending on whether you are Sunni or Shi'a."

"Which is just as well, because the schedule isn't ready," muttered Dawn.

This meeting was beginning to get interesting.

"Some other things y'all should know," Dr. Cecily went on. "The Ministry of Education is all-powerful, and the school and staff have to follow their rules or the school will be closed down."

Dr. Cecily explained how the Ministry of Education's rules would affect us and I made a mental list. In England, I was called Schindler because of my love of making lists, but judging by the following, I was in no danger of being given that nickname here in Bahrain.

1) Israel was completely missing from the curriculum, and must never be mentioned by us. We must act as though it didn't exist.
2) The Holocaust must never be referred to, as the government does not recognise that it ever happened. It must be skipped by all History teachers.
3) School textbooks sometimes had pages glued together to protect students from 'offensive material'.
4) In textbooks containing photographs of people dressed scantily, or wearing shorts, expect to find clothes added and coloured in by hand.

Joe, Jake, Colton and I gaped and exchanged

more glances. Was this for real? What were we doing here in this strange place? But there were more surprises:

5) The older generation are highly respected. (I hoped that would stand Joe and me in good stead in the classroom.)
6) Bribery is commonplace. Both students and their parents have been known to offer money, goods, even cars, in exchange for higher grades.
7) Never complain about being kept waiting, it's very rude.
8) Boys and girls do not 'date'. Instead, they go out in groups, chaperoning each other. At discos, girls and boys dance separately, protected from each other by a barrier.
9) Hand-holding by members of the opposite sex, or any public signs of affection, even between husband and wife, are frowned upon.
10) However, hand-holding by members of the same gender is perfectly acceptable. Men often walk along holding hands.

By now, Joe, Jake, Colton and I were listening with our mouths hanging open, but there were even more extraordinary customs to observe:

11) Never, never show the soles of your feet, as it's regarded as a terrible insult.

12) Beware, many Muslims believe that Western ladies are easy because of the way they dress. (Andrea snorted at that one. Joe said, "Do you mean they're not?" and received another kick from me under the table.)
13) Never pass anything to anyone using your left hand. The right hand is used for eating and drinking, whilst the left is reserved for bodily hygiene and thus considered unclean.
14) Never compliment anybody on a possession, as Muslims will feel obliged to give it to you, whatever the value.

Jake leaned into Joe. "Nice watch," he said, pointing at Joe's shiny new timepiece. We'd never bothered with watches in El Hoyo, but felt we needed them now.

"Thank you, it's new..." said Joe, then started laughing as Jake opened his palm, ready to accept the gift that Joe was supposed to make.

"I really like this," said Colton, fingering Joe's shirt collar.

"Okay, y'all," said Dr. Cecily, frowning at the hilarity at our end of the long table. "Why don't you go off and take a look round the school and find your own classrooms."

She closed the meeting and we all wandered off.

"Well, Miss Daryna told me that I'm a floater

and I haven't been given my own classroom," said Joe. "Makes me feel like something left in a lavatory," he added under his breath. "Let's go and find your room in the Middle School."

I agreed, picturing my classroom to be similar to the many I'd taught in, back in the UK. How mistaken I was.

We passed Brent in the corridor, scribbling in his notebook.

"Hi, Brent," said Joe. "Have you found your classroom?"

"Hi. No, I'm a floater," said Brent, not looking up. He frantically flicked the pages in his notebook. "Excuse me, please, what are your names, please?"

We passed through the double swing doors into the Middle School. The ground floor housed all the Grade 6 classes, so I knew my classroom would be somewhere here.

The first room was a small staffroom. A bank of elderly-looking computers lined the walls. In the centre was a large worktable. Every chair was occupied by an Arabic member of staff, all women, all veiled. They were all speaking at once and the noise level was high. I understood not a word and hurriedly backed out.

The first classroom was large, the walls decorated with maps and bulletin boards. A foam mattress leaned against the back wall.

"Well!" I said. "This must be the Geography room, but if my classroom is anything like this, I certainly won't complain. They even provide a bed for naps between lessons!"

We walked further down the corridor and found my classroom. 'Miss Vicky Grade 6 ENGLISH' was signed above the door. It was sandwiched between the Principal's office and another that housed the school's computer control system.

"Well, this is it!" I said to Joe. "This is going to be my home for the next year." I opened the door and looked in.

"Oh my..."

"Oh!" echoed Joe.

The room was tiny and bleak. At the front stood a ramshackle teacher's desk with a whiteboard behind. The room had no cupboards, just an ancient bookcase with bowed shelves. The battered students' desks had already been set out. They were of the 'combo' type, with a writing surface fixed to the chair. I counted twenty-two. They were so closely packed that I wondered how the children would reach the ones at the back without having to climb over the ones in front. I could already see that I wouldn't be able to wander around the classroom to check on pupils' work. In fact, there wasn't even space for me to write on the whiteboard, as the front desks nosed up against the wall.

"There must be some mistake," I said. "Perhaps they're just storing extra desks in here."

"Well, at least you have a classroom," said Joe. "At least you're not a floater, like me. And those two big windows let in lots of light."

That was true. The barred windows had no blinds and looked out onto the courtyard.

"I think you wan' to cover those windows," said a voice from the doorway. "You buy paper, you stick it all over windows!"

Joe and I swung round to see who was speaking...

SHISH TAOUK

Nadia calls this delicious dish, 'It's Thyme for Kebabs'. It is best barbecued but, alternatively, it can also be grilled and should take the same amount of time. Do leave time to soak the skewers, if you're using the wooden ones, to prevent them from catching fire.

Traditionally, this dish is made with chicken breasts, but thigh meat is really tasty and your friendly butcher will bone these for you. The longer you leave the meat to marinate, the more tender and delicious it will be.

Ingredients (Serves 8)

4 boneless, skinned chicken breasts, diced into 2½cm (1 inch) cubes

6 boned chicken thighs, cubed as above

FOR THE MARINADE:

6-8 garlic cloves, peeled and pounded until creamy

Juice of 4 lemons

1 handful fresh thyme

1 tsp cayenne pepper

A few glugs of olive oil

Lots of crunchy salt

Method

Have your barbecue coals ready, and your wooden skewers soaking in water.

Thoroughly mix the marinade ingredients in a small bowl.

Place the breast and thigh meat in 2 separate bowls. Share out the marinade ingredients between them and mix well.

Allow to marinate for at least 15 minutes, but the longer the better.

Thread the breasts and thighs on separate skewers.

Place the skewers on hot, white coals.

Regularly baste and turn, until cooked through and golden (takes about 8 minutes).

Serve in a wrap of hot flatbread with a drizzle of tahini sauce.

5
FRIENDS

In the doorway stood a figure, the owner of the voice. She smiled shyly and stepped forward.

"I'm Hawa," she said. "I teach Grade 6 Math, an' my classroom is opposi' yours. I am the *meanest* teacher."

We smiled at each other, and I sensed a friend and ally. Hawa was petite, graceful and dressed in a beautiful, shimmering turquoise *abaya*, her *hijab* decorated with sequins and pearls. In all the time I spent in Bahrain, I never saw her wear the same outfit twice. Joe and I introduced ourselves.

"The meanest teacher?" I asked.

"Oh yes!" She giggled, and her pretty oriental eyes shone. "You see! You see!"

Hawa looked more like a butterfly than the meanest teacher, but I didn't say so.

FRIENDS

"You say I should cover the windows?" I asked.

"Yes. When the High School come out for their break, all the kids, they not listen to you, they watch big kids. An' big kids, they knock on glass and make bad faces. Better you cover the windows with paper."

"Well, I'll leave you to it," said Joe. "I'd better go and explore the High School. I'll see you both later."

He left, and Hawa and I got to know each other better.

Hawa was Malaysian and had already worked at ASS for four years. She had settled on the island, her husband worked in Manama, and her children attended the British School. I explained that Joe and I were British, but lived in Spain.

"You not work in Spain?"

"No, we were supposed to be retired."

"You do nothing?"

"Er, well, I wrote books."

"What the name of your book?"

"Chickens, Mules..."

"Chicken? You write abou' chicken? And mule? Wha' is mule?"

I tried to explain, then fired questions at her.

"Are all the classrooms so small?"

"Oh yes, on this floor, all small. Except for the Arabic Geography teacher. She has a big, BIG room, and a bed. Sometime she lock room to take a nap." She clapped her hands and giggled. "You see! You see!"

"But there's no space in here!"

"No space, yes. Every year the same-same."

"And where are the books? No paper? No exercise books?"

"The students, they buy all tha'. Not a' first, you nee' to nag them, then they buy later."

"And what about our timetables, the schedule?"

Hawa shrugged. "Schedule not ready."

Poor Hawa answered my onslaught of questions as best she could. My heart sank with each reply. This was not what I'd expected at all.

"How can we prepare our lessons with no books and no schedule?"

Hawa shrugged again, so I tried a different tack.

"What are the kids like?"

"Some very good, some very bad. Mos' very, very lazy! You see! You see!"

"How good is their English?"

"Most is okay. You see!"

"What is the Middle School Principal like?"

But Ms. Hawa didn't get the chance to respond. Raised voices from the room next door made us both stop and listen.

"Tha' Mr. Brewster," she whispered. "With Datu. He the computer guy. They try fix the schedule. I don' know who the lady voice is."

"I do. That's Miss Daryna, the High School Principal."

Just then, my mobile phone rang. It was Joe.

"How are you getting on? I can't find a staffroom that isn't full of people, but I've met a teacher called Rashida, and she's shown me a place where we can sit outside in the shade. I'll meet you at the main door, okay?"

The argument next door was getting more heated, although I couldn't make out any actual words. Hawa excused herself and slipped into her own classroom. I shut the door on my own dismal little classroom and went down the corridor to meet Joe. We crossed the courtyard together, the sun blinding us and making us squint. The heat was unbearable.

"It's here," he said, rounding the corner behind one of the administration blocks and pushing a gate open. We walked down a narrow alley, flanked by the school perimeter wall on one side and the classroom block on the other. Around two corners the alley opened out a little and I saw two rows of old chairs, facing each other. Someone had constructed a temporary roof that provided much-needed shade.

"This is Smokers' Corner," said Joe. "Rashida told me it's for staff to use if they want. Imagine providing a smoking area for teachers! You wouldn't get that in the UK! Anyway, it's a private area for all staff, whether they smoke or not."

"So who is Rashida?" I asked.

"I think she teaches Algebra in the High School. She's Lebanese and has worked here for years. She borrowed my pen... Actually, I don't think she gave it back."

Joe and I were just comparing observations when Joe's phone rang. It was Colton, telling us that Jasim and the school bus were waiting to take us to the bank. ASS insisted we open bank accounts for the payment of our salaries.

The bank was cool, modern and airy. We had to wait a long time, as accounts needed to be opened for each new teacher. It was the turn of a fellow teacher, Barry. Older than most, he was talking incessantly to the bank teller. Barry, who sported huge yellow teeth and wafted bad breath as he spoke, never stopped talking.

"I'm just a dude," said Barry, leaning in to the poor bank-teller, who recoiled from the blast of toxic odour directed at her. "I'm just a dude from the good ol' US of A, here to instruct kids in your country. Before I came here, I was..."

"Get on with it!" muttered Joe.

FRIENDS

But Barry was in full swing and unlikely to be stopped easily.

"And then, of course, before Saudi, I..."

"Oh, for heaven's sake!" said Joe through clenched teeth, scratching himself down below.

"I'm just a dude, but I always think..." Barry droned on. And on.

Joe's impatience rose in a crescendo, and he pushed his way out through the bank's entrance doors to cool his temper with a breath of fresh air, quickly returning when he discovered there wasn't any outside.

"Get on with it!" repeated Joe in a voice loud enough for Barry to hear.

It had the desired effect. Barry signed the last paper and vacated his seat. Joe and I were next and were soon clutching our new bank account number. As we waited for the last few, I noticed most of the bank staff's name tags read 'Kalifa'.

"That means they're related to the King," whispered Jake. "I don't know if it's true, but somebody told me that the King gives all the best jobs to his friends and relations."

Back at the hotel, we felt exhausted and settled down to take a nap. I was just dozing off, when the telephone rang.

"Hi! Jake here! Fancy coming down to our room? We've got some beer and wine and a few people here. Come and join us!"

"Tell him we'll be there in an hour," said Joe, half-asleep.

"Jake? We'll be there in an hour."

"Aw... Can't you come now?"

Reluctantly, we got up, splashed warm water (cold tap-water doesn't exist in August) on our faces and knocked on Jake's door. The apartment was filled with other new teachers who all stopped talking and spun round to look at us as we entered.

"Sorry about that," said Joe to the room. "It's not often I get a chance for a spot of afternoon hanky-panky with Vicky. We were just getting into it when Jake called."

My jaw dropped with horror and embarrassment.

"But we weren't doing anything!" I squeaked.

Everybody was silent, staring at us, probably imagining us oldsters in the throes of passion, and not enjoying the image.

Only Jake and Colton roared with laughter; they already understood Joe's warped sense of humour. Later, whenever they got the chance, they would harmonize 'Afternoon Delight' in our hearing, much to my chagrin and Joe's amusement. Actually, they both had excellent voices, but the song always made me wince.

In spite of Joe's bad behaviour, we had a good time and stayed late, after most of the other guests had left. There were six of us, and we were to spend a lot of time together in the future. There was Jake, and his beautiful girlfriend, Emily. Emily held a British passport but had been raised in America and no traces of an English accent remained. She would teach in the Elementary school. She had made friends with another Elementary teacher, Allison, a lovely redhead from Iowa. Then there was Colton, and finally, Joe and me. We sat round the big polished table in Jake and Emily's suite, and laughed the night away. It felt like a scene from 'Friends', except that Joe and I were so much older.

"So," I said after a few glasses of wine, "who knows why the Three Fat Ladies hate Miss Daryna? They've hardly met her!"

"I think I know," said Jake, who always seemed to know everything that was going on. "I think Dr. Cecily was expecting to be given the job of High School Principal. And they used to have a really easy time with the last Principal, so I think Miss Daryna's arrival has really ruffled their collective feathers."

This confirmed what I had suspected and filled in a few more gaps.

"And what do you think of Barry?"

Everyone groaned. "Hali-Barry?"

It was an apt name, the halitosis being Barry's chief trait. Nobody remembered exactly where in the States he hailed from but, during the previous year, he had been teaching in Saudi Arabia. Apparently, he had left under 'mysterious' circumstances that were never properly explained.

"Hey, I'm just a dude..." said Jake, imitating Barry perfectly, hands shoulder-height, palms exposed, exactly as Barry often did.

"He's creepy," said Emily.

"Yes, he stares at you, then corners you and tells you his life history," said Allison. "And all the time he's talking, he's kinda undressing you with his eyes."

"Hey, he'll be a member of your faculty," Colton happily pointed out to Joe. "He teaches Math, doesn't he?"

Joe shuddered. "And what do you think of Brent?" he asked.

We all agreed that Brent was very peculiar. All of us had spelled our names for his notebook several times.

"Well, school starts on Tuesday. I wonder how many kids will turn up?" someone asked.

I tried to imagine myself teaching a class of Arabic kids, with no schedule, no books, no paper, in a classroom the size of a cupboard, but failed miserably.

Back in our room, a scribbled note had been pushed under our door.

FRIENDS

Vicky! I've found something out! Come over for a coffee when you can. D.

I looked at my watch. It was too late now, but I was very curious to hear what Daryna had discovered.

ARABIC SALAD

Nadia says, "I serve this lovely, fresh salad with meat, fish, chicken, baked potatoes and falafel. But, sometimes, without telling anyone, I just make a huge bowl of it and eat the lot entirely on its own!"

Ingredients (Serves 4)

1 red onion, peeled and very thinly sliced.

Juice of 1 lemon

3 tomatoes, cubed

2 small Middle Eastern cucumbers, cubed

1 small Cos lettuce, chopped

1 small green pepper, seeded and thinly sliced

1 tbsp chopped fresh parsley

1 pita bread, cut into squares and fried in olive oil

For the dressing:

3 tbsp olive oil

3 tbsp lemon juice

1 garlic clove, peeled and crushed

1 tsp sumac (from Middle Eastern shops, and many big stores)

1 tbsp chopped fresh mint

Salt

Method

Macerate the red onion in the lemon juice for 10 minutes.

For the dressing, put the oil, lemon juice and garlic in a small bowl, and stir well.

Now add the remaining ingredients.

Place all the vegetables into a bowl.

Just before serving, add the fried pita bread, and pour the dressing over it.

6

THE WORM

Early the next morning I tapped on Daryna's door. She appeared in a pink fluffy bathrobe and tugged me inside. I shivered. Daryna always kept her air conditioning set at 'Very Cold'.

"I guess I like it that way because I'm from Canada," she said. "And your room temperature is like Spain."

"So what did that note mean?" I asked, when she'd made coffee. "What did you find out?"

"The schedule! You know the schedules aren't ready?"

"Of course, everybody's talking about it. What's the problem?"

"A Worm! A *Worm* is the problem!"

I looked at her blankly. A Worm?

THE WORM

"The reason the schedule is not ready is because the staff member who was in charge of time-tabling last year didn't get his contract renewed."

"So?"

"So, he infected the system with a worm. A virus or something. And he's the only one who knows the password to the school's set-up. He's left the island, and the school can't fix the program."

"Oh my! That's illegal, isn't it?"

"Oh yes! It's all being kept hush-hush because it would reflect badly on the school. We don't want the parents or the students to know about it. Mrs. Sherazi made him a promise that she wouldn't call the police if he handed over the password."

"So has he agreed?"

"No! He has not! This is one very disgruntled ex-employee!"

"So what's going to happen?"

"Mrs. Sherazi is going to offer him money to come back and fix it. Miss Naima from the office is going to meet him secretly somewhere. I'm assuming he's agreed to come back to the island. We'll just have to wait and see. All the students are arriving on Tuesday expecting their schedules, and the teachers can't function without theirs. I've been closeted in the central computer room with

Datu and Mr. Brewster, trying to get our heads round the problem."

"Yes, my classroom is next door, I heard you."

"Mr. Brewster is being a bit obstructive. I gather he fell out with the last Principal, so he's probably suspicious of me. He's supposed to be a bit of an expert with computers. The Middle School is going to be easier to sort, because it's much smaller than the High School. We have a real problem on our hands with the High School."

We chatted on. I asked Daryna whether she was pleased with her staff so far. Had she met them all? What were her first impressions? It was then that I learned, nice as she was, Daryna was not the best judge of character.

"Oh, I have two favourites already," she said happily. "That nice Barry, I think he's going to be an asset to the school, and he's such a gentleman, so attentive! And Brent, a very intelligent young man with credentials as long as your arm!"

Daryna had a way of accompanying her words with actions, like a Kindergarten teacher. "As long as your arm" was illustrated by shooting out one arm to emphasise just how very long Brent's credentials were. Unfortunately, she knocked over the table lamp and spilled her coffee in the process.

I had news for her, too. I explained why she wasn't popular with the Three Fat Ladies, which bothered her not at all. Daryna was one of those people who never bares a grudge, dare I say, a rare quality for us women. I'm ashamed to confess I've been known to harbour a grudge for years, until I can't even remember why I disliked that person in the first place.

The few days before school started flashed past in a haze of heat and activity. Every morning we waited in the hotel lobby, shadowed by Toothy, the porter, who bowed and scraped, offering to carry our school bags, hoping for a tip.

Jasim was usually late, but nobody ever complained, probably for three very good reasons.

First, Jasim was popular. Everybody liked him. He reminded me of the genie in Aladdin because they shared the same broad, friendly, grinning face.

Second, Jasim had a dark side. His driving style reflected his mood, and a journey with an unhappy Jasim was not an experience anybody, except Joe, enjoyed.

And third, nobody would be foolish enough to argue with Jasim, who was built like a brick outhouse. Like the genie in Aladdin, he had huge forearms, and stood with his arms folded. When not driving the bus, he would join the security team at the school gates, his powerful muscles rippling under his uniform.

Each drive with Jasim was an adventure. Every morning we greeted him and clambered onto the school bus for the first of our twice-daily fairground rides. Jasim would accelerate away, tyres screeching and sending up plumes of sand that obscured a bowing and waving Toothy.

Few journeys on the school bus were uneventful. For instance, Jasim had two mobile phones that often rang simultaneously. As his passengers held their breaths, Jasim would clamp a phone to each ear and fire off a stream of Arabic, whilst steering with his elbows.

He regularly drove at oncoming traffic, ignoring their flashing headlights and horns, at the last moment suddenly diving down a side street. Traffic lights meant nothing to him, stopping only if obstructed by other vehicles.

Joe, smiling broadly at the conclusion of each journey, would shake his hand and say, "That was awesome, Jasim! Thank you!"

The rest of us would emerge trembling.

During those days without students, we familiarised ourselves with the school and I prepared my classroom. Joe, of course, was a 'floater', with no classroom of his own, so he had little to do except chat with other members of staff. Having no schedule, he had no idea what classes he would be teaching and therefore was unable to prepare for them.

Once home again, we waited for nightfall when the shops would open, then purchased teacher stuff: cardboard, red pens, files and folders. I bought coloured gift-wrapping paper and, as Hawa had advised, pasted it on the windows of my classroom, blocking out the view of the courtyard. I would also have bought a fish and fishbowl if I'd had enough space in my classroom.

Tuesday loomed, the first day of school, and still we had no schedule. The veteran teachers, led by the ever-resentful Three Fat Ladies, blamed Daryna. Even the new staff blamed Daryna, having listened to the Three Fat Ladies. Only a few knew the truth but we weren't permitted to discuss it. The villainous Worm hadn't kept his assignation and the computer program was infected beyond repair. Daryna, Mr. Brewster and the administration staff were attempting to assemble the schedule manually. The task was enormous and hugely complicated.

Suddenly it was Tuesday morning, the first day of the new school year. We rose at 5.30 a.m., as we would every school day in the future. I couldn't eat any breakfast, partly due to the early hour, but mostly because of my nervousness. Being Ramadan, it was our last chance to eat something until late in the afternoon, when we returned from school. My stomach churned and the toast Joe made me tasted like sawdust. I couldn't swallow. Even Joe was unusually quiet.

Jasim was late. By the time we arrived at ASS, the street outside was filled with parked cars disgorging students. I gaped. Many of the cars were chauffeur-driven, and all were glittering, expensive vehicles: Mercedes, Range Rovers, Ferraris, Rolls Royces. Not a camel in sight. Jasim somehow barged his way through the shiny cars and dropped us off at the front gates.

The courtyard was thronging with students of all shapes and sizes. Tall young men shouted and called across the yard to each other. Pretty, veiled teenage girls stood in huddles, whispering and giggling behind their hands, or texting on their iPhones and Blackberrys. Younger students kicked empty Coke cans, rough-and-tumbled, or chased one another. Nobody seemed to be in charge and everything appeared disorderly.

We fought our way to the clocking-in machine and punched our cards for the first time. It was 7.15 a.m. and the machine was unforgiving. Because it was after 7 a.m., it stamped the time in red. Three red 'lates' meant we would be deducted a day's salary. Not a good start.

We all headed for the classroom block, the students staring curiously, standing back, creating a path like the parting of the Red Sea. Brent strode ahead, alone. Hali-Barry was talking loudly to Andrea and her beautiful roommate, Saja. Neither appeared remotely interested.

"Good luck!" I whispered to Joe.

"Good luck!" he answered, and we pushed through the swing doors into the school building.

The first thing I noticed was a chair, occupied by an Indian lady in a sari, in the corridor.

"Welcome to your firs' proper day at ASS!" said a voice at my elbow. It was Hawa, dressed in sky blue, her veil decorated with tiny feathers and butterflies.

"Who is the lady in the chair in the corridor?" I asked, unlocking my classroom.

"Tha' is Hall Monitor," explained Hawa, her brown eyes twinkling. "She keep order in the corridor." She clapped her hands. "You see soon!"

My classroom was dark and stiflingly hot. I switched on the lights and air conditioning. I checked that the desks were lined up in neat rows, and sighed deeply. *Bring it on*, I thought. I was as ready as I ever would be. Then the bell rang, and a huge roar of youthful voices rose from the courtyard. I heard the students stampede to the entrance doors, shouting, pushing, jostling. I braced myself.

"OUT! OUT! All Middle School students go back out to the courtyard!" bellowed a voice that I recognised as belonging to Mr. Brewster, the Middle School Principal.

"Awww..." yelled the kids, but obediently spilled back outside.

The lower part of my classroom windows were papered over, so I needed to stand on a chair to see what was happening outside. With difficulty Mr. Brewster and his Deputy divided the students into groups of twenty.

"GROUP #1!" roared Mr. Brewster. "Group #1 go to Math with Miss Hawa."

Group #1 picked up their school bags and headed for the doors.

"GROUP #2! Go to English with Miss Vicky."

I hurriedly jumped off the chair and stood by the classroom door, ready to welcome them, and was almost bowled over by the mob of children intent on reaching the best seats, those in the back row. Chairs overturned and small fights broke out. I waited until each student was seated, aware that first impressions are all-important. At last they settled, eyeing me suspiciously.

"Look at my classroom!" I said. "I expect you to come into my room QUIETLY, not knocking over desks, not charging in like a herd of wildebeest!"

Some kids pulled faces at each other, others fell silent, others grumbled.

"What is a wildebeest?" asked a cheeky-looking boy.

"It's an African wild animal," I said shortly.

"Mees called us animals!" said a moon-faced boy, eyes wide.

I sensed I'd already made a *faux pas,* but blundered on.

"Now, I want you all to stand up and go *quietly* out into the corridor, then come back in again sensibly. This time, I want you to sort yourselves out into alternate rows of boys and girls."

"Mees? What we do, Mees?"

"I'm not sitting next to a boy!" exclaimed a girl wearing a *hijab.*

"Sit next to a *girl?*" asked the cheeky boy. "Not me!"

Things were not going at all well, but I knew I had to follow through. "Into the corridor, all of you!" I repeated.

"Aww... Mees!" complained the class, but they did as they were told, much to my relief.

"You! All you! Go back in classroom!" shrilled a voice outside. It was the Hall Monitor. "You not allowed in hall in lesson time!"

"But the Mees told us to come out!"

"It's okay," I explained to the Hall Monitor, "I sent them out. Now, class, go back in. And quietly!"

From the corner of my eye, I saw a black-robed, shadowy figure watching the whole scene. Somehow, I sensed this lady was no idle spectator. This lady was going to feature in my future.

TRUE FALAFELS

"Whatever you do, don't ignore this recipe!" says Nadia. "If there's only one recipe you do in this book, do this one!"

I agree with Nadia; true falafels, unlike the horrid versions from supermarkets, have to be gloriously spicy. They must have a crispy-on-the-outside crunch with a light-and-fluffy-on-the-inside bit-of-give.

Ingredients (Serves 4-6)

175g (6oz) dried chickpeas, soaked in cold water for 24 hours

85g (3oz) dried fava beans, soaked in cold water for 24 hours

A handful each of fresh parsley and coriander leaves

2 tsp each of ground cinnamon, ground cumin, ground coriander

1 tsp ground allspice

1½ tsp each of salt and freshly ground black pepper

1 tsp cayenne pepper (optional)

2 garlic cloves, peeled

1 tsp bicarbonate of soda (providing lightness to the falafels)

¼ green pepper, seeded and very finely chopped.

2 tbsp flour

3 tbsp sesame seeds

Groundnut oil (for deep frying)

Method

Drain the chickpeas and fava beans.

Chop the parsley and coriander, then whizz in a blender until fine.

Add the chickpeas, fava beans, spices, garlic, baking soda, green pepper and flour. Blend until it is a smooth paste.

Stir in the sesame seeds and leave to rest for about an hour in the fridge.

Gently heat the groundnut oil in a deep-fat frying pan. (Test for heat by dropping a small amount of the mixture into the oil - if it sizzles, it's ready.)

Gently add 1 tbsp of the mixture at a time, as many as possible, without overcrowding them.

Wait till they float to the top, then gently turn them over.

Fry for a couple of minutes until they are golden brown.

Drain on kitchen paper.

Serve with pita bread, tahini sauce and pickles.

7

GIVING UP

The class filed back in, a little more orderly this time, with no chairs knocked over, although I noticed the moon-faced boy attempting to trip the girl in the *hijab*. It was only when they were seated once more that I saw a flaw in my plan to separate them. More than three-quarters of the class were boys. I gave up with the seating plan.

"Good morning, everybody," I began, standing at the front in the only tiny space available in the room. Thanks to the Worm, I had no class list, so I had to improvise.

"My name is Miss Vicky. Please call me 'Miss Vicky', not 'Miss', and I shall attempt to take your names, one by one."

I turned to the cheeky boy, who was now sitting in the front row.

"What is your name?"

"Mees? My name is Mohammed, Mees."

I wrote it down and looked at the next boy. "Name, please?"

"Mohammed, Mees."

"Hmm... Two Mohammeds in this class? And you?" I asked a third boy.

"Mees, Mohammed, Mees."

This was getting ridiculous. Three Mohammeds?

"Okay," I said, "how many Mohammeds do we have in this room?"

A forest of hands were raised. I should have asked who *wasn't* called Mohammed. I tried asking for their second names, but the strange words and spellings just confused me further. The children were becoming bored and fidgety. I gave up with the class list.

"Mees, where are our schedules, Mees?" asked the cheeky boy. "Where do we go next lesson?"

"Er, they're just being finished." I said. "You'll be getting them soon. And please call me 'Miss Vicky', not 'Mees'."

"Sorry, Mees."

"Mees, what you want us to do, Mees?"

I sighed and gave up with the 'Mees'.

"Right!" I said brightly. "I'm going to tell you four things about myself, and then I want each of you to tell me four things about yourselves. Okay?"

"Yes, Mees."

"Number #1. My name is Miss Vicky, and this is my first year at ASS."

"Where ALL STUDENTS SUCCEED!" shouted the class, making me jump.

"Number #2. My husband teaches Physics and Maths in the High School."

"Mees? Does he, Mees? He might teach my brother!" said a girl.

"Oh, really? What's your brother's name?" Silly question.

"Mohammed, Mees."

"Number #3. I'm British, but I live in a little village in Spain."

"Mees! Spain won the World Cup, Mees!"

"Yes, I know, I was there at the time."

"Mees? Which football team do you support, Mees?"

I opened my mouth to answer, but the class had dissolved into a shouting match, each boy yelling out the team he supported, and leaning over to punch any boy within range who didn't agree.

"Mees! Liverpool is the greatest!"

"Mees! Mees! Manchester United!"

"No, Mees! Arsenal!"

"Mees! Chelsea!"

GIVING UP

It seemed that Arabic kids knew more about English football than I did. I was just trying to regain order, when a pale face appeared briefly at the little window in my classroom door. It was female, black-veiled, and I guessed belonged to the shadowy figure I had seen earlier in the corridor. Who was she?

"Number #4. My hobbies are reading and writing and I love animals."

Hoots of derision from the class.

"Mees? Reading and writing is boring, Mees!"

"Mees? Why you like animals, Mees? Animals are dirty!"

"Animals are ugly, Mees!"

I gaped at them. Perhaps I hadn't heard right.

"Don't you have pets?" I asked.

"No, Mees!"

"Not even camels?"

"No, Mees!"

"My father and my uncle have falcons, Mees. But they're not pets."

I gave up on animals. In desperation, I hit on a sure-fire subject, one that I knew was of interest, one that my pupils in England adored talking about.

"What is your favourite food?" I asked.

"Mees," said a sweet-faced girl patiently, "it's Ramadan. We don't talk about food in Ramadan."

Again, I gave up. Enough class discussion, I

would quieten them down by getting them to write.

"Okay, I want you to get out paper and pens. Write your name at the top of the paper, then write four good sentences about yourselves."

"Mees, we didn't bring paper and pens today."

"Why not?"

"We never do anything on the first day of term. Not many kids come to school because of Ramadan."

Mentally I threw in the towel yet again. Luckily, the bell rang, and my charges departed, only to be replaced by another batch of rowdy Mohammeds. I fervently hoped that Joe was faring better.

After nearly four hours of solid 'teaching', without so much as a sip of water, I closed the classroom door behind the last Mohammed. My voice, unaccustomed to such heavy usage, had deteriorated into a rasping croak. I had an hour before my next lesson, valuable time to prepare for tomorrow. Then I had to attend a meeting where all the Grade 6 teachers would meet each other. Finally, back to the hotel.

I sighed and tried not to think of our home in

the village of El Hoyo, where the only people I met were villagers, where I could eat and drink what I pleased, and nobody was called Mohammed.

I was just straightening the desks, when somebody tapped on the door.

"Come in!" I rasped.

The door opened, and a black-robed figure swept in. I recognised it immediately. It was the shadowy figure I had seen in the corridor, when I had sent my first class out. I examined her face, and was certain that it was the same face I had seen peering into my classroom.

"Can I help?" I asked.

"Miss Vicky? I am Fatima's mother."

"Oh, hello, I'm very pleased to meet you."

I smiled and offered my hand but quickly dropped it when she made no move to reciprocate. Her hands remained hidden in the flowing folds of her *abaya*. This lady had a pale, waxy complexion, her face framed by a black *hijab*. Her narrow, colourless eyes drilled into mine. Her voice was accented, but she spoke English well.

"I'm so sorry," I began, "I'm not sure which one is your daughter. I met three classes for the first time today."

"Fatima was in your first class. She is an exceptional student." The pale eyelids twitched.

"Well, I look forward to getting to know her," I said. "But the class lists haven't been finalised yet. Mr. Wayne may be teaching her, not me."

"No, I have spoken with the school's owner, Mrs. Sherazi, and also Mr. Brewster. They have both promised me that *you* will be teaching Fatima."

"Oh."

Was this a compliment? I wasn't quite sure, but I felt most uncomfortable.

"Fatima's education is extremely important, and English, in my opinion, is the most important subject."

"Er, yes, English is very important."

"So I came here to introduce myself, and to let you know that you have my full support in giving Fatima the best education possible."

"Er, thank you."

"One more thing," she said, her cold eyes boring into me. "Please do not call my daughter a wildebeest *ever* again."

She bowed briefly and swept out of the room, not allowing me to explain that I hadn't exactly called her daughter a wildebeest.

The words Fatima's mother had uttered weren't threatening, but I was left with the distinct impression that I was being warned. I shook my head to clear it. I didn't have the time to worry about a parent just now.

GIVING UP

Somehow I got through the last class, and headed to the Geography room for the meeting. The Arabic teacher sat in her upholstered teacher chair, her hands folded in her lap, while the rest of us sat at the students' desks.

"You meet Fatima's mother already?" whispered Hawa, rolling her eyes.

"Yes. I wasn't sure what to make of her."

"Tha' woman! Everybody has heard of tha' woman!" All the little butterflies pinned to her *hijab* trembled in sympathy as she spoke. "Tha' woman, she make life miserable for all the teachers in the Elementary school las' year. Me, I not let her bully me!"

I believed her. The clenched fists and grim look of determination didn't fit with the delicate, exotic butterflies dancing around her head, but I sensed a huge inner strength, and began to understand why she described herself as 'the *meanest* teacher'.

Mr. Brewster entered at that point, and the meeting began. All the Grade 6 teachers were present and we introduced ourselves to each other. I already knew Hawa, and had shaken hands with the Arabic Geography teacher. I also knew young Mohammed, the Science teacher, who was a quiet, gentle, bespectacled young man from Lebanon. He rarely spoke, and telephoned his father every evening. Like many of the new staff, this was his first teaching job, and the first time he had left his own country. I knew he was sharing a hotel suite with Brent, the strange TOK teacher, and wondered how compatible they were.

My eyes searched the room. It was Mr. Wayne that interested me most, because he was the only other Grade 6 English teacher. I assumed we would be working as a team.

"The only person missing is Mr. Wayne," said Mr. Brewster, looking around. "Ah, here he is!"

Wayne's athletic outline filled the doorway. Very tall, he was an African American, like Mr. Brewster. He was thirty-something, with the physique of a weight-lifter, but it wasn't his bulk that was remarkable. It was the multi-coloured clothes he wore. It started from his feet, encased in yellow, patent leather shoes with black stitching, went up to faded jeans (with designer slashes), continued with a purple shirt under an orange cardigan, and was topped off by a lime green felt hat. His style definitely made a statement, although I wasn't sure what statement it made. So this was the other member of my team?

"Cool!" breathed Wayne.

"Wayne, welcome!" said Mr. Brewster, clapping him affectionately on the back. "Take a seat. We've heard a lot about you. Welcome to ASS!"

"Where ALL STUDENTS SUCCEED," chanted the other teachers without much enthusiasm.

GIVING UP

Mr. Brewster waxed lyrical, describing Wayne's many talents as described by his former employer. I listened carefully, but it seemed that Wayne hadn't actually been a schoolteacher before. Oh well, it had been a long time since I'd been in a classroom too, so probably we were on the same level.

"Mr. Brewster, he don' like women very much," whispered Hawa from behind her hand. "I been here many, *many* year, and he not listen to women! He only make best friend with the men! You see!"

"Is Mr. Brewster married?" I asked from the corner of my mouth.

"Yes! He choose a wife las' year from village in Thailand."

That surprised me.

The meeting wound up, and I tried to chat with my team member, before I caught the bus, but didn't make much headway. Wayne was leaning back in his chair, long legs stretched out, chin resting on his chest, absorbed with texting on his mobile. I stepped over his legs and sat in the vacant chair beside him.

"Hi! We should have a chat about what books and stuff we're doing this year," I said.

"Cool..." he purred, but didn't look up.

For the hundredth time that day, I gave up, and made my way back to the waiting school bus, via the clocking-in machine. I caught sight of Fatima's mother hovering around the admin block and gave her a brief smile, which wasn't returned. It had been a very long day, and it hadn't finished yet...

MEJEDDARAH

"Mejeddarah is a humble pleasure of a dish, consisting of fragrant basmati rice, brown lentils and masses of fried onions gently spiced with cumin and black pepper. In our family, we serve it with a chunky tomato and cucumber salad and thick, creamy yoghurt," writes Nadia. "It's really important for this dish that you have a good heavy-bottomed pan with a tightly fitting lid, otherwise the rice and lentils will burn and there will be no saving them!"

Ingredients (Serves 4)

125g (4½oz) brown lentils, washed

2 onions, peeled and chopped

4 onions, peeled and sliced

1 tsp each of ground cumin and ground cinnamon

Plenty of salt and black pepper

6-7 tbsp olive oil.

150g (5½oz) basmati rice

A pinch of granulated sugar

Method

Place the lentils in 250ml (9 fl oz) of water, bring to the boil, then turn down the heat.

Cook until almost tender and the water has been absorbed: about 20-30 minutes. Add more water if they begin to dry out.

Meanwhile, gently fry the chopped onions and spices, with ½ tsp black pepper, in 2 tbsp olive oil.

When the onions are a deep golden brown, mix with the rice and add some salt and pepper.

Add the rice and onion mixture to the cooked lentils, adding water until it is 1cm (½ inch) above the top of the rice. Check the seasoning, then cover with a tight-fitting lid.

Cook on a very low heat for about 15 minutes, until small holes appear in the rice surface.

Meanwhile, in a large frying pan, Heat 4-5 tbsp olive oil.

Fry the sliced onions for a few minutes, then reduce the heat a little.

Sprinkle the onions with sugar and cook until they are dark brown.

Turn the rice and lentils into a bowl and top with the fried onions.

8
ADJUSTING

Joe was already on the bus, looking haggard. I slipped into the seat beside him.

The bus was unusually quiet, all the teachers looking exhausted and more than a little shell-shocked. Jasim started the engine and drew away from the school, homeward bound.

A few blocks from the school, some roadworks were underway. Indian workers were paving the sidewalk with red bricks, and a No Entry rope was stretched across the road. Jasim ignored it, driving through and snapping the barrier as the workers leaped aside in alarm.

"How was your day?" I asked Joe at last.

"Diabolical."

"Oh dear, why?"

"Well, the schedule isn't finished yet, so I was

given a class to look after. About twenty of them. None had any books or paper or anything."

"Ah, that's exactly what happened to me!"

"Miss Daryna said that we were supposed to start teaching right away. But the students I was given were all different ages, ranging from 14 to 19. Only two of them were doing Physics."

"So what did you do?"

"Well, first I had a chat with them. Then some got out their Blackberrys and sent texts to their friends. Some just sat around, playing cards or listening to music on their iPods. I just let them get on with it. Luckily I had my Ibsen Plays with me so I sat and read."

"So what was the problem?"

"Well, you know how immersed I get when I'm reading?"

"Yes..."

"I didn't notice the class go all quiet. Miss Daryna must have been passing and heard the noise. Anyway, she came in and bawled at them. She said playing cards wasn't allowed, and they weren't supposed to have iPods or Blackberrys in the classroom. She said I should be teaching them, but how could I?"

"Did the kids behave after that?"

"As if!" Joe snorted. He scratched his nethers. "Some of them escaped, I don't know where they went. The rest just carried on playing cards and stuff."

"And the rest of the day?"

"All the same. The students just wandered around doing whatever they liked. Sometimes, when some escaped, the Hall Monitors brought them back, but they soon slipped out again. Miss Daryna came back in once, and I didn't even notice. She confiscated their playing cards and stuck them right under my nose. Gave me a shock, because I was so immersed in Ibsen."

I laughed. "Well, let's look on the Internet tonight. We should be able to find some general knowledge quizzes or something to occupy them tomorrow."

"The whole thing is just *chaos*," said Joe, giving himself another hearty scratch. "You can't run a school without a timetable. I honestly don't know if I'm going to last the course. The thought of the months ahead makes me want to book the next flight back to Spain."

Judging by the snippets of other conversations on the bus, everybody had had a bad day. And they all blamed one person for the absence of a schedule. The Principal, Miss Daryna. I'd been sworn to secrecy about the evil Worm, so I couldn't defend her.

"This wasn't what I was expecting at all," Joe grumbled, and lapsed into silence.

I knew what he was thinking about, and so was I. I pictured our garden in Spain. Swallows swooping and wheeling in the sky, cicadas chirruping busily in our grapevine. Village cats with their new litters of kittens would be hiding from the heat, coming out to play and hunt in the cool of the evening. Our neighbours, the Ufartes, dancing flamenco in the street. And we'd given all that up for this? Was it really worth it?

Jasim dropped us off at the hotel, and I marched past Toothy and headed straight for Daryna's room. I wanted to know if the schedule problem had been fixed.

"Come in!" she called when I knocked on her door. "How has your day been?"

I told her the condensed version and she sympathised.

"I'm afraid the Worm has gone underground," she said. "He's refusing to communicate at all now, and we're no nearer to completing a schedule. I've spent all day trying to get the teachers to teach something, anything! The students aren't stupid, they know the school isn't running properly. Did you know the last Principal let them run wild? There used to be fights and stampedes in the corridor! Honestly, they were allowed to do as they pleased. I've promised Mrs. Sherazi that I'm going to crack down. She wants me to stop the students wandering around the

ADJUSTING

school, or playing cards, or listening to music when they should be learning."

I didn't mention Joe's tale of woe. Secretly I wondered how successful she would be with improving discipline in the school.

Daryna laughed. "Never mind," she said brightly, "I don't mind being the ogre. That's my job and it's what I'm paid for."

I certainly didn't envy her the job.

"Anyway," she went on, "I didn't tell you about my shopping yesterday. I was just picking up a few things from the supermarket last night, and guess who popped up and gave me a hand?"

"No idea..."

"That nice Barry. He carried the shopping bags all the way to my room, which was very kind of him. The trouble was, I couldn't get rid of him afterwards, he just wouldn't go."

Hali-Barry? I remembered what the other female teachers had said about Hali-Barry, and how they disliked his attentions. Perhaps Hali-Barry was trying his luck with the Principal?

The Worm never surfaced, and we lurched through the remainder of August and the first week of September without a schedule.

My team member, the colourful Wayne, asked

me for ideas to occupy our classes until a structured timetable was in place, so I shared the resources and worksheets I had created. The Gin Twins had sent me a wonderful parcel of workbooks from England, exercises on punctuation, grammar and creative writing, which probably saved my sanity. I tore the staples out of the workbooks and took them up to the photocopying room, a few at a time.

"Leave them there," said the grim-faced Indian who operated the giant photocopying machines. "When do you want them?"

"For tomorrow, please."

The next day, I went up to collect them, but was disappointed.

"Sorry, sorry," said the Indian, not looking apologetic at all. "They're not done yet."

So I ran back down the stairs, desperately thinking what tasks I could set my classes that day. This happened every day and having anything photocopied seemed an almost impossible dream.

One hot, airless day I was sitting in Smokers' Corner, the only place where we could escape the oppressive building. I liked the regular group that congregated there. It was an assortment of male Arabic staff, Colton, Rashida and young Mohammed from Lebanon. Even Jasim, the bus driver, would sometimes come and sit for a while.

The folk there always made me laugh and helped me forget my troubles. It was also the best place to garner gossip. Some smoked, some didn't, but I always felt I was amongst friends.

Joe was there and we'd been laughing hysterically at Colton's latest tale about his hometown, Boise. The story involved the Boise River, an inflated tractor tyre and a girl with a glass eye.

"Hey, how's it going in the Middle School?" asked Colton, when we'd all stopped laughing.

"Terrible!" I said. "It's bad enough killing time because we can't do anything without a schedule. And I'm sick of not being able to get any photocopying done. I take my stuff up there, and he never does it. And that photocopying man is so grumpy!"

"Hey, d'ya have some that needs doin' right now?" asked Colton. "Give 'em to me."

I pulled some sheets out of my bag and handed them over.

"I need 120 of those. It's a lot, I know, but I always do some for Wayne's classes, too. I don't think you'll have any luck though. There were piles of stuff waiting to be photocopied when I went up just now."

Colton just smiled and walked away. To my astonishment, he returned ten minutes later, with all my photocopying completed.

"How did you do that?" Joe and I asked, astonished.

"Hey, it was easy!" said Colton. "I just slipped him some *baksheesh*. 1BD does the trick every time."

It had never occurred to me to tip the photocopying man. The next time I went up, I tucked a 1BD note, just visible, under the top sheet. It had an instant effect.

"Thank you, Miss," he said, grinning so broadly I thought the top of his head might come off. "You wait here, I do them now."

It worked like a dream and I never had to wait for photocopying again. The photocopying man's face lit up whenever he saw me approaching, as though I was his most beloved aunt.

Ramadan stretched ahead, and I often looked longingly at the padlocked canteen doors and the empty cold-water dispenser in the staffroom.

Mr. Brewster called the occasional meeting, although there wasn't much to discuss. Until we were allocated our permanent classes, we were all merely marking time. But these meetings held another source of annoyance for me.

"I'd like to congratulate all of you for coping so well," said Mr. Brewster. "Particularly Wayne, who has produced all kinds of English worksheets for his classes. He is an example to us all."

Inwardly I seethed, but said nothing.

ADJUSTING

Mr. Brewster also had the unfortunate habit of talking for far too long about very little, making chopping motions with his hands to emphasise each point, and constantly repeating himself. Although I liked him, I found it hard to concentrate, especially after a long day in the classroom, and without any refreshment.

Worse still, he often made the Middle School teachers late for Jasim's bus, and the other passengers were forced to wait until he closed our meeting. Joe and I devised a plan. Joe would call my mobile phone if we were late, and I would look up and say, "I'm sorry, the bus is waiting for us."

Then Hawa and I, and all the teachers who took the bus, would stand up en masse and leave. That cured the late meetings as well as the impatience of our fellow passengers who had been kept waiting.

There were fewer regular passengers on the bus now. Jake, Colton, Emily and Allison hired a car, which they shared, and we missed their nonsense on the bus. Daryna caught a separate bus, probably wisely, as conversation often centred around her latest rule enforcements. This left a hardcore of passengers: the awfully strange Brent, Hali-Barry, Texan Andrea, her exquisite roommate, Saja, quiet, young Mohammed, Hawa,

Ibekwe from Ghana, Joe, myself and sometimes a few others.

Andrea was feisty and streetwise, and although she'd never taught before, was full of confidence. By contrast, her roommate, Saja, was a tiny, delicate Iraqi girl, gentle, quiet and friendly. She had moved to America with her family when she was very young but still understood and spoke Arabic fluently. Students were supposed only to speak English at school but, understandably, reverted to their native tongue whenever possible.

Saja enjoyed an immense advantage over the rest of us in understanding Arabic. Her students didn't know she could understand them, and were probably horrified when they found out.

Andrea's story was also interesting. She'd met and fallen for an Arab in Texas, and had applied for the job at ASS to be near him when he returned to his home in Bahrain. Her Arab boyfriend was a wealthy Sunni who lived in a luxury compound with his extended family. We, however, felt sure there was no future in their relationship, and she probably did, too. We guessed he was already betrothed to a cousin, a common Arabic practice that keeps the money in the family. We could see her boyfriend's family compound from our hotel window. However, although he lived so close, we never met him, and

ADJUSTING

heard that he refused even to be seen out with her. Perhaps their cultural differences meant he shouldn't be seen with a Westerner? Instead, he visited her secretly, often very late at night.

Every week we were told that our new apartments were almost ready to move into. But six weeks later, we were still residents of the hotel. I didn't mind. Our rooms were cleaned, and the sheets and towels changed daily. In my whole life I had never had so few chores. And no bills! Apart from food and mobile phone bills, everything was paid for. Were we grateful? Yes. But were we happy? I'm afraid not.

Anyone working in a Middle Eastern country for the first time is bound to suffer from culture shock. But when you come out of retirement, and your home has been a tiny Spanish village, it's very hard. We weren't accustomed to being surrounded by so many people, as our village has only a handful of permanent residents.

Although we lorded it in a hotel suite, we had no outside space, apart from the rooftop pool. We missed our garden and the ability to sit outside or stroll around the village. Being outside for long in the Bahraini summer was impossible as the heat sapped our strength and the sun scalded our skin.

But most of all, Joe and I missed the wildlife. We'd seen no animals and no birds, except for some exhausted-looking pigeons and a few seagulls. Surprisingly, there were no flies, but there were no other insects to be seen either, not even an ant. Jake and Emily visited the Bahraini Zoo and were astounded to see one of the exhibits, a dog in a cage, with a sign proclaiming 'Domestic Dog'.

Any waste ground was just an expanse of sand. No weed had the strength to survive in such dry, barren conditions. Neither did any weed dare to poke its head out from between the cracks in the red-bricked sidewalks. (Colton informed us that the reason every pavement was identical was because one of the King's relations had secured the contract.) We saw no trees, apart from ornamental ones, carefully tended by servants.

And then there were the strange customs and rules. I was terrified of making a silly mistake, like passing something using my left hand, or inadvertently showing the soles of my feet. I already knew that my clothes were not really suitable. Either they were too hot, or the sleeves were too short, revealing too much arm. I promised myself, as soon as Ramadan was over, to go clothes shopping.

SPICED LAMB AND DATE TAGINE

Although this fabulous recipe is best cooked in a traditional tagine or other clay dish, like the Spanish *cazuela*, it may also be prepared in a heavy-based pan.

Ingredients (Serves 4)

1kg (2¼lb) leg of lamb

A dollop of butter

2 tbsp olive oil

1 medium onion, peeled and thinly sliced

2 tsp each of ground cinnamon and ground ginger

500ml (18 fl oz) water

3 tbsp chopped dates

Salt and black pepper

2 tbsp runny honey

2 tbsp lemon juice

To serve:

8 fresh dates, stoned

55g (2oz) whole shelled almonds, toasted

1 tbsp sesame seeds, toasted

Method

Cut the lamb into even cubes of about 4cm (1½ inches) or ask your friendly butcher to do it for you.

Melt the butter and oil together in a tagine, *cazuela* or heavy-based pan. Seal the meat on all sides.

Add the onions, cooking them really slowly, until translucent.

Add the spices and stir until their aroma is released.

Add the water and chopped dates.

Season well, cover and allow to cook for 1-1½ hours until the meat is soft. (If you are using a *cazuela*, use aluminium foil to create a lid.)

To finish, stir in the honey and lemon juice.

Scatter on the fresh dates and sprinkle on the toasted almonds and sesame seeds.

Serve with crusty bread to mop up the juices.

9

CRAZY TEACHERS

Smokers' Corner was a sanctuary, a place to hide away from the hustle and bustle of the main school building. However, it wasn't always peaceful.

The school was in the midst of several surrounding mosques and the call to prayer regularly filled the air. In the building, the walls muffled the sound, but at Smokers' Corner it was a different story. First one, closely followed by another two, so loud that we couldn't speak until all three had finished. They were always live, never recorded, and they seemed to compete with each other. Sometimes one of the chanting elders would dissolve into a coughing fit, and Joe and I avoided looking at each other, afraid we might laugh and look disrespectful.

The Arab staff who frequented Smokers' Corner were equally noisy. They loved to bawl politics at each other or discuss English soccer. Saeed, in charge of maintenance and stationery, suffered from a serious stutter and usually sat, quietly smoking, not joining in with the conversation. But sometimes his face would flush, his fists would ball, and one foot would begin tapping. Suddenly, he would leap up and lean over Yussef, or Essam, or Jasim, his cheeks inflated, as he tried to force the words past his stutter.

The first time Joe and I witnessed an argument, the red faces and clenched fists, we honestly thought they were all going to come to blows. The 'fights' were always in Arabic and we understood nothing. It was only when we listened carefully that we realised what the topic of the argument was centred around.

Saeed: Arabic-Arabic(stutter)Arabic

Yussef: Arabic

Essam: Arabic

Saeed: Arabic...**M-M-M-Manchester United!**

Even quiet, young Mohammed, his spectacles flashing as he became animated, was drawn into these 'fights', which dissolved as quickly as they erupted.

Saeed loved to fight physically, too, or at least demonstrate his strength. He adored Jake, but had a strange way of showing it. Whenever he encountered him, whether at Smokers' Corner or in a school corridor, his eyes would light up and he'd hold out his hand for shaking. But this was no gentle hand-shake. Instead, Saeed would seize Jake's hand in a vice-like grip and twist his arm behind his back. Jake played along at first, and it became a contest. Saeed never said a word, and his expression never changed, apart from a twinkle of pleasure in his eyes as he wrestled Jake to the ground.

As time went on, the well-meaning assaults became more violent. Jake began to avoid Saeed, sending students to the stationery office on his behalf, unwilling to risk serious injury.

But perhaps the loudest, most strident person at Smokers' Corner was Rashida, the Lebanese Algebra teacher. Rashida used the five-minute break between lessons to smoke half a cigarette, hide the other half in a groove in the wall, and then hurry back to her class. During her free periods, she would often fall asleep in Smokers' Corner, and we tried in vain to conduct conversations over the noise of her steady snoring. She was not popular for many reasons, the main one being her miserliness, which was legendary.

"I have forget my cigarettes," she would whine, looking imploringly at the smokers, until somebody gave her one, usually Colton. I could see into her bag, and knew she was not telling the truth.

Saeed needed to collect 50 fils (about 85p or 1$) from each of us as a deposit for our keys.

"You not want 50 fils from little me?" wheedled Rashida, wearing her most winning smile.

"Everybody must g-g-g..."

"Get 50 fils?" Joe helpfully suggested.

"No, g-g-g..."

"Give you 50 fils?" I tried.

"No, everybody must g-g-g-go to the auditorium for a meeting with Miss Daryna after school. Rashida, please give me 50 fils."

Rashida nipped off the end of her cigarette, surreptitiously hid it in the wall, and marched away, a determined look on her face. I happened to be there, with Saeed, when she returned later in the afternoon.

"Here! I have for you the 50 fils," she said, and dropped a handful of coins into his outstretched palm.

"Th-th-th..."

"Thank you?" I suggested.

"No, th-th-th-that's a miracle," he said and even Rashida smiled.

Rashida smoked her half-cigarette and strode away, to be replaced by Joe and Colton.

"That Rashida!" complained Colton, "She's just asked me if I can spare some some small change for a phone call."

"That's strange. She just asked me, too," said Joe.

"And me," said Essam.

It seemed that everybody had contributed toward Rashida's key deposit, except Rashida.

Rashida was in her late 50s and had left her husband back in Lebanon, attracted by better wages in Bahrain. She called him daily and her booming voice, like the prayer chants, halted all conversation in Smokers' Corner.

"Hey, were you having a fight?" Colton asked, when she'd concluded a particularly loud and aggressive-sounding call.

Rashida frowned. "No," she said, shaking her head. "I just suggest to my husband what he make for his dinner today."

Rashida was mannish, and rather unkempt. She wore her hair scraped back, and her make-up must have been applied in the dark with a spade. Her English was quite good, but her taste in Western clothes was questionable. Somehow she poured her ample backside into trousers much too small for her and would plonk herself in a chair, knees wide apart. She also had the disconcerting habit of standing up, bending from the waist, and digging into her bag on the ground. For maybe a minute, somebody, usually Joe, would have Rashida's huge bottom blocking out the light, inches from his nose, while she rummaged.

"Somebody tell me you write a book?" she once asked me.

"Yes," I said, not elaborating.

"Chickens," she said. "You write about chickens?"

"Well, not exactly... It's about our life in Sp..."

"You give me book?"

"Er..."

Because I'd only brought two copies of my first book, *Chickens*, with me to Bahrain, I couldn't hand them out freely to anybody who asked.

"Good. You bring me book tomorrow."

I hoped that she'd forget but she nagged me about it every day until I was forced to hand over a copy. I forgot all about it until a week later, when I was astonished to find a Middle School teacher reading my book.

"Where did you get that from, if you don't mind me asking?" I said, but I'd already guessed.

"Oh, Rashida from the High School sold it to me."

Rashida loved to talk, and she always assumed I wanted to chat about chickens.

BEAUTIFUL BEETROOT DIP

When the purple of the beetroot is puréed with the tahini and lemon juice, this dip is transformed into an almost neon pink. Try this with white fish, chicken or even in a cheese sandwich.

Ingredients (Serves 6-8)

3 large beetroot, cooked

1 tsp salt

2 garlic cloves, peeled and crushed (optional)

60ml (2 fl oz) lemon juice

125ml (4 fl oz) tahini

55ml (2 fl oz) warm water

Method

Mash the beetroot to a purée, or leave a bit more texture (your choice).

In a separate bowl, add the salt, garlic, lemon juice, tahini and water.

Mix until smooth and creamy.

Add more water if the tahini becomes sticky, and keep stirring.

Stir in the beetroot.

Serve with warm pita bread, or crisp Cos lettuce leaves, to dip and scoop.

10

BENNIGANS

"I hate this place!" Joe wailed, his elbows resting on the table, his head buried in his hands.

We were still living in the hotel but I knew it wasn't the accommodation that was troubling him.

"I can't teach Maths and Physics with half-classes and classes that keep changing all the time. When are they going to sort this schedule out? Every day it's a fight with the kids and Miss Daryna. Doesn't she realise how hard it is to teach when you don't have a syllabus? If ever I get hold of that Worm, I'm going to grind it into the sand with my heel."

"Cheer up," I said. "Ramadan is nearly over. Then we've got a week off, and by the time school starts again, it will probably all be sorted. Life won't be so bad then."

By now we were into the second week of September. The sun was still fierce, but we were growing accustomed to it. Often the air above the city was hazy, filled with pollution and sand, blurring the silhouettes of the domed mosques and skyscrapers.

There was an atmosphere of suspense. Everybody seemed to be marking time, waiting. The ninth month of the Islamic calendar, Ramadan, was drawing to a close. The fasting from dawn to sunset would soon cease, the shops would open during the day, and celebrations would begin.

My students told me that, during Ramadan, they were all expected to read the Quran through at least once. Every day they rose just before dawn to eat *suhoor*, the last thing to pass their lips until sundown. They couldn't wait for the end of Ramadan and *Eid-al-Fitr*, the 'Festival of breaking of the Fast', to begin, and neither could I.

But first we had to wait for the Islamic elders to declare the crescent moon visible.

I parted the curtains, trying to spot the moon through the pollution haze. I remembered nights when Joe and I had gazed up at the clear night sky in Spain, and marvelled at the billion stars glittering above. Was this moon, that the Islamic clerics were currently studying so carefully, the same friendly moon that hung above El Hoyo? It was hard to believe.

I dropped the heavy curtain and walked over to Joe. I sat beside him and put my arm around his shoulders.

"It's not just the chaos at school," he said. "I'm so miserable that I've put you through this. I've dragged you out here, and for what? Money, I know, but was it worth it? If I could just whisk ourselves back to Spain, I would. Right now."

"It's not so bad…"

"It is! And I have it easy compared with you. You have class after class, it's relentless! You have to prepare lessons for yourself as well as that idiot, Wayne. You get no recognition for it and you don't even have time to write!"

A hammering on the door made us both jump and our thoughts were pushed aside.

"Come in, it's open!" I called, thinking it was Colton or Jake.

The door opened, and Toothy sprang into the room.

"*Eid mubarak!*" he cried and stretched his hand out toward Joe.

"That means 'Happy *Eid*'," I said. "Ramadan must be over! He's waiting for a tip."

Joe rummaged in his pocket and handed Toothy a couple of BD. Toothy bowed himself out of the room, and Joe and I looked at each other, our faces wreathed in smiles.

"No school for a week!" said Joe, and we danced around the room.

Then the door crashed open, and this time it really was Colton and Jake.

"Hey! Have you heard? Ramadan's finished!"

"Fancy celebrating?" asked Colton. "You know that place behind the hotel, Bennigan's? It's an Irish pub, and it's OPEN!"

We couldn't have vacated the room faster if we'd been chased by a herd of rabid camels.

The bus passed Bennigan's every day, but I'd never given it much thought, as it was shuttered up during Ramadan. Now a green neon light was flashing a welcome and the doors were open. The four of us skipped in.

I'd be lying if I said that Bennigan's was exactly like an Irish pub. It wasn't. The building did not remotely resemble an Irish pub, but we liked it. Big green cutouts of shamrocks were pasted in odd places, and a television was mounted on almost every wall.

Judging by the hubbub, the other customers were mostly from the American Naval Base, although there were also several Arabs. Bennigan's staff were not Irish, but Filipino, and utterly charming. They learned our names that first evening, and never forgot them.

"Sir Joe, wha' you like to drink?"

"Oh, a beer for me, a white wine for Vicky, and whatever Jake and Colton want." Such ordinary words, but in such surreal surroundings.

Soon we had glasses lined up on the table in front of us and the party really began. We were so unused to alcohol, it went straight to our heads. Everything was hilarious.

I remember that night with huge affection. It was exactly what Joe needed and the birth of the Bennigan's Working Men's Drinking Club (BWMDC), of which I, being female, was an honorary member. It was that night that I discovered I could bark like a Jack Russell, and became known as Dogsbody. Being with Colton and Jake, so full of intelligence, nonsense and energy, was like being with two bright puppies. We loved it.

Bennigan's became our meeting house, a precious place to escape from other staff, from school, from Bahrain. If anybody wanted to join us, we'd politely chase them away. Bennigan's was ours, where we shared memories, secrets, hopes and dreams. If any of us was having a tough time or had a difficult decision to make, we'd call an Extraordinary BWMDC Meeting at Bennigan's and all four of us would be there.

The next morning, we had the luxury of staying in bed because there was no school. I carefully opened my eyes. It felt as if six midgets were wrestling behind my eyeballs. Of course! *Eid* had started! Bennigan's! The formation of the BWMDC!

I opened the curtains and saw the bright lights of the stores and restaurants opposite, all open for business. I groaned. I'd promised myself to go clothes shopping after Ramadan. Now all the shops and malls were open, I had no excuse.

Hailing a taxi in Manama is easy, but choosing which mall to shop in isn't. Should I go to the Dana Mall or Marine Mall? Or the Lulu Centre near the Pearl monument? In the end, I decided on the City Centre mall, just because it was the biggest. Saeed had recommended it when I had enquired at Smokers' Corner.

"City Centre is the best. At City Centre you can get l-l-l..."

"Lots of things?"

"No, l-l-l..."

"Lovely things?"

"No, l-l-l-lost, because it is so big."

"Yes, I like City Centre the bestest," said Rashida, who had just woken herself up with an elephantine snort. "You can go to the Food Hall and try all the samples. Sometimes I go there when I do not want to cook for my own self. And I do not spend one fil!"

City Centre was everything that I'd been

promised, and more. I'd never seen such a huge, glitzy mall. The marble floors stretched away in every direction, numerous escalators rose to brightly lit upper floors, shop windows glittered with designer merchandise. Shopping here was going to be easy, wasn't it?

I'm not a city gal, and shopping fills me with dread, but I was confident that I'd find everything I wanted. I needed some outfits for school, with sleeves that covered my arms.

With Joe trailing behind me, I rifled through racks of clothes, trying to find something suitable, which turned out to be a much harder task than I'd imagined. To my surprise, everything on display was low-cut, skimpy, glittery, or a combination of all three. Rack after rack of strumpet-wear. How was that possible when Muslim ladies are dressed from head to toe in black, with only their faces (or just eyes) showing? Who buys these clothes?

We deduced something that day. Outwardly, Muslim ladies are the picture of anonymity and decorum, but underneath those veils...who knows what saucy show-girls are lurking?

The telephone rings and I pick it up. It's my son.
"Mum? Is that you? How's Bahrain?"

"Hello! Oh, it's fine. Taking a bit of time to settle in, but Bahrain is a nice place, and the Bahraini people are really friendly and helpful. Some things take a bit of getting used to, like weekends being Friday and Saturday. Hey! I thought you were on holiday with Hannah in the Seychelles?"

"Yes, we are."

"Are you having a good time?"

"Fantastic!"

"What are the Seychelles like?"

"Perfect! We're staying in a lovely place, the beaches are fabulous, the food's great. Beautiful weather. Really enjoying it."

"Oh, good!"

"Oh, and by the way... Hannah and I just got married."

"Y-you WHAT?"

"Hold on, Hannah wants a word."

I hear him pass the phone to a giggling Hannah.

"Hello, Mother-in-law!"

"Oh my G... It's not a joke then? You just got married?"

Laughter in the background. "Yep! We just didn't want any fuss, and it's like paradise here, so we just went ahead and did it!"

"Well! Congratulations!"

For once, I'm struggling to find words. I'm

delighted, but profoundly shocked. It takes a BWMDC Extraordinary Meeting before Joe and I can fully absorb the news.

How we enjoyed that week of *Eid!* The school's promise to move us into our new apartments didn't materialise, but that didn't matter to us, although poor young Mohammed was beside himself. Each day living with Brent was torture for him.

We got lazy about cooking, ordering fast food that arrived on a scooter, delivered by an Indian. We swam in the rooftop pool, unless Brent was there first, and explored our surroundings. We spent far too much time at Bennigan's, and revelled in the fact that we didn't need to rise at 5.30 in the morning.

All good things must inevitably come to a close, and Sunday, 19th September 2010 arrived much too quickly. Now we would start teaching in earnest. The schedule for the Middle School was complete, although the High School only had a makeshift timetable with which to work.

Jasim was already parked on the sand outside the hotel. We all piled onto the bus, Mohammed sitting as far from Brent as possible. Texan Andrea and her roommate, Saja, chatted, heads together.

Ibekwe, oblivious, hummed songs to himself. Jasim raised a can of Coke, glugged a mouthful, accelerated across bumpy sand and into the morning traffic.

We picked up Hawa who was already waiting outside her apartment block. Today she wore scarlet, her *hijab* embroidered with tiny pink flowers and intertwined leaves.

"Goo' morning, everybody!" she called as she settled herself.

"Morning, Hawa," we chorused, and held on tight as the bus lurched away again and joined a busy main road. I was lost in my own thoughts when Jasim, twisting the steering wheel, veered into the oncoming traffic. Some teachers closed their eyes, others, like me, gripped the handrail tighter. Joe laughed. Without slowing the bus, Jasim hurled his empty Coke can at an open trash bin on the opposite pavement, missed, shrugged, then swung the bus back into the correct traffic lane.

"Bad luck, Jasim!" Joe shouted and Jasim smiled at him, gold teeth glinting, in his rear-view mirror.

I wondered if I'd ever get used to Jasim's erratic driving.

As usual, there was a distinct lack of camels, but Mercedes, Ferraris and Range Rovers were plentiful outside the school. Today there were many more vehicles. Ramadan was over, and school was beginning in earnest. Jasim barged the bus through the traffic and pedestrians, scolding parents for blocking the main entrance.

We clocked in (black for once) and made our way into the school building. Pots of pink and red petunias had been placed around the courtyard, adding a welcome splash of colour. As the students waited outside for the first school bell to ring, I made my way to the staffroom, where Mr. Brewster was holding a hurried meeting.

SFEEHA (MIDDLE EASTERN LAMB MINI-PIZZAS)

Nadia says this is her Auntie Jamileh's recipe, with a few little added ingredients of her own. Joe and I were often served these little pizzas at staff meetings. It's a delicious lunch with a salad, and any leftovers (unlikely) may be stored in the freezer.

Ingredients (Makes 20-30)

For the topping:

350g (12oz) minced lamb

2 tsp each ground cinnamon and ground allspice

3 tbsp pine nuts, lightly fried

2 handfuls chopped fresh parsley

2 tsp pomegranate syrup (from Middle Eastern shops, online or large supermarkets)

1-2 tsp salt

1 tsp freshly ground black pepper

1 medium onion, peeled and grated

2 tomatoes, very finely chopped

4 tbsp tahini

2 tbsp lemon juice

FOR THE DOUGH:

1 tsp dried yeast, dissolved with a pinch of caster sugar.

450g (1lb) strong white bread flour.

1½ tsp fine salt.

125ml (4 fl oz) olive oil

175ml (6 fl oz) plain yoghurt

125ml (4 fl oz) warm water

Method

Place all topping materials in a bowl and mix until almost a paste. (Nadia recommends using your hands.) Place in the fridge.

Leave the yeast for 5 minutes or until it starts to bubble.

Place the flour and salt in a large bowl, making a well in the middle. Add the dissolved yeast, oil and yoghurt and mix well.

Continue kneading, (a dough hook saves a lot of work) and adding a little warm water, until the dough is smooth and elastic.

Roll the dough into a ball, place in a bowl, cover it and

leave it in a warm place for 2 hours or until the dough has doubled in size.

Punch it down and leave for another 20-30 minutes.

Preheat the oven to 230ºC / gas mark 8 / 450ºF.

On a floured surface, roll out the dough and divide it into about 30 pieces.

Roll each out into a rough circle.

Flatten a spoonful of the lamb mix onto each circle, right to the edge.

Place the sfeeha onto a baking tray and then into the oven for 20-30 minutes. The dough should still be pale.

11

CHILDREN AND CHICKENS

"Welcome back," said Mr. Brewster, looking round at us all. "Just two main points this morning. Firstly, we've had a delivery of some new overhead projectors. The little portable ones that you can link to your computers. There are not enough for everybody, so we'll have to share. I've labeled them with the names of those who are getting them. Please collect them on your way out."

I was near the projectors, and flicked my eyes over the labels. I immediately saw I hadn't been allocated one, although Wayne had. In fact, it seemed as though only the male teachers had been allotted one.

"Secondly, we've been warned that the

Ministry of Education is making a surprise inspection."

Ah! That explained the sudden appearance of the petunias outside.

"Please make sure your classrooms are in order, and that your bulletin boards are looking attractive. We can all learn a lesson from Wayne, whose boards are already looking wonderful."

I looked around for Wayne, but he wasn't in the room. The school bell shrilled and we all turned to leave.

"Oh, and please collect your class lists," shouted Mr. Brewster.

I grabbed my stack and quickly scanned them. Fatima's name jumped out at me.

"Miss Vicky!" called Mr. Brewster. "Wayne has phoned in sick. Would you mind finding some work for his classes and starting them off?"

Look after my own back-to-back classes *and* Wayne's? This was going to be a heavy day.

"You see wha' I say?" said Hawa as we hurried to our rooms. "Mr. Brewster, he like men best. I not get projector either."

A boisterous rabble of kids was rioting outside my classroom, waiting for me to open the door.

"Right, class!" I shouted above the din. "I'm going to unlock the door now, and I want you to come in *quietly*, and find a seat. You may sit where you like, just for today. Tomorrow you'll have a seating plan. I need to go and sort out Mr. Wayne's class, so you can talk quietly amongst yourselves while you wait for me."

I unlocked the door and stood back as they surged into the classroom like a tsunami. Then I ran down the corridor to speak to Wayne's class and give them some work. On my return, I heard my class long before I saw them.

I paused in the doorway, surveying the scene. One boy was wearing the wastepaper basket on his head and dancing between the desks. Another two were doodling on the whiteboard, using permanent markers. A wrestling match was taking place at the back of the room, complete with cheering spectators. My carefully pasted paper had already been torn from the windows and three boys were leaning out, bawling at others still outside in the courtyard.

Just one girl sat still and upright, in the front row, hands clasped primly in her lap. Fatima. I was just opening my mouth to yell at the class when a flinty voice beside me stopped me in my tracks.

"Miss Vicky? I was just checking that Fatima had found the correct classroom. I see she has. I sincerely hope this is not an example of your teaching methods."

Fatima's mother. Why did she always turn up at the most difficult times? I opened my mouth to explain that I'd been sorting Mr. Wayne's class, but didn't get a chance to speak.

"Fatima's education is *extremely* important. She cannot work in this kind of environment."

"I..."

"Please make sure that Fatima is given homework tonight."

Parting shot delivered, she swept away, black robes swishing with disapproval.

A flashback of Spain crowded into my mind. I saw Joe and myself on our roof terrace, a glass of Paco's wine in our hands, heads tipped back to watch a pair of eagles soaring above the mountaintops. The valley bristling with green pines, and bee-eaters chattering in the almond trees. Impatiently, I banished the memory, together with the wave of homesickness, and took a deep breath.

Ten minutes later, order in the classroom was restored. I discovered that I was already familiar with many in the class. Cheeky Mohammed, moon-faced Mohammed, the chubby girl Zainab, Ahmed, Yasir.

And Fatima.

Another boy was proving to be even cheekier and louder than Mohammed.

"Please don't interrupt when I'm speaking," I warned him. "Only one person speaks at the time in my classroom. What is your name?"

CHILDREN AND CHICKENS

"Mees, Mustafa Kamel, Mees."

I scrutinised his face to check he wasn't joking. He wasn't.

"And your name?" I smiled at a tiny girl with a long, thick plait that hung down her back. She remained staring down at her desk.

"What is your name?" I asked again.

No reply.

"Mees!" said cheeky Mohammed, "that's Huda, and she doesn't speak."

"You mean she doesn't speak English?"

Huda's fingers gripped her pencil so tightly I thought it would snap.

"No, Mees! She doesn't speak, Mees."

Great! That's all I needed. A mute in the class as well.

"Never mind," I said. "I'm sure she'll speak when she's ready."

I turned my back to write the day's vocabulary list on the board, which was a mistake. Mustafa Kamel knocked cheeky Mohammed's pencil-tin to the floor with a crash. Ahmed ripped some more paper off the window glass. Yasir made a face at Zainab and was rewarded with a slap.

Only Fatima, in the front row, was neatly copying the words into her exercise book.

"Who emptied a bottle of Tippex over my desk?" I asked, horrified at the sticky white pool beginning to congeal.

"What's Tippex, Mees?" asked Yasir.

"Tippex, White-Out, Blanco, whatever you want to call it!" I snapped.

"Mees! It was Huda, Mees!" yelled Mustafa Kamel, making the class shout with laughter.

Huda shrank even more into herself, her face expressionless, her eyes still fixed on her desk. I knew she hadn't moved. I couldn't prove it but I was pretty sure the culprit was Mustafa Kamel.

I learned a lesson that day, one that helped me through the rest of those torrid days. Every morning, before school began, I wrote the day's vocabulary list on the board. That way I needn't turn my back and I could police my pupils as they copied from the board.

"Miss," said Fatima, just before the bell rang. "You've spelt 'colour' wrong."

She was right, of course, and I was wrong. I'd automatically spelt it the British way, but as we were in an American school, I should have written 'color'. From that day on, Fatima delighted in catching me out with British/American spelling.

I had a precious free period and made my way to Smokers' Corner, hoping Joe would be there. Joe, Saeed and some others were roaring with laughter at another story Colton was relating about floating down the Boise River.

"Hey, so my buddy Tucker, he hates the cops, 'n they're on every bridge lookin' down, checkin' out if we've got beer, which ain't allowed. Well, my buddy Tucker, he just flips over onto his stomach, 'n' when we go under this bridge, he pulls his shorts down 'n' moons some at the cops."

"Did he d-d-d..." asked Saeed when the story was over.

"Do it again? Yeh! Loads of times!"

"No, did he d-d-d..."

"Drown?" suggested Joe, rather unhelpfully.

"No, did he d-d-d-drink Coors? You said the Coors factory was nearby?"

Alcohol was a subject of fascination to our Muslim friends, most of whom had never let a single drop pass their lips.

"When you take alcohol," asked Yussef, the Egyptian Information Technology teacher and father of newborn triplets in Cairo. "When you drink, how do you get home?"

Joe and Colton looked puzzled.

"Bennigan's isn't far away," said Joe.

"No, I mean, don't you fall over? I was told that your legs don't work after drinking alcohol."

The High School bell rang and, being the only Middle School teacher there, I was left alone. I got my books out to plan the next day's lessons, just as Rashida arrived. With a chipped fingernail, she retrieved her half-smoked cigarette from the groove in the wall and sat down, knees wide apart.

"How are your chickens?" she asked as usual.

"Er, I don't know," I replied. "I expect they're fine. Our neighbour in Spain is looking after them while we are away."

Rashida fumbled in her bag and brought out a small mirror and a pair of tweezers. She leaned her head back, and began plucking hairs from her chin, holding the mirror to study her work.

"You remember I tell you about our chickens? In our balcony in Beirut?" she asked, after a plucking pause.

"Oh, yes."

"My husband, he tell me that our grandson, he just loves the chickens!"

I smiled and waited for her to continue.

"My little grandson, every day he ask, 'Grandfather, Grandfather, please can we buy a husband for the chickens?' So my husband, he say, 'Yes'."

"Did he get one?"

"Oh, yes! A very, very beautiful husband for the chickens. Many, many colours. And the chickens, they love their new husband!"

"That's nice!"

CHILDREN AND CHICKENS

"No, my husband say it now a *big* problem..." Rashida plucked a few more hairs, and shook her head.

"Why?"

"The chicken husband, he have very bad attitude, very bad. Now, he not let my husband go into the balcony! He want to fight all the time."

"Oh dear..."

"The chicken husband, he love my grandson. He not start a fight with my grandson, but he hate my husband."

Memories of our feisty little cock in Spain came flooding back. Cocky had been a nightmare, and I sympathised.

"And the chicken husband, he crowls so loud! He crowls all through the day and he crowls all through the night. My husband, he not sleep, and the neighbours, they are calling him, asking if it his chicken crowling all the time."

"What did he say?"

Rashida brushed cigarette ash from her knee and chuckled.

"My husband, he tell neighbours it not his chicken. But the security man, he know we have chickens in our balcony. My husband, he say the chicken husband must go, but when he say that, my grandson, he cries, cries very much."

I could see that this was a difficult problem, and wondered how it could be resolved. I opened my mouth to speak, but Rashida had already fallen asleep, mouth wide open, hands resting on the mirror and tweezers in her lap.

On the bus home that day, I noticed that Hali-Barry was missing.

"He's bought himself a jeep," said Andrea, in her Texan drawl. "At least we won't have him breathing all over us anymore. Do you know, he asked me on a date the other day? The thought of it!"

As the days rolled by, I slowly shaped a workable routine for myself. It was exhausting, as every class produced work and homework to be assessed. Apart from planning lessons, I usually had 80 assignments to grade daily. Wayne was frequently absent, which meant extra work for me. Mr. Brewster still sang Wayne's praises at every opportunity, and I gathered that they were socialising together, out of school. But I was coping, and in spite of myself, I was growing fond of my unruly charges, even Mustafa Kamel and cheeky Mohammed.

Joe, however, was not adapting so well.

LEBANESE MINTED LIVER

Nadia says, "If you don't fancy liver and hummus, try this Lebanese recipe, which is so easy to make and has a really unique flavour. The original doesn't use wine, if you prefer you can replace it with vinegar. Be really careful not to overcook the liver, because it will absolutely ruin the dish."

Ingredients (Serves 4-6)

450g (1lb) liver, sliced (calf's or your choice)

Salt and black pepper

2 tsp olive oil

25g (1oz) butter

1 onion, peeled and thinly sliced

2 garlic cloves, peeled and chopped

125ml (4 fl oz) white wine or white wine vinegar

1½ tsp plain flour

1 tbsp dried mint, crushed

3-4 tbsp cold water

Fresh coriander, chopped

Method

Season the liver with salt and black pepper.

Heat the oil in a heavy-based frying pan, then drop in most of the butter.

Once melted, flash-fry the liver on both sides. Remove from the pan and set aside.

Add a little more butter if it needs it, then fry the garlic and onion until soft.

Now pour in the wine and let the alcohol burn off a little.

Add the flour and stir for a minute or so, then add the mint and water, letting it bubble for a few minutes.

Add the liver to the sauce, and, if necessary, add a little more water.

Allow to simmer for a few minutes until the liver is just cooked. Pierce with a sharp knife to check whether it is cooked through.

Sprinkle with a little freshly chopped coriander and serve.

12

BRENT

To Joe's frustration his schedule was still being chopped and changed. Every week different faces appeared in his classes. Worse still, the students were beginning to see through his fierce exterior and were taking advantage.

"They actually bring their breakfast to eat during my lesson," he complained. "And if I'm in the Science lab, they make tea on the Bunsen burners."

"Well, stop them!" I said.

"I can't. They're very polite, and they always make some for me, too. I haven't the heart to shout at them."

"Are they doing any work?"

"Huh! A handful, maybe, but the rest just use my lessons as a social gathering. When I do a head count, I always find twice as many kids as I should have because they invite their friends from other classes."

"It can't be that bad."

"It is. It *is* that bad. I'm telling you, Vicky, if things don't improve, I think we need to leave, go back home to Spain at Christmas. I think I'll go insane if I have to stay here. I can't teach teenagers who don't want to learn, I'm getting too old for this."

I truly sympathised. These children, whom we were supposed to be teaching, had little desire to learn. Why should they? They came from rich families with secure futures. For them, attending school was compulsory, but actual learning, getting an education, wasn't important at all.

However, we had signed contracts to work for a year. We couldn't just pull out. Rumours abounded of past teachers who simply disappeared, unable to take the stress. A little heap of keys were found on the desk, and the teacher vanished, never to be seen or heard from again.

But I felt the school had been good to us. We were well paid and provided for, even though the work was gruelling. I wasn't ready to give up.

But Joe became steadily more downhearted. Had it not been for Colton, Jake, and Bennigan's, our oasis in the desert, I think he would have booked an immediate flight home. As it was, I was determined to jolly him along, at least until Christmas.

So I was pleased when Joe made an announcement, particularly as it concerned his beloved sport, football.

"I've volunteered to help with the after-school soccer club," he said, rare, genuine pleasure in his eyes. "You know Jane, the Physical Education teacher at the High School?"

Yes, I did know Jane. American, built like an Olympic shot-putter. She was, in fact, the Athletics Director for the entire school. Her husband was a quiet, hen-pecked chap who taught PE in the Middle School.

"That's good," I said brightly, trying not to calculate the years since Joe had last played soccer. Of course, back in Spain, he'd kicked a ball round the village square with the Ufarte boys and Geronimo, but that probably didn't count. It might do him good to thunder around a proper football pitch with the High School boys soccer team. Perhaps it might cheer him up and he'd forget about booking a flight home to Spain. Unfortunately, it didn't go well.

Joe played a lot of football when he was younger and is a qualified referee. He turned up at the gymnasium, looking the part, shiny new whistle in hand. He ran on the spot, warming up, then practised a few intricate ball skills, hoping to impress the watching ASS High School 1st team with his fancy footwork.

"Your team is over there," said Jane.

But Joe was now practising his header techniques, bouncing the ball on his head and concentrating on keeping it in the air.

"MR JOE! Your team is waiting for you over there!"

"Right!" said Joe, eager to begin coaching the senior boys. He gathered up the ball and looked around.

"Over there," repeated Jane and waved a muscular arm at the far corner of the gym where a group of ten-year-old girls stood watching curiously. Joe had been given the Grade 6 girls' team.

He didn't mind. The football pitch was in the gym, it being much too hot to play outside, and the girls were enthusiastic. At the end of the session he was exhausted, but had to wait until the last child was collected by her parents. It was only then that he realised he had no money for a taxi, no phone, and nobody left to give him a ride home.

Sighing, he set out on the long trek back to the hotel. The sun beat down relentlessly, his new trainers gave him blisters, and he had brought no water.

BRENT

Of course I was oblivious to all this. Had I known about his predicament, one word to Jake or Colton would have sent them speeding out in their car to collect him. Joe finally arrived home, almost crawling. His head was as red as the Bahraini flag, his heart raced and his body shook. I believe any longer in the sun would have made him seriously ill.

"But did you enjoy the session?" I asked, much later, when he'd sufficiently recovered to tell me all about it.

"Yes," he said, "I did enjoy it. The girls were super. Apart from the walk home, the only thing I objected to was one of the parents. There was this mother, on the sidelines, all dressed in black. I could see her shaking her head at every decision I made and she watched her daughter like a hawk."

"What did the daughter look like?"

"Oh, you know, dressed like all the others, in a tracksuit with long sleeves. Nice looking girl, very determined. Wasn't wearing a *hijab*, had long, very curly hair and a pale face. I'm sorry but I don't recall her name, there were too many to remember."

He didn't need to. I knew exactly who he was describing. Joe had met Fatima - and her dreaded mother.

Unfortunately, Joe's soccer coaching experience didn't last long. He'd bitten off more than he could chew, even with the Middle School girls' team and, much to my relief, resigned.

Luckily it was a Thursday evening, the beginning of the week-end. A visit to Bennigan's would revive his spirits. A raucous BWMDC meeting, followed by some rest, saw Joe well on the road to recovery. By Sunday, the start of the new week, he was almost his miserable old self again.

Daryna, on the other hand, was struggling with demons of her own.

"So many problems!" she confided. "I've fallen out big-time with the Three Fat Ladies and I'm getting really negative responses from all the teachers about my new rules."

Of course I already knew about all the ructions at the High School through Joe, Colton and Jake. The new rules were a frequent topic of hilarity at our Bennigan's meetings. The latest was The Coffee War. Mrs. Sherazi, the owner, had informed Daryna that members of staff were no longer permitted to drink coffee in the classrooms.

"Personally, I don't care if they drink coffee or not," said Daryna. "But if it's what Mrs. Sherazi wants, well, she's the boss..."

Mr. Brewster had issued the same edict but the Middle School staff simply continued with their coffee habits, but furtively. Most of the High School staff did, too. Only one silly young teacher insisted on having a permanent mug of coffee on her desk and in full view. Not only that, but she would teach her lessons, coffee in hand, frequently taking sips. It was only a matter of time before Daryna caught her coffee-handed. Daryna reprimanded her. The young teacher complained that she was being picked on. The Three Fat Ladies sided with her and the whole matter was completely blown out of proportion.

And then there was The One-Way Rule. To reduce congestion during lesson breaks, Daryna devised a system whereby students moved in one direction along corridors and staircases. Joe, Colton and Jake had described it in great detail at Bennigan's, using ashtrays, beermats and matchsticks. Of course, they added their own personal touches with proposed traffic lights, parking bays, and no-entry signs.

In reality, the traffic police had already been appointed. Hali-Barry had assigned himself the task and loved to stand at strategic points, bawling instructions and blasting bad breath at the students. Jake had a gift for mimicry, and his arm-waving performances had the whole of Bennigan's laughing.

"What am I to do about Brent?" asked Daryna, one day. "The man's completely insane! The students and parents complain about him all the time. He loses their work, and do you know, he wastes 40 minutes every lesson just taking the register! He insists on spelling each name out loud, God only knows why... I've had to take some classes away from him. But you won't believe the latest drama!"

I was all ears. Nothing that Brent said, or did, surprised me anymore. Daryna shook her head in disbelief and launched into the latest tale.

Brent had been allocated one of the brand-new projectors. Being a 'floater', he had no classroom of his own and therefore nowhere to store it. Daryna suggested he keep it in one of her cupboards, in the Principal's office, which he did. Brent needed the projector, came to collect it, and opened the cupboard. No projector. Brent's reaction was as unpredictable as ever.

"Where's my projector?"

"I don't know, when did you last see it?" asked Daryna.

"It was in this cupboard!"

"Are you sure? Perhaps you forgot to put it away?"

"NO! It was here! I ALWAYS put it back in here!"

"Well, that's very strange..."

"Somebody has stolen it!"

"Brent, nobody has keys to this office apart from me, you and Mr. Saeed from Stationery. This room is always locked."

BRENT

"YOU took it!"

"Come on, Brent, why would I want to take your projector?"

"YOU took it!"

"Oh, for goodness sake..."

"You STOLE it!"

"Brent, I've been overseas for the past few days." This was true. Daryna had been away on school business. "How could I take your projector, even if I wanted to?"

Daryna paused in her story-telling, rolled her eyes at me and flung her arms out in disbelief, knocking over a pile of papers that fluttered to the floor.

"Did you ask Saeed in Stationery about it?" I asked, helping her pick them up.

"Oh yes, I spoke to him right away. Of course he hadn't taken it. Why would he? So off Brent goes, fuming and telling anybody that will listen how the Principal stole his projector. And then the Three Fat Ladies take up the story and spread it around. Honestly! This place!" Daryna was laughing. The whole affair was so ridiculous it was funny.

The mystery of the disappearing projector was solved a week later. Saeed had taken it upon himself to check every classroom. Another teacher (named Malaria, or Asthma, or Cholera, I don't exactly remember) had found an unattended projector and borrowed it.

"I ch-ch-ch-checked the serial number," Saeed told Daryna, "and it was B-B-B-Brent's."

Brent hadn't put it in the cupboard after all, and nobody had stolen anything. Daryna was innocent, but few people were ever aware that her name had been cleared.

Another week began and the usual crowd was waiting in the hotel foyer for the school bus. I glanced at my watch.

"Jasim's very late today," I said.

"Aw, you know what he's like," drawled Andrea. She looked tired, as though she'd not had much sleep.

"We're going to be really late," I said. "I dread to think what my class is getting up to."

I could only imagine what Mustafa Kamel and cheeky Mohammed were doing in my absence. They were hard enough to control when I was in the room, but left unsupervised... The hands on my watch ticked round, and still Jasim didn't appear.

"I'll go outside and see if he's coming," said Joe, pushing through the hotel swing doors.

"Where's Brent?" somebody asked.

We all looked round. Brent wasn't there.

"I saw him earlier," Ibekwe commented. Ibekwe, from Ghana, taught Biology, and was always the first person in the foyer waiting for the bus. "He went outside."

"No sign of the bus," said Joe, returning, accompanied by a surge of heat.

"Was Brent out there?"

"Nope."

"Bus? Bus for school? Bus gone!" said Toothy, popping up from behind the reception desk like a jack-in-the-box.

Everybody swung round to the desk.

"The bus has come and gone?"

"Are you sure?"

"We're 25 minutes late already!"

"That's ridiculous! Jasim wouldn't leave with an empty bus."

"Not empty," said Toothy, and held up one brown finger. "Not empty, one man."

Brent! Brent had boarded the bus and allowed Jasim to drive away without telling him that we were all waiting inside!

"That Brent! What a moron!"

"What was Brent thinking? Why didn't he call us?"

"What a stupid thing to do!"

"I'm not walking to school in this heat!"

The outrage was palpable.

I shook my head in disbelief and pulled out my mobile phone.

"Daryna? That idiot, Brent, has let Jasim drive

away without us. Can you send Jasim back again, please?"

We eventually arrived at school flustered and annoyed. Jasim informed us that Brent had told him to drive on and he'd assumed we'd already gone to school by other means. We clocked in, and our cards were punched in bright red ink. I sprinted to my classroom, hardly registering the shadowy figure of Fatima's mother in the corridor. I was relieved to find Mr. Brewster in the classroom doorway, overseeing my bunch of hooligans.

"I'm so sorry," I said, breathless and sweating. "The bus left without us."

"That's okay," said Mr. Brewster. "Could you pop into my office for a moment when you finish your classes? I need a word with you."

SHEIKH-AL-MAHSHI

Nadia says that this is known throughout the Arab world as 'the king of the stuffed ones'.

Ingredients (Serves 2-4)

4 small aubergines

4 green peppers

Olive oil

1 large onion, peeled and finely minced

1 large garlic clove, peeled and finely chopped

2 tbsp pine nuts

900g (2lb) minced lamb (not too finely minced)

2 tsp ground allspice

A bunch of fresh parsley, chopped

Salt and black pepper

2 tbsp tomato purée

600ml (1 pint) water (or enough to cover the vegetables)

Method

Preheat the oven to 190ºC/gas mark 5/375ºF.

Remove the leaves and make a slit down one side of the aubergines from top to bottom. (If the aubergine is curved, make the slit on the concave side.)

Scoop out the flesh, leaving a 5mm (¼ inch) shell all the way around. Discard the flesh.

Cut round the tops of the peppers, leaving 2.5cm (1 inch) uncut so that you can re-attach it. Scoop out and discard the seeds.

In a large pan, fry the aubergine and pepper shells until they begin to brown, and remove from the pan.

Add a little more oil to the pan and fry the onion and garlic until they're soft. Remove from the pan, then fry the pine nuts. Remove from the pan.

Next fry the lamb, with the spice, until it just begins to brown.

At the end, throw in a big handful of parsley and stir.

Now add the onions and garlic back, together with the pine nuts, salt, and plenty of black pepper, and mix together.

Fully stuff (without pressure) this mixture into the aubergines and peppers.

Close the lids on the peppers. and arrange the aubergines and peppers together in a shallow ovenproof dish.

Mix the tomato purée, seasoned with salt and pepper with just enough water to cover the vegetables.

Pour this over the vegetables and bake until tender, about 30 minutes. (The sauce should reduce to halfway down.)

Sprinkle with the remaining chopped parsley.

13

A HORRIBLE DAY AND SHOPPING

There wasn't time to wonder what Mr. Brewster wanted to talk about. I had my lesson to sort and, thanks to Brent, I wasn't at all prepared. I hadn't written the day's vocabulary list on the board (again, thanks to Brent) and I couldn't do it now. Turning my back on the kids for any length of time was not an option. But I needed to get the class focused as soon as possible.

"Right, class," I said. "Please get out your 'Shiloh' books and turn to the next chapter."

The class groaned.

"Mees, Shiloh is a stupid book, Mees!"

"Mees, we don't want to read about a stupid dog, Mees."

Only Fatima sat, her back ramrod-straight, book open, pen poised ready to take notes.

A HORRIBLE DAY AND SHOPPING

'Shiloh' would not have been my choice of a class text. It is about a small boy who rescues a beagle, (or 'bagel' as most of the class spelled it), and because few of them liked animals, it wasn't a popular read. I rummaged in my bag for my own copy and couldn't find it. Impatiently, I turned my bag upside down and the contents spewed out on my desk. *No time to tidy it up now,* I thought, *must get on with this lesson before they start playing up.* I ignored the mess on my desk, grabbed my copy of 'Shiloh', and began to read.

I couldn't really blame the class for not being interested in the story. It is set in West Virginia, a lush green, mountainous place, totally unlike the flat desert that is Bahrain. The text was peppered with unfamiliar American words that needed explaining.

"What does 'buckshot' mean?" asked cheeky Mohammed.

"Does anyone know?" I asked the class.

"Does it mean 'tired'?" asked Zainab.

"No...but a good try," I said. "Anybody else care to guess?"

I looked round the classroom, but even Fatima shook her head. Huda shrank into herself, terrified that I might ask her.

I always tried hard to make my lessons lively, so I seized a board-pen from the pile of junk on my desk and quickly drew a big cartoon rabbit on the whiteboard, its paws held up to crying eyes. Then I drew a shotgun, with dots to show buckshot leaving the barrel and landing on the rabbit. I used a red marker for drops of blood, knowing that kids love gore. The shotgun interested the boys hugely.

I was just calming the class again, when there was a tap on the door. Before I had the chance to call 'Come in', the door opened, and Mrs. Sherazi entered, her face fixed in an artificial smile, synthetic black hair cascading over her shoulders.

Why was the school owner visiting my classroom? I wondered.

The children fell silent, aware that something unusual was happening. Little Huda's eyes were like satellite dishes.

I opened my mouth to say 'Good Morning', but nothing came out. Mrs. Sherazi ignored me, and came deeper into the room, but not before she'd taken in the disgraceful pile of junk on my desk and the drawing of the gun and sobbing bunny on the board.

To my horror, a procession followed her: Mr. Brewster, four men in suits, three ladies in *abayas* and *hijabs*, and two men carrying photographic equipment. My classroom was so cramped, I was backed up against the window to make room for the visitors. I was painfully aware of the chaos on my desk and the drawing on the board.

A HORRIBLE DAY AND SHOPPING

Two of the ladies began firing questions at the class, none of which I understood as I spoke no Arabic. The suited men picked on individual kids and asked more questions. I was relieved that none asked Huda anything, as they would have a long wait for an answer. The photographers' cameras flashed. Mrs. Sherazi's fixed smile never wavered, although it never reached her eyes. At last, as suddenly as they'd appeared, they departed.

"Who were they?" I asked the class, who looked as shocked as I was.

"The Ministry of Education," said Fatima primly. "They are inspecting the school."

"Oh! And what did they ask you?"

"Mees, they ask if we like the school, Mees," said Mustafa Kamel.

"And if we like our lessons," said Zainab.

"And if we like *you*, Mees," said cheeky Mohammed.

I changed the subject. I didn't want to hear the replies the children had given.

At last the end of the day arrived, but instead of meeting my friends at Smokers' Corner, I had to report to Mr. Brewster's office. The door was open, and Mr. Brewster and Wayne were chatting and laughing together. Wayne looked at me.

"Hi, Babe," he said, then to Mr. Brewster, "I'll see you later tonight."

They high-fived and Wayne sauntered out of the office.

I am NOT your babe, I thought, and walked in.

"Ah, Miss Vicky," Mr. Brewster began, "I'm afraid I've had a complaint from a parent."

It didn't need the Brain of Bahrain to work out who had complained.

"Fatima, she's in your class?" he asked, eyebrows raised, as if he didn't already know.

"Yes..."

"Her mother says you are not setting enough homework."

"I..."

"Fatima's friend is in Wayne's class, and she's told Fatima that they have an hour's English homework every night."

"But..."

I was fuming. I knew that Wayne ordered his classes to copy great chunks from the textbooks, and I didn't see the point of that. He didn't even grade it, he just stamped it with a rubber stamp as 'Checked'.

"I set my classes meaningful homework three times a week," I said, through clenched teeth.

"Well, could you step it up to every day in future?"

Great! More grading. Could this day get any worse?

A HORRIBLE DAY AND SHOPPING

It could.

"Oh, the Ministry visit today went well, I think," said Mr. Brewster, swiftly changing the subject, probably aware that I was far from happy.

I left before the subjects of untidy teachers' desks and tragic bunnies could be raised, and went straight to Hawa.

"You see, I tell you tha' woman is *bad!*" said Hawa, rolling her eyes. "She better not try bully *me!*"

I believed her. Hawa looked small and delicate but I knew that beneath her beautifully embroidered clothes beat the heart of a cockerel.

"Hah! Soon we have Parents' Conference, then we see!" She clapped her hands, bedevilment in her eyes.

But it was the email that arrived that evening that was the final straw that broke the camel's back and drove me to call a BWMDC Extraordinary Meeting.

"dear Ms. vicky,
Fatima did not understand today your lesson on reported speech. She needs clarification and explaination. Please repeat it tomorrow, and why do you not give a quiz today like in Mr. Wayne's class?
Fatima's mother"

Thankfully, the Bahraini people we came to know were utterly charming, friendly, supportive people, not at all like Fatima's mother. When Daryna had a small crisis at the shopping mall, they couldn't have been kinder.

Daryna was always beautifully dressed and enjoyed shopping for clothes. One day she was browsing happily from store to store when she suddenly realised she'd lost her handbag. It was black, and contained everything: phone, credit cards, ID, passport, wallet... Panic set in.

She forced herself to get a grip and thought hard. When did she last have it? She didn't believe it'd been stolen. No, it was more likely that she'd put it down somewhere. But where? And how would she get back to the hotel with no money?

She approached a salesgirl behind the counter and explained her problem. Although the girl didn't know Daryna from a piece of toffee, she insisted on giving her 10BD (approximately £17, or $26) from her own purse, more than enough for a taxi home. Daryna gratefully accepted.

She thought hard again. Ah, the phone! She made her way over to one of the security guards and told him the sorry tale. Again, the security guard couldn't have been more sympathetic or helpful. He agreed to keep calling her phone,

A HORRIBLE DAY AND SHOPPING

while Daryna attempted to retrace her steps once more.

"God bless that nice man!" said Daryna, as she relived the incident. "Do you know, he called my phone about 50 times! Well, about an hour later, I walked into the store where I first thought I'd lost my purse, walked about, and then - all of a sudden - dee-dee-dee diddlededeedee, I heard the familiar music. It was my phone! I followed the melody to the sweater pile, just where I'd been standing two hours before, and there, sure enough, was my purse, ringing! My purse was black, and I'd put it down on a pile of black sweaters. I must have held up a sweater to look at, then put it down on top of my purse. Then I must have picked up my shopping bags and walked away. But everything was there and nothing was missing."

"What a relief!"

"Yes, it was. So I thanked that wonderful security guard and gave the nice salesgirl her 10BD back, and all was well."

Shopping was never a problem for Joe and me, because we had a nearby Cold Store, or mini-supermarket. But carrying the shopping home was a problem. We usually had to buy heavy bottles of water, as Bahraini water is unsafe to drink, and lugging it home across the sand, in the searing heat, was exhausting.

One of the Middle School teachers overheard Joe moaning about it, and interrupted.

"Hey, I've got a cart at home that we never use. A kinda trolley thing, do you want it? It's just taking up space. You're welcome to it if you want it."

Joe accepted, and the next day she produced the trolley. Trollster, as we christened it, entered our lives. Trollster was a very sturdy trolley and much bigger than we'd imagined. It had a metal frame, four large stable wheels, and folded up when not in use. Joe was looking forward to his maiden voyage.

"I'll stock up on everything," he announced. "We need water, milk, everything."

Joe often went shopping for groceries alone because I was weighed down grading my pupils' work and couldn't afford the time. Off he went, pushing Trollster in front of him. All went well as he traversed the sand, and from my vantage point on the 7th floor, I saw him cross the busy road with no problems. Unfortunately, the return journey was much more hazardous.

Twenty minutes later I watched him exit the Cold Store, Trollster packed with groceries. He pushed it to the kerb, waited for the traffic lights to change and the road to clear, then attempted to negotiate the kerb-stone. Trollster lurched sideways, spilling toilet rolls and cans into the road.

Colton arrived, looking for Joe, and joined me at the window. We watched the little figure stamp its foot and hurriedly retrieve the fallen items. The traffic lights changed to green and the traffic roared towards him.

With just moments to spare, he hauled Trollster back on the kerb. Again he waited for the lights to change and this time reached the opposite kerb without further mishap. He just managed to pull Trollster up onto the pavement before the lights changed and the traffic bore down on him again.

"Awww... That was tricky..." chuckled Colton.

We watched as Joe and Trollster bumped across the red-bricked sidewalk, until that gave way to compacted sand. Joe pushed confidently and Trollster behaved quite well until the hard sand gave way to soft. Now Joe was struggling. Shoulders stooped, rear-end raised, he shoved Trollster forward. Then something caught the front wheels. Joe was pushing so hard that he projected himself over the handlebar, headfirst into the groceries. Joe and Trollster fell sideways in a jumble of wheels, arms, legs and shopping.

"Oh no..."

"Hey, I'll go and help him, silly old fool," said Colton and bounded out of the room.

Joe picked himself up, brushed himself down and repacked Trollster before Colton reached him. Pushing Trollster through the soft sand was clearly impossible so he tried pulling instead. I watched as Trollster balked and bounced, the wheels leaving tracks in the sand. Joe, pouring sweat, bald head ruby-red, fists clenched on the handle, was clearly struggling.

Where are the camels when you need one? I thought.

Colton, the knight in shining armour, arrived, and together they dragged Trollster home, up the lift and into our room.

"Trollster hates sand," Joe muttered.

"Sir Joe," asked the Filipino barmaid in Bennigan's later, "why you look so red? Wha' you been doing?"

"Oh, just a spot of shopping," sighed Joe and took a deep draught of his cold beer.

Joe wasn't the only one with a red face that weekend. Joe was out visiting Colton in his apartment and I was marking assignments at the dining room table. There was a knock on our door, which I opened, and found Daryna holding a white plate with a circle of plump, rosy strawberries, carefully arranged.

A HORRIBLE DAY AND SHOPPING

Perhaps I'm wrong, but I think school Principals are rarely popular with their staff. Poor Daryna was placed in a difficult situation. She was compelled to execute Mrs Sherazi's often eccentric edicts, but blamed for the peculiar rules she was expected to enforce. The Coffee War was a good example, and she lost many friends over that. If people, instead of being poisoned by false accusations from the Three Fat Ladies, had bothered to get to know her better, they'd have found a very sweet lady with the best of intentions. Yes, she made hasty decisions. No, she wasn't always a good judge of character. But she was one of the most well-meaning and generous people I have ever had the good fortune to meet.

And that day was a good example. Daryna had bought strawberries, and thought Joe and I might enjoy some. She spent time picking out the most perfect, washing them and arranging them, Martha Stewart-style, on a plate. Satisfied with the arrangement, she crossed the hall and knocked on our door.

"Hi, Daryna," I said.

"A treat for you!" she said, smiling and stepped forward, offering out the plate.

Unfortunately, her sleeve caught on the door handle. The strawberries hurled themselves at me and the plate clattered to the ground. Had Toothy been at the reception desk below, watching footage from the surveillance camera, he would have had a good laugh.

"Come into my room," she said, when we'd cleared up the mess and stopped laughing. "I've got things to tell you!"

SHAWARMA

Okay, I confess, I had no idea what 'mastic' was, except as builders' putty stuff, but Nadia Sawalha's mum, Bobbie, enlightened me. Mastic is Arabic gum (not gum Arabic), and it's the resin from the mastic tree. Bobbie says the flavour is quite delicate, and mastic looks like cloudy sugar crystals about the size of round rice. It can be bought in small packets, online or from Turkish shops. She suggests that if you can't get it, just leave it out, as it can't be replaced by any other flavour. Nadia claims that this delicious dish is divine when cooked on the barbecue (BBQ) - a minute or so each side. If a BBQ is unavailable, then a really hot grill will do.

Top Tips

Grind the mastic finely between 2 spoons with a little sugar.

Instead of pita bread, warmed tortilla can be used to wrap the ingredients in a tight hold-in-your-hand roll to eat.

Ingredients (serves 4-6)

450g (1lb) leg of lamb meat, cut into thin strips

2 tbsp cider vinegar

Juice of 1 juicy lemon

1 tsp finely grated lemon zest

1 tsp each of ground cinnamon and ground allspice

1 tsp each of salt and black pepper

½ tsp ground cardamom

3 pieces mastic (optional, see above)

1 small onion, peeled and grated

1 small tomato, chopped

3 glugs of olive oil

5 tbsp finely chopped fresh parsley

Method

Place the shawarma ingredients in a bowl and leave in the fridge for 24 hours. Every now and then, give it a good stir.

Remove from the fridge 1 hour before you need it. Allow to drain in a sieve or on a rack. Cook over a barbecue (or under a hot grill) giving each side a minute or so. Nestle the lamb into warmed pita bread, or onto a warmed tortilla.

Add the salad and drizzle tahini sauce all over.

14

BASKETBALL

"It's Hali-Barry," said Daryna, settling herself on the sofa.

"What about him?"

"I'm getting as many complaints from parents about him as I'm getting about crazy Brent."

"Why?"

"Why? Where shall I start?" She sighed and started counting the points on her fingers. "He shouts at the students. All his lessons sound like a slanging match and you can hear him several classrooms away. And the swearing! I've warned him, and my deputies have warned him, but he just carries on using bad language round the students."

"You can't curse and swear round students! That's really unprofessional..."

"I know! And he makes inappropriate comments which upsets some of the girls. He's had his first written warning about that. Then there's his halitosis. I presented him with a big jar of mints. He said, 'I don't need those,' and I said, 'Believe me, Barry, you do!' But he's still blasting that awful breath over the kids."

"I think he needs to see a dentist."

"He sure does! But I can't force him to go. But that's not all..."

"Oh my, what else?"

"Well, he's always *there*, if you know what I mean. After school he's *there*, ready to take me home. If I go shopping, he's *there* ready to carry my bags. He's always in my office. He's always a step behind me."

"He's desperate for a ladyfriend, you know..."

"Yuk! I know that now. I thought it was innocent, that he was just being helpful, but then he came up here earlier, and asked what I was planning for the Winter Break. I said I wasn't sure, and he suggested I might like to book a double room and go on a Nile cruise with him. Can you imagine?"

"What? Has the man got the hide of a rhinoceros?"

"Ha! I think so! Anyway, how are things with you?"

"Well, they would be fine, except for Fatima's mother."

"What is she doing now?"

"She's always in the building, snooping on me, and I'm getting emails from her nearly every day. Do you know, I don't think I've had a complaint from a parent before, ever, but this woman never stops. She questions every single thing I do with the class. I'm dreading the Parents' Conference."

I recalled the latest email...

"dear Ms. Vicky,
The literary analysis for the story 'Eleven' is about symbolism, I am wondering if you will explain this concept to the students or not?
Fatima's mother"

Huh! It was hard enough just to get the children to learn their vocabulary lists, or even string a sentence together correctly. And she wanted me to launch into an in-depth lesson on symbolism?

Our memories of Spain were beginning to blur and become a little less painful as Joe and I immersed ourselves in the daily life of the school.

Fatima's mother continued to stalk me. Mr.

Brewster continued to sing the praises of the wonderful Wayne. Joe's students continued to waste his time, and their own. Brent never ceased to astound us, and Hali-Barry sniffed after Daryna, or any other female with a pulse. Hali-Barry had got so bad that Andrea and Saja refused to share an elevator with him.

Joe was just managing to keep his head above water, teaching Physics and Maths. Two and a half months into the academic year and the High School schedule had still to be finalised. Keeping the students in his classroom, and without their friends from other classes, was another major obstacle. The Hall Monitors frequently brought escapees back, often students that Joe hadn't even noticed were missing. He described how some of the High School Monitors actually carried sticks.

"So there I was, writing this equation on the board, and my door flies open. In comes Mr. Hussein, the Hall Monitor, pushing Ali in front of him, poking him with his stick and bawling at him. I couldn't believe it! Then Ali answers him back, and Mr. Hussein clips him round the ear and yells at him to sit down and behave. I called Mr. Hussein over and very quietly said, 'Mr. Hussein, you cannot treat students that way you know,' and he just grins at me. So I look at Ali, and he's grinning, too. Then Mr. Hussein says,

BASKETBALL

'It's okay, Mr. Joe, Ali is my son.' Well! This school is just crazy..."

In our little mountain village in Spain, children rule. They run wild in the streets, get up to all sorts of mischief and are regarded as little angels by their doting parents. And they are. Joe and I have always found Spanish kids to be delightful, polite and charming.

Now we had the opportunity of comparing Arabic kids with their Spanish counterparts. To begin with, their life-styles were massively different. In Spain, kids' lives are governed by the seasons and their huge families. Fiestas, football, grape-pressing, endless summer weeks romping in the village, days on the beach, Christmas...all important times for Spanish children.

In Bahrain, however, the children we taught came mostly from very wealthy families. They enjoyed the latest material possessions, were waited on by maids and chauffeured to school in luxury cars. Unlike Spanish kids, they lived indoors most of the time. For the majority of the year, Bahrain is simply too hot for kids to play outside. There are no nice beaches and certainly no countryside. So for Bahraini kids, leisure time is usually spent in the city malls, meeting friends, eating fast food and spending money.

Most of our Spanish neighbours have never been out of Andalucía or left Spain. They have never been on a plane and have no desire to. Bahraini families, however, spend the long summer-break travelling, and many of the kids in my class had regularly visited Europe and America.

In spite of their dreadful behaviour, both Joe and I became very fond of our pupils. My Mohammeds were the bane of my life. Joe had Talal, and a bunch of lads bigger, stronger, taller and hairier than he was, who tormented him on a daily basis. But basically, they were nice kids, just very spoiled.

Just how badly behaved these kids could be was illustrated at the basketball championship. ASS was hosting the championship final that year. There was a crowd of thirty or forty ASS students on the sidelines, mostly senior boys, bellowing for their team. ASS was up against a team from a neighbouring school. The aged gymnasium rang with the cheers, boos and screams of the spectating boys and it was clear that the visiting team's spectators were already intimidated.

"Talk about a scary tribe!" said Jake, telling us about it later at a BWMDC meeting. He shook his head at the memory. "Anyway, across the gym sat the awful Miss Jane, the Athletics Director."

Joe and I nodded. The same Miss Jane who organised the after-school football club.

"The awful Miss Jane was perched up on the

score box, and it turned out that she had as little idea about sportsmanship as the kids did. She was yelling and heckling with the best of 'em."

"Another Stella, Sir Jake, Sir John?" asked the Filipino barmaid, interrupting Jake's juicy tale. "Coors Light for you, Sir Colton?"

"Hey, funny isn't it?" said Colton, when our glasses were refreshed. "Funny how the kids can barely understand basic classroom instructions, like 'get your books out', but..."

"But know everything about the rules of basketball," finished Jake, "a hundred times better than the poor, underpaid Indian referee who was calling for a fair game."

"What happened next?" I asked.

"Well, our kids played real dirty. They threw elbows, charged, grabbed, everything you hate about an unfair athlete."

"Some of the other school's team just had enough," Colton added. "They started to throw elbows back."

"Hey, I didn't blame them!" Jake cut in.

Colton agreed. "It was a really filthy game. Finally, the ref called a technical on our star player, Talal. As soon as that happened, a boy from the other team shoved Talal, 'n' that cleared the stands."

"All the ASS kids jumped up and surged onto the court, yelling and pushing," said Jake.

"One minute we were just observing the incredibly awful basketball and worse crowd behaviour, and then, teacher mode kinda kicked in. I didn't know I could run hurdles, or jump anything as high as a chair," he said. "I'm telling you, I have *never* jumped so fast over anything higher than my waist, trying to put myself between our students and the other school's team."

"Hey, we just didn't think," said Colton. "We just went for it!"

"Anyway," said Jake, "the other teachers followed us, and it was just one almighty brawl. Punches, foul language, and the worst cowardice I've ever seen. I personally shoved five students to the ground only to have them pop right back up and give me a look as though I just told them Jesus was better than Mohammed."

"Course, the students didn't listen to us. Do they ever? It sure took a while to clear the gym." Colton grinned over his beer glass.

"And that Jane, our wondrous Athletics Director, she never left the safety of her three-foot-tall box, and her yelling was more abusive than the kids'! A couple of the other team's boys were punched in the face and had to be treated with ice. Anyway, we finally managed to clear the gym of our students and the other team packed up their things."

"And we thought that was the end of it," laughed Colton.

"But being ASS..."

"Where ALL STUDENTS SUCCEED!" Joe and I chanted.

"Yep, being our school, that wasn't the end of it."

"It was like a really bad teen drama," said Colton.

"Yep, our students were waiting outside. I felt like a song-and-dance number should break out any minute. Unfortunately, it did not. We had to escort the other team down the street. We were followed by our students all the way. And where was our Athletics Director? Nowhere to be seen!"

It wasn't really funny, but Jake acting out the scene, blow by blow and hurdling over bar stools, had us convulsed with laughter. And it wasn't funny that ASS was banned from taking part in the basketball championship for the next two years, either. But it was a great night at Bennigan's.

Unfortunately, the evening was spoiled by yet another email from Fatima's mother:

"dear Ms. Vicky,
are you going to give the students a spelling and vocabulary test tomorrow? Also I notice that Mr. Wayne's class are up to page 103 in shiloh and they

done the evaluating exercise in the big yellow book already. when will you be doing it? I looking forward to the parents conference.
Fatimas mother"

Aaaargh!

On the day of the Parents' Conference, the kids were allowed home early, and the parents queued outside our classrooms. The mothers were black-robed, wearing *hijabs*, the men in white robes with red-and-white chequered head-gear. I couldn't help feeling a little intimidated. I ran my eye down the line, looking for Fatima's mother, but didn't see her. I guessed she was bullying the Music teacher, who was the only teacher brave enough not to award Fatima an 'A'. Fatima, one of the brightest in my class, certainly deserved her 'A' grade from me, but perhaps she was not so gifted in other subjects.

Then I heard Hawa's familiar voice floating out of her classroom.

STUFF YA POTATOES!

Nadia says, "They're *delicious*, especially with buttered cabbage and onions sitting prettily alongside them."

Ingredients (Serves 2 big eaters)

8 potatoes, peeled (Maris Piper are good)

Sunflower oil

Butter

Olive oil

2 tbsp chopped fresh coriander or parsley

For the filling:

4 tbsp pine nuts

1 medium onion, peeled and chopped

1 tsp ground cinnamon

2-3 tsp ground allspice

225g (8oz) organic minced lamb (not lean - fat adds flavour)

2 tomatoes, finely chopped

Salt and black pepper

3 tbsp tomato purée

300ml (½ pint) lamb stock, hot

Method

Preheat the oven to 180ºC/gas mark 4/350ºF.

Cut off the top of each potato. Core each potato leaving a 1cm (½ inch) shell.

Fry the potatoes in a little sunflower oil, and a knob of butter, until they are golden brown, then set them aside.

Heat some sunflower oil in a heavy-based pan and fry the pine nuts until coloured, then set them aside.

In the same pan, fry the onion until soft, adding more oil if necessary.

Now add the spices and fry until their aroma is released.

Stir in the lamb, tomatoes and pine nuts and season well.

Fill the potatoes with the lamb mixture, leaving a 1cm (½ inch) gap at the top. Lay them side by side in an oven dish.

Mix the tomato purée with the hot lamb stock.

Pour around the potatoes until they are halfway covered. Add hot water if necessary.

Cover with foil and bake for 45-50 minutes or until tender.

For the last 15 minutes, remove the foil and drizzle with olive oil.

Serve sprinkled with coriander or parsley.

15
PARENTS' CONFERENCE

I paused in the corridor, pretending to fiddle with some papers, and listened. Hawa was annoyed, that was evident, and it wasn't difficult to work out who she was talking to.

"Wha' you want? You wan' your daughter be robot? Fatima good girl, but she must no' work all day and all night!"

"Fatima likes to work."

"But she little girl! She mus' have time for hersel' sometime! Why you no go easy on her? Time enough later for her to work, work, work!"

I slid into my classroom, dreading my turn with Fatima's mother. I was also worried about how exactly I was going to tell the mother of Abdul and Abdulaziz that her twins shared a brain cell.

PARENTS' CONFERENCE

However, the majority of parents were charming and supportive. I often forgot *not* to shake hands with the fathers, but my loose Western behaviour seemed to be forgiven.

However, I encountered another problem. A mother would smile, bow her head and ask the question that I found hard to answer.

"How is my little Mohammed doing?"

Oh dear, which Mohammed?

I peered into the mother's face, searching in vain for a resemblance to any of my pupils. Her face, however, was too covered to be of any help.

"Which class is your Mohammed in?" I asked.

"Your class, Mees."

"Yes...but I teach five classes."

"Your English class, Mees."

"All my classes are English." I smiled helpfully.

"My Mohammed has black hair and brown eyes."

That would describe them all.

"What is his middle name?" My eyes desperately scanned the columns of names in my grade-book.

"This one, Mees." A soft hand emerges from the loose robe and a manicured fingernail points at a Mohammed on the page.

Of course that doesn't really help either. I knew all my Mohammeds when they were in front of me, but I couldn't remember all their second names. Their surnames weren't any help either, as some shared the same surname and could only be identified through their middle names. It was all too bewildering.

This scenario played itself out a few times before I solved the problem. Now the conversation went more along these lines:

"How is my little Mohammed doing?"

"Mohammed? Oh, he's doing fine. Can be a little chatty at times, but when he applies himself, he does really well." The problem only reared its ugly head again when parents asked to see their Mohammed's grades.

Later I heard that Joe had experienced the same Mohammed problem. One parent waited patiently while Joe scrutinised his grade-book. Finally the parent pointed to one Mohammed with a row of straight 'A's.

"I'll take that one," he said, which had them both laughing.

A few parents were shocked that I hadn't awarded their little darlings an 'A' grade.

"Mees! I think you make a mistake. Why you give Ahmed 'F'?"

"I'm sorry, it's no mistake. Ahmed never does any work in class, in fact he doesn't even bring any books, or paper or anything to write with."

Ahmed's mother takes off her Gucci shades,

PARENTS' CONFERENCE

leans forward and stares at me. "But Ahmed is very smart boy!"

"Yes, I'm sure he is, but he refuses to do any work. He never does his homework, and doesn't even write down the weekly vocabulary. That's why he always scores zero in our Thursday quizzes."

"But, Mees! When he see his mid-term grade, he cry!"

"I'm sorry, but you must explain to Ahmed that he needs to make an effort in class. I can't give him a better grade until he produces some work."

"But, Mees! His father be angry! And we having new baby in family." She coyly pats the folds of her robes, in the stomach area. "Perhaps he need extra help?"

"I'm sorry, I'm sure Ahmed is a smart boy. He just doesn't do any work..."

Her eyes narrow as she tries another tactic. "All other teachers, they give my son 'A'."

"Really?"

Later on, between parents, I popped across to Hawa's classroom.

"Hawa, did you give Ahmed an 'A' for Maths?"

"Ahmed?" she snorted. "Tha' boy lazy, very lazy! I give him 'F'. His mother tell me you give him 'A'!"

"Did she really? Well, I didn't. He got an 'F' from me too."

"You see Fatima's mother yet?" Hawa rolled her beautiful oriental eyes. "Tha' woman!"

"No, I still have that treat in store."

Slowly the line of parents waiting to see me depleted, until only a couple were left. To my huge relief, Fatima's mother was not there.

Mr. Brewster stuck his head into my classroom, his eyebrows raised in enquiry. "Ah, Miss Vicky, would you mind popping into my office briefly before you leave?"

Yes, I would mind.

"No problem, Mr. Brewster."

The last parent departed, and I was disappointed that Huda's parents hadn't attended. I wanted to know why she never spoke and perhaps find clues to start her talking. I also wanted to know why their daughter always handed me an empty homework book. I'd asked her many times but, of course, she never answered. I gathered my bags and tapped on Mr. Brewster's door.

"Ah, Miss Vicky, come in. Here's the problem. Fatima's mother has requested that Fatima should be moved to Mr. Wayne's class."

"Has she? Well, good! I think that's an excellent idea." Brilliant! No more being stalked by Fatima's mother. No more daily emails of interrogation and complaint. Perfect!

Mr. Brewster shook his head. "No, I told her that Fatima can't move classes. We can't pander to parents or they'll be asking to change classes all the time."

I sighed. No reprieve for me then.

A bell signalled the end of the Parents' Conference and my mobile shrilled. Three messages had been sent simultaneously. Joe, Colton and Jake, all calling for an Extraordinary BWMDC Meeting. It seemed we all needed to discuss our first Parents' Conference and share our stories.

The meeting opened with Joe, Colton and Jake comparing notes about the parents of students they shared, followed by my ranting about Fatima's mother. However, soon the discussion deteriorated into another of Colton's Boise River tales.

"Hey, so me 'n' my buddy Tucker were floatin' down the Boise River in a tractor inner-tube, and the current had gotten mighty strong. We get swept along, 'n' next thing we know, we get caught in these overhanging branches. Before we know it, our case of beer tips into the water. Well, we all jump in to rescue it, 'n' so does everyone else, folks we don't even know…"

By late October, the weather had become a

little more bearable. We still hadn't moved to our new apartments, but living in the hotel was hardly a punishment.

We held a pizza party to celebrate Colton's birthday, on the hotel roof, under the stars. Brent, as usual, was in the pool, swimming up and down, up and down. We ignored him. It was a perfect vantage point to enjoy the Manama cityscape. The lights of the elegant towers of the Financial District buildings twinkled against the dark sky. It was a world away from our mountains in Spain, but nevertheless, beautiful in a different way. The celebrations were fun, until Hali-Barry arrived uninvited and broke up the party.

Back in Spain, Sue and Juliet, the Gin Twins, arrived for their annual visit, determined to continue the tradition even though Joe and I were in Bahrain. How I envied them! I so wished I could be in El Hoyo, pouring the gins, slicing the bright, yellow lemons and listening to the latest gossip from England. Much later I got the full, unabridged version of their visit, but for now, I had to content myself with their emails.

"Did you get the keys okay?" I wrote. "And how are the chickens?"

"No problem with the keys," came the reply. "And the chickens are fine, they're looking really good, all six of them."

PARENTS' CONFERENCE

"Good, but six chickens? Are you sure? We have eight chickens."

"Nope, just sent Juliet out to count again. Definitely six chickens."

Oh dear. So we'd lost two of our girls. How sad. Well, they were elderly and they couldn't live forever.

Whenever the Gin Twins come to Spain, it's a kind of tradition that they take over the kitchen and cook up a humungous curry, and this year was no exception, even though we weren't there. It's a pleasure to cook using all locally grown ingredients. Beautiful glossy green, red and yellow peppers, onions and tomatoes all succumb under the knife and are tossed into hot, fragrant olive oil. I can almost smell it as I write.

This year was no different, and the Gin Twins chopped, sliced and sang along to a 60s CD at the top of their voices while the level on the gin bottle dropped at regular intervals.

"I think I'll pop outside to take a few photos of the street," said Juliet, during a lull in cooking duties.

She pointed her camera this way and that, capturing the window boxes, the little white houses and towering mountains. Then, through the viewfinder, two figures appeared. *Oh good,* she thought, *some colourful locals in my picture,* and carried on snapping. But the figures loomed larger.

"*Hola,*" said Juliet, which is about as far as her Spanish stretches.

Instead of passing, the two men halted. They clearly took her greeting as encouragement and rattled a reply in Spanish. Juliet was floundering. Having exhausted her minimal Spanish vocabulary, she was in need of assistance.

"Sue! Come out here! I need your help!"

In a mixture of Spanish, French and energetic hand-signals, the Gin Twins learned that the most insistent of the two, Luis, wasn't a local at all. He was a relative of Marcia's, from the shop, and just happened to be visiting. Luis's eyes lit up in his pasty face and his lecherous grin revealed gold teeth that glinted when he realised that the Gin Twins were man-less, holidaying alone. The other introduced himself as Juan.

Somehow the Gin Twins were prevailed upon, chiefly by Luis, to halt their curry-cooking and were steered down the street to Juan's cottage.

"They gave us wine and meaty things," said Juliet, shuddering. Being vegetarian, she found the offerings particularly unappetising. "And then I made the big mistake of plonking myself down on the sofa."

"I sat on that sofa, too," recalled Sue.

"Well, Luis starts leaning in, getting all close,

you know, touchy-feely... So up I leap up off the sofa and start wandering round the room, pretending I'm looking at Juan's photos and stuff."

I'm already laughing. "Did that stop Luis?"

"Sort of. He gives up on me and moves in on Sue. Instead of getting up, she stays rooted to the spot."

"I did not!"

"You did! The trouble was, we were both extremely pickled and I think they knew it..."

"Then, the next day," said Sue, "after we'd had some more gins, they turned up *again* and started banging on the door. They wouldn't go away!"

"We refused to open it. We just pretended the music was turned up too loud to hear them knocking."

"But then they started shouting from the street. So we sneaked upstairs and onto the roof terrace..." By now, both Juliet and Sue were creased up, laughing at the memory.

"Then we thought they might see us, so we dropped down on all-fours..."

"Haha! I can remember crawling round that terrace, giggling hysterically, wishing they would go away and leave us in peace!"

"I also remember that curry we cooked was one of the most awesome we ever made. And the accompanying singing was of the highest order!"

The Gin Twins had a good time, in spite of being pursued, and I was ridiculously jealous of them being in Spain, even for that short time. However, I was comforted by the fact that they'd already booked flights to Bahrain for February. I couldn't wait to see them and show them around ASS, the island, and Bennigan's.

September, October, was it really November already? So much had happened, and yet we had no idea that events in other parts of the world were bubbling, poised to erupt, and would affect us hugely. Back then, we had never even heard of the Arab Spring, a term that was soon to become a household phrase.

THE GIN TWINS' CHUCK-IT-ALL-IN CURRY

Juliet: Well, I think we use about two onions chopped and softened in the pan with about 3 cloves of garlic crushed and added to the onion.

Then you need 4 chicken breasts, chopped into cubes, add to onion and cook all over. Then we add a tablespoon of curry paste and a few teaspoons of curry powder. Also need a couple of red peppers!

We then add some water, a tin of chopped tomatoes and a large glug of wine!

You need to peel 4 medium potatoes and dice them and add to pan, along with some chopped cauliflower, carrot and whatever other veg is in Vicky's fridge.

Oh, add a tin of sweet corn too. The whole lot is left to simmer for a few hours. Add water or more curry powder if necessary!

Ok, Sue, have I forgotten anything? Oh yes, you need to drink gin.

Sue: And top tip for cooking rice, wash rice thoroughly

in a sieve under running water until water is clear. Place washed rice in bowl and cover well with water. Leave for up to an hour. Drain then cook in boiling water for about 10 minutes. Perfect fluffy rice every time!

Health warning on curry cooking, avoid cooking poppadoms after drinking gin...

Juliet: Forgot to say we add whole chilies and if we can't get them, then chili powder!

Sue: Absolutely!

Juliet: Had to add that, it's been bugging me! We couldn't have a Fail in the curry department!!

16

THE TREE OF LIFE

"dear Ms. vicky,
I wonder why you minimized the work and do not give a comperhension today like in Mr. Wayne's class?
Fatima's mother"

Blissfully unaware of the imminent birth of the Arab Spring, we toiled on at school, day after day. I tried hard to make my lessons as interesting as possible but it was an uphill task trying to stimulate the imaginations of my ten and eleven-year-old students.

One day, I handed out sheets of word-puzzles that I'd bribed the photocopier man to reproduce.

"Okay," I said, passing round the papers, "I'd like you to do this sheet, and then this sheet..."

"Mees..." asked Mustafa Kamel, looking puzzled. "Mees, eef you think it's sheet, why you want us to do it?"

The kids made me laugh, but also exasperated me. At the start of every week I gave them a list of twenty vocabulary words to learn. Every day we'd practice those words, in sentences, making them familiar. Their homework, on Wednesday, was to revise the words in preparation for the Thursday quiz.

The quiz questions were always the same: 'Make up your own sentence using the word ---.' But grading those completed quizzes over the weekend was a trial. Of course, Fatima's answers were flawless. Those from the boys, however, were disappointing. For example:

Fatima: There were <u>various</u> potted plants in the room.
Ahmed: My computer has a <u>various</u>.

Fatima: The seal was wet and <u>sleek</u>.
Cheeky Mohammed: My sister like to play hide and <u>sleek</u>.

Fatima: The little <u>fairy</u> waved her magic wand.

Mustafa Kamel: If you want to go acros the water jump on a <u>fairy</u>.

Joe was still battling with his own students, very few of whom ever did a stroke of work, and still treated his classes as social gatherings. Making his way to the classroom was his first hurdle, as he ran the gauntlet of passing boys in the corridor who insisted on shaking his hand. Then the first portion of the lesson was taken up with yet more hand-shaking. Every male student walked to the front to shake Joe's hand, which was very time-consuming.

"Meester Joe, how are you?" Shake, shake.

"Good morning, Talal. I'm fine, thank you. And you?" Shake, shake.

"Good morning, Meester!" Shake, shake.

"Good morning, Mahmoud." Shake, shake.

"How are you, Meester?" Shake, shake.

"Fine, Isa, and you?" Shake, shake.

And Joe's grade-book was laughable, empty rows of boxes showing absences both of students and assignments.

"Talal, where is your homework?"

"Oh, Meester! Sorry Meester! I forget to bring it."

"Mohammed? Where's your homework?"

"Meester, sorry, Meester. I'll bring it tomorrow, I swear to God!"

"You kids are impossible! How do you think you're going to pass your exams?"

Joe often growled at them, showing his teeth, but that only made them laugh. Thanks to their ubiquitous smartphones, his snarling was captured and within minutes appeared on Facebook and YouTube entitled something like, 'My physics teacher growling'.

"Meester!" said Noor, knowing she was next to be asked for her homework. "Can I have a Hall Pass and go down to the school entrance? I've phoned my driver to bring in my homework."

And if they could steer Joe away from quadratic equations or Newton's Laws, they invariably did, (although I hardly blamed them). Aware of his passion for soccer and Formula 1, they'd deliberately initiate discussions.

"Which team you support, Meester?"

"My team is Liverpool," Joe would say, "but I love seeing Arsenal play."

"Meester, I can get you tickets for the Formula 1 in March."

"Thank you, Talal! That would be great! How many of you have been to the Formula 1 races?" he asked the class.

Most of the boys shouted, "I have, Meester!" or, "Meester, I go every year!" while the girls shook their heads.

"You wouldn't believe the noise those cars

make!" said Joe. "They just *scream* round the track." He proceeded to execute a pretty good imitation of engines roaring round the circuit. Yet again, his rendition was captured and broadcast on the Internet almost before he'd passed the finishing line.

Attendance at school was poor, but on one day it was practically nonexistent. Joe and I were concentrating on preparing lessons, in our hotel, when a text arrived from Jake.

"Have you looked out the window?"

We hadn't, the heavy curtains being closed. We parted them to see fat raindrops hurling themselves against the glass, running down in zig-zags, collecting the desert sand as they coursed. Rain? Rain in Bahrain? It was the first rain we'd seen since leaving Spain.

Bahrain is rarely rained upon. I once asked my class if it ever rained in Bahrain, and they all yelled, "No, Mees!" So I should have been prepared for their reaction when it did. The rain fell all night and it was still raining when Jasim collected us with the school bus the next morning.

Bahrain is not built for rain. The roofs are flat and have no gutters. The roads have no slope, nor drains. Therefore it wasn't long before many streets became impassable and were transformed into rivers of dirty, standing water. The water level soon reached the doors of parked cars.

None of this bothered Jasim, who happily sloshed his bus through the lakes, spraying plumes of filthy water at any unfortunate pedestrian, soaking him further still. When we reached ASS, the short walk from the bus to the administration block to clock in, drenched us. With hair plastered to my head and water running down my back, I entered the Middle School building.

Very few High School students had turned up, rain being an event big enough to warrant staying at home, whether the roads were passable or not. And my classes were also depleted. About two-thirds of my kids did actually appear, although I wished they hadn't bothered. Any teacher will tell you that kids are affected by adverse weather. Normally good classes turn wild when the wind blows strongly, and naughty children become naughtier. That day, even Fatima couldn't concentrate, and cheeky Mohammed, Ahmed, Mustafa Kamel and the others were practically swinging from the rafters.

The rain stopped during the day, and the sun came out again. Smokers' Corner was ankle deep in water, but one of the Nepalese staff, responsible for cleaning and maintenance, had thoughtfully placed lumps of wood for us to use as stepping stones.

Young Mohammed was there, chain-smoking

and tapping his pointed shoe nervously. I knew he was still in a world of pain, living with crazy Brent.

Rashida was also there, her ample derriere parked in a damp chair.

"What rain!" she said, slapping her knees. "I have no students!"

"My classes are awful," I said. "They're like a bunch of hyperactive chimps today."

"And how are your chickens?"

"I've no idea. Our neighbour doesn't give us updates."

"You remember our chicken husband? The one that crowled all day? And the neighbours, they complain?"

"Yes, I remember. Your husband wanted to get rid of it, but your grandson cried. What happened? Does your husband still have it?"

Rashida swung round to young Mohammed and held out her hand. "Mohammed, give me cigarette."

Obediently, Mohammed gave her a cigarette. Rashida lit up and inhaled deeply.

"No, he does not have it." She exhaled and the smoke drifted lazily around her in the moist air. "My husband, he tell my grandson if he agree to let chicken husband go, he buy for him six new baby chicklets."

"To keep on the balcony?" I remembered they occupied an apartment on the eighth floor.

"Yes," Rashida nodded. "My husband say he sell eggs to the neighbours and security man. Then they not complain." She flicked the ash away into the water, where it hissed briefly, and continued. "My grandson, he say 'yes' because he want the six baby chicklets. And my husband, he take chicken husband to the kill shop. How you call it?"

"I'm not sure, perhaps 'slaughter shop'?" I was sure shops in Beirut were very different from the European ones I was familiar with.

"The slaughter shop man, he look at our chicken husband, and he say, 'That is fine bird. That is very fine bird. I weigh your bird, and I give you another, exactly same weight, for your oven. I take your fine bird and put it in my farm. Your fine bird will be chicken husband in my farm and will make more fine birds.' My grandson, he is very happy, because chicken husband does not die." Rashida cackled so much at her own story that she sent herself into a coughing fit.

I'm sure the thirsty plants welcomed the rain much more than Joe and I did, particularly Bahrain's famous Tree of Life. According to official websites, the Tree of Life is a miraculous mesquite, 400 years old and surviving in the desert without any apparent water supply.

THE TREE OF LIFE

According to the same sites, it stands alone in the sand, majestic and mysterious. Local inhabitants believe it stands on the actual location of the Garden of Eden and possesses magical youth-giving properties. The Gulf News proclaims it to be 'ranked fourth in the Official New Seven Wonders of Nature Campaign'.

To be honest, Bahrain is rather short of tourist attractions. I guess the malls and shopping are a big draw, and there is the fort, museum and the King's camels. But as far as I knew, there were no nice beaches or historical sites to visit. Check any Bahraini tourist site, however, and you will read that The Tree of Life should not be missed.

Joe and I declined Colton and Jake's kind invitation to see The Tree of Life. I was weighed down with mountains of grading and Joe felt his added bulk would prove too much with four others in the hired car. So Colton, Jake, Emily and Allison set off, eager to view this legend.

"Huh!" said Jake afterwards. "We set out late in the morning in the general direction of the Tree, and our first problem was the traffic congestion. You know what it's like here in Manama. Traffic backing up, not moving, an accident, whatever."

"Was the Tree signposted?" I asked.

Jake spluttered. "It was not! We drove for about thirty minutes until we finally saw a poor excuse for a sign pointing down this road. Great, we thought. Finally something that made sense. Directions to Bahrain's most famous place of interest. What we didn't know was that the Tree was going to be an hour's drive on unmarked paths. That one sign, at the beginning, was our only reference point. Following the best off-roading one can get in a compact car, we spent a good portion of the day searching and scanning the horizon for this great spectacle."

"But you found it?"

"Yep. After four hours we arrived with pomp and circumstance at the location of Adam's greatest sin. We also discovered one of the biggest misconceptions surrounding this 'magic of nature'. It isn't just one tree at all. The whole day we kept seeing a group of trees and shrubs in the distance, but we all wrote them off because we were looking for, I quote, 'a single majestic tree standing alone in the desert'. It turned out that the group of trees we'd been staring at for the past four hours was actually where we needed to be. Sadly, we had been close to it all along."

"What was it like?"

"Was *this* supposed to be The Tree of Life? What a crock of horseshit. It was a dead tree! The massive dead thing that it was, had a green iron fence surrounding the base of the trunk. But the branches reached so low you could easily climb up and walk along the entire tree. People had carved their names all over it. It was sad to see so many of the large branches broken off and lying nearby. And you should see the trash! It's just not maintained."

"Was it really dead?" asked Joe.

"No, but if they don't start looking after it, it soon will be."

"What a pity..."

"Yep, it was a sad sight. Not what we expected at all. And to make matters worse, we parked in a deep pile of sand and it took fifteen minutes, and a lot of pushing and coughing, to get the car out."

"So you wouldn't recommend a trip to see The Tree of Life?"

"No. Don't bother. Seriously, don't bother."

Apparently the day's rain had delayed our move to the new apartments, but we were assured, yet again, that we'd be moving within a week. Of course, that didn't happen. Six months had passed and we were still firmly ensconced in the hotel. The new apartment block was so close we could see it from our hotel room, but we were no closer to actually moving in. The six of us laid bets as to when we would move, each putting 500 fils into the pot, winner takes all.

Allison: 9th December
Me: 29th December
Colton: 1st January
Emily: 7th January
Jake: 20th January
Joe: (ever the pessimist) 1st April, (April Fools Day)

Our friends, being American, invited Joe and me to our first ever Thanksgiving celebration. The gang cooked up a feast and we ate until we nearly burst.

I remember that evening with great affection as all six of us sat around the dining table, giving thanks in the traditional American way. Later we were joined by Kent, another American teacher from a different school, and we played silly games until we all crawled off to bed.

November closed, and now none of us could think of anything but the approaching Winter Break.

JAKE'S DAD'S THANKSGIVING SWEET POTATO WONDERFUL

Jake's Dad says, "You will need a greased 9 x 13 baking pan (glass is nice)."

Ingredients

7 lbs (3 kilos) of sweet potatoes

⅓ cup of brown sugar (could add more, depending on how sweet you like it)

1 stick of butter (softened but not melted)

1 10.5 oz (300g) package of miniature marshmallows

½ tablespoon of cinnamon

(Salt to taste…approx 3 teaspoons)

1 teaspoon of nutmeg (optional)

¼ cup of sliced almonds to add texture and some interest.

(Optional…but a very delicious addition, is to add a

streusel type topping. You can buy a packaged mix at most US grocery stores.)

Method

After rinsing off potatoes, slice up sweet potatoes into thirds (each section about ½ the size of a green pepper). With skin still on, boil potatoes for approximately 15 minutes. Stick fork in potato for softness.

Remove from heat when fork enters with no resistance, but potato should not fall apart.

With potatoes still in the pan, pour out hot water and add cold water with just a few cubes of ice to help cool potatoes enough to be able to peel them. Let cool in pan for two or three minutes.

Begin to pull off peel and place potatoes in large mixing bowl. (Peel should come off easily.)

Once all potatoes are peeled and placed in large mixing bowl, start to mash using a potato masher.

Once most of the chunks are gone, add brown sugar, butter, cinnamon, salt, nutmeg, and sliced almonds.

Continue to use a potato masher and a large spatula to stir the potato mixture until fairly smooth.

When finished mixing in all ingredients, spread out half of the mixture into the baking pan.

Smooth out the top of mixture using a spatula.

Sprinkle half of the marshmallows over the mixture and finish covering with the remaining potato mix.

If you are going to use a crumbly topping (streusel), apply it as the top layer at this time.

You may even want to add some more almonds as part of the topping.

Be careful, you want to have room to put on the final layer of marshmallows. The top of the mixture should never be above the top of the baking dish. Leave baking dish uncovered.

Bake at 350°F degrees for approximately 15 minutes.

Take out mixture and add final layer of marshmallows. Bake mixture for another 5-10 minutes…just enough time to get marshmallows on top time to brown.

Take out and let cool for 10 minutes…time to serve the WONDERFUL!

17

WINTER BREAK

The 9th of December was the last day of the school term, and then we would have three glorious weeks off. As the end of term approached, I wasn't surprised to find an email waiting in my inbox.

"dear Ms. Vicky,
are you planning to give the students assignments for the winter break? Mr. Wayne's class have been given extra vocabulary.
Fatimas mother"

Nearly everybody had plans to spend Christmas elsewhere. Colton, Jake and Emily were going back to the States, and Allison planned to visit Vietnam. Hali-Barry went somewhere, but

WINTER BREAK

without Daryna, who could not be persuaded to join him on a romantic Nile cruise.

Joe and I were amongst the very few to stay behind in Bahrain. We figured it would be more sensible to save the airfare rather than rush back to Spain. El Hoyo would be cold and I was secretly afraid that, if we returned to Spain, I'd never be able to drag Joe back to Bahrain again. Spending the Winter Break in Bahrain would give me a chance to write with few interruptions, a real luxury for me, as I hadn't written a word since we'd arrived in the Middle East.

Before they left for their travels, Jake and Colton made a rather exciting discovery.

"Hey," said Jake, "you'll never guess what we've found! There's a place by the Gulf Hotel. Looks like a kinda windowless concrete cube, but guess what's on sale!"

"Camels?"

"Nah! Booze! Beers, wine, spirits, everything!"

Joe brightened visibly. "What? You can buy slabs of beer and bring them home to drink?"

"Yep!"

"Wow!"

Suddenly Christmas in the Middle East didn't seem so depressing. We loved going to Bennigan's, but it was expensive, and it would be nice to entertain our friends at home sometimes.

"Hey! We'll take you in the car and show you. You coming, Dogsbody?"

I certainly was. We piled into the car, and, sure enough, in the shadow of the Gulf Hotel, very close to the King's palace, was a small, unmarked, grey, windowless building. On either side of the entrance, arms folded, guns in their holsters, stood two uniformed security guards. I got out of the car, and, always on the lookout for a photo opportunity, whipped out my camera. The security guards closed in immediately.

"No photos, no photos," they said, waving their hands at me.

I quickly put the camera away, suddenly noticing a sign that forbade the taking of photographs, by order of the King. Later, we were told that the King not only owned the Gulf Hotel, but also Bennigan's, and the liquor store, too.

Another sign stated that no Muslims were permitted to buy alcohol, which was odd as we saw several Arabs in *thobes* and headdresses exiting with laden shopping carts.

The liquor store was an Aladdin's Cave of booze. Sparkling bottles of wine and spirits, and cans of beer, all stacked from floor to ceiling, under fluorescent lights. We loaded our trolleys and made our way to the checkout, where an Indian took our money and packed our purchases. It was illegal to have alcohol on public display in

Bahrain, so our purchases were hidden in large, black, plastic bags for us to take out. The black bags were instantly recognisable, which rather defeated the object, I thought. The six of us partied that night.

Sadly, we waved our friends goodbye as they left on their travels.

Young Mohammed stayed and was celebrating because his unstable roommate, Brent, was also away for the holiday. Mohammed acquired a spring in his step and Joe's mobile phone buzzed with messages inviting us to his room for Turkish coffee. The hotel seemed very quiet and the corridors echoed. We missed our friends but we didn't miss the booming voices of the Three Fat Ladies and Hali-Barry.

The ASS teachers may have disappeared, but weekends in the hotel were always busy. Male Saudi Arabian visitors drove across the causeway in their expensive cars, intent on drinking alcohol and finding women, itches they could not scratch in Saudi. It was common knowledge that Bahrain was Saudi's playground. Saudi Arabia's stifling laws were abandoned and carousing Saudis filled the bars to overflowing. According to hotel staff with whom we chatted, prostitution was a thriving industry in Bahrain.

We were told that complete Saudi families would cross the causeway at weekends. At night, husbands locked their wives and children into their hotel rooms, while they went out and partied. I dreaded to think what would happen if a fire broke out, as the wives and children would not have been able to escape.

Joe and I referred to the weekends as 'the Saudi Invasion', unaware how prophetic that phrase would soon prove to be.

Meanwhile, we developed a comfortable routine. During the day, I wrote, and Joe read, or watched movies on the projector we'd borrowed from the school. Joe was in charge of shopping, and even used Trollster to replenish his beer stocks when they ran low. In the evenings, we either cooked or ordered in food.

Ordering take-aways was a luxury we were denied in Spain, El Hoyo being so far from the nearest town. Here, in Bahrain, we had plenty of choice but ordering wasn't always easy. The order-lines were manned by Indians, whose accents seemed to grow thicker on the phone, and I usually left Joe to make the call.

"Hello, may we place an order, please?"

"Good evening, sir! It is delightful that you are calling us."

"Er, thank you. May we place an order, please?"

"Oh, yes, sir! You like to order pizza?"

"Yes, please. May we have two 'Meals-for-Two', please?" Joe asked.

Our plan was to order double portions so that we could reheat for the next day.

"Sir, you are wanting two pizza?"

"No, we'd like two 'Meals-for-Two', please, like you advertise. That's four pizzas altogether."

"Sir, you are wanting four pizza? Which size are you wanting?"

"No, two 'Meals-for-Two', please."

"Ah, you are wanting two pizza?"

"No, two 'Meals-for-Two'. Four pizzas. Like you advertise on your menu."

"Sir, may I suggest to you our very good offer? We can give to you our very special 'Meal-for-Two'. If you order, you will receive also one pasta pot with two toppings, two breadsticks, two wraps and two colas."

"Good! That's exactly what we want! Two of those, please!"

"Sir, you are wanting two colas?"

"Yes! I mean, no, we want four."

"Ah, I am understanding the sir now. You are wanting two 'Meals-for-Two'. With cola."

"Yes!" By now Joe's face is an interesting shade of red, and a vein is visibly throbbing on his temple.

"Certainly, sir. And the pasta has two

toppings. Which delicious toppings would the sir like?"

"Anything! Anything! Surprise me."

"Very good, sir. One thing more... Which crust is the sir wanting?"

"Which crust?"

"Yes, sir. We have Italian crust, pan crust, thick crust, thin crust, extra-deep crust or stuffed crust."

"What? Oh, I don't know... Here, Vicky, take the phone. I give up."

"Hello?" Surely ordering pizzas couldn't be that difficult.

"Good evening, Madam."

"You spoke to my husband, you are delivering two 'Meals-for-Two' to us."

"Madam is wanting two pizza?"

"No... Oh, never mind." I switched off the phone and looked at Joe. "Have a look in the freezer, see if there's something we can eat tonight."

Sometimes it was easier to eat at Bennigan's. Every time we entered the building, the Filipino staff treated us like long-lost friends.

"Sir Joe! How are you? Miss Vicky! How are you?"

They always reserved our favourite seats, and knew our regular drinks. Every hour, they would line up and perform a dance routine, (always YMCA), but as most of their customers had left for Christmas, Joe and I were usually the only spectators.

It was at Bennigan's that we first became aware of the birth of the Arab revolution, although it was so distant from us, it hardly registered. On the 18th December, we watched rioting on the Tunisian streets played out on Bennigan's flatscreen TVs.

Apparently, the police confiscated the fruit and vegetable stall belonging to a young, unemployed graduate. In despair, he set fire to himself, which sparked off violent clashes between furious protesters and the authorities. Interviews showed demonstrators decrying the high level of unemployment, inflated food prices, the lack of freedom of speech, dreadful living conditions, police brutality, and corruption. Shop windows were broken, cars smashed and set on fire, teargas deployed, and scores of people were arrested.

We soon forgot all about it, enjoying our quiet winter break. Christmas was a low-key affair for us. Some of the big stores displayed a few Christmas goodies, and the Bennigan's staff wore little red Santa costumes, with tiny mini-skirts and Santa hats to mark the occasion, but that was about it. Very different from Christmas celebrations in the UK, or our village in Spain.

As the New Year approached, the ASS staff returned in dribs and drabs. The Islamic New

Year, *Al-Hijra*, had already passed without us really noticing, although it is an important time for Shi'a Muslims. The Shi'a believe that New Year marks the anniversary of the murder of the Prophet Muhammed's grandson, along with his family and followers. Our school stood in a staunchly Shi'a area, and to demonstrate their period of mourning, black flags were draped from the buildings.

During this time, both men and women perform public enactments of grief. This includes beating their chests continuously, or worse still, using bunches of chains attached to handles, and flailing their own backs, which soon become raw and blooded. The extremely devout will incorporate razor blades and knives in the chains.

I never witnessed this, nor did I want to, but the boys in my class showed me how it was done, and one proudly showed me the bruises on his chest.

In contrast, our Western New Year celebrations were much lighter. The only damage we did to ourselves was to our livers and involved a heavy, but very enjoyable, session at Bennigan's.

Colton would be the last of our group to arrive back in Bahrain, late at night. Kent was with us that night, and for some reason, the six of us decided it would be a really great idea if we all hid in Colton's bed to surprise him when he came home, and entered his bedroom. We knew what time he was expected, so we lay there, under the covers, giggling like schoolgirls, waiting to hear his key in the lock.

Unfortunately, things didn't quite go according to plan. Colton phoned Joe from the airport.

"Hey, you guys still up? I don't have my keys, can I come and collect my other set from your room?"

"Of course," said Joe, and relayed the message to the rest of us in Colton's bed, in a stage whisper.

"Right!" said Jake, the natural leader. "Joe, you and Dogsbody go back to your room and wait for him. We'll stay here in his bed. Don't say a word about us being here, he'll never suspect!"

It seemed like an excellent plan. The prank had been salvaged. However, Colton took a long time to arrive, and Joe fell asleep on the sofa in our apartment. Jake, Kent, Emily and Allison had fallen asleep in Colton's bed.

At long last, Colton knocked on our door. I let him in, poker-faced. Joe woke up with a start and sat bolt upright.

"Colton, my mate! Did you get a fright when you saw the others in your bed?"

"You what? The others are in my bed?"

"Honestly, Joe, you are hopeless! You've spoilt it now! You weren't supposed to tell him!"

Colton, always a quick thinker, understood the situation immediately. "Hey, never mind, we can do a double bluff... I'll put on my Green Man suit, 'n' get into bed as if it's the most natural thing in the world."

Off he went and changed into his stretchy, pea-green lycra suit. It covered every part of him: face, hands, feet, everything. When Joe and I stopped laughing, the three of us tip-toed to Colton's room. Quietly, we let ourselves in. By now it was daylight, and the sun streamed in through the windows. Colton eased open the bedroom door, pulled back the bedcovers and got into bed, ignoring the four dozing occupants.

"Aaaah!" yelled Kent, and rolled out onto the floor.

"Aaaah!" shrieked Allison, sitting upright, eyes huge over the covers.

"Aaaah!" screamed Emily, and catapulted out of the bed.

"%*$#!" shouted Jake, leaped out of bed and leaned against the wall, clutching his heart.

Joe and I laughed until tears ran down our cheeks. Success!

Later that day, we caught up with everybody's travel tales. Jake's was probably my favourite story.

SAMBOUSEK
SPINACH KISSES

As Nadia says, "This recipe will make loads of pastries, but none of them will ever make it to the freezer!"

Ingredients Makes 30-40 pastries)

FOR THE DOUGH:

10g (¼oz) dried yeast

A pinch of caster sugar

300ml (½ pint) warm water

500g (1¼lb) strong white bread flour

1 tbsp fine salt

6 tbsp olive oil

Melted butter, for brushing

FOR THE FILLING:

500g (1¼lb) fresh spinach, washed and thoroughly dried

2½ tsp fine salt

1 medium onion, peeled and finely chopped

2 tbsp olive oil

2 tbsp sumac (from Middle Eastern shops)

Large handful of pine nuts

Knob of butter

5 tbsp lemon juice

1 tsp freshly ground black pepper

Method

Place the yeast and sugar in half the warm water and leave until it bubbles.

Put the flour and salt in a large mixing bowl, making a well in the middle. Add the oil and yeast. Knead the dough for 15-20 minutes until soft.

Add the rest of the water bit by bit; you may not need all of it.

Place the bowl in a warm spot, with a cloth over it, for 1½-2 hours, until double in size.

For the filling, put the spinach with 1 tsp of salt into a bowl. Rub them together until the spinach reduces down, then chop. (Don't cook it.)

Fry the onion in the oil until transparent, then stir in the sumac.

Mix the (uncooked) spinach with the onion.

Fry the pine nuts separately in the butter until light

golden brown. Stir these into the spinach with lemon juice and pepper.

Preheat the oven to 180ºC/gas mark 4/350ºF and grease a couple of baking trays.

Knead the dough a little and divide it into about 30 pieces. Roll them out into 7½cm (3 inch) rounds.

Place about 1 tsp of the spinach filling into the middle of each circle. With your finger, wet the edge of the circle and fold over the pastry, pinching it closed.

Place the pastries on a baking tray and brush with butter. Bake for 20-30 minutes, until light golden. ("God, these are good!" says Nadia.)

18

CONFRONTATIONS

"dear Mr Brewster,
I would like to draw your knd attention that ms. Vicky didn't give the students a comperhension test on the last day. When you have a close look given to the work in Mr. Wayne's class, you will feel you are in another school and this is not the same standard.
Fatima's mother"

Jake is a natural storyteller, which is why he was such a popular history teacher. I never tired of his anecdotes and as always, he acted out the story.

"Only my mom knew I was coming home for Christmas, because I wanted it to be a surprise. My dad and the rest of my family had no idea," said Jake, a grin lighting up his face. "So, I waited for my dad to get home from work, ran upstairs and Skyped him. He was on our main computer downstairs. Anyways, we chatted, and he never caught on that I was upstairs. Then I beckoned Julia, my three-year-old sister, who climbs up onto my lap. She says, 'Hi, Daddy!' and he looks puzzled. He says, 'Jake, how are you doing this?' then his eyes tear up, and he turns to my mom. 'Where is he?' he asks. 'Course she's grinning like a Hallowe'en pumpkin and points up. Then I hear him pelting up the stairs. Greatest surprise I have ever executed!"

Our friend, Kent, now a fully-fledged BWMDC member, had also not announced his homecoming. He laid down and hid amongst the wrapped gifts under the Christmas tree, then jumped up, nearly giving his grandmother a heart attack.

On the first day of the new term, Jasim and the school bus arrived on time. The automatic door system of the bus seemed to have developed a fault, but Jasim had a solution. We all climbed aboard and the door refused to close, so Joe jumped up to wrestle with it. Jasim waved him away and lifted a long stick from the floor. Expertly, he prodded the door closed, without even leaving his seat.

The school looked the same, apart from Arabic

graffiti that had appeared on the outside walls. However, the area looked different. The usual black Shi'a flags had multiplied and were draped from buildings surrounding the school. We already knew that the school stood in a fiercely Shi'a area, although the owners of the school were Sunni. We'd been warned not to wander out alone, as Westerners were not popular and considered spies for the government. In some Shi'a areas there were no street lights, as the residents wouldn't accept them.

We punched our cards into the clocking-in machine, black ink, on time, and made our way across the courtyard. Progress was slow as all the students wanted to shake Joe's hand.

"Good morning, Meester Joe!"

"Good morning, Ali."

"Good morning, Meester Joe! You are the best!"

"You're not getting an 'A', Talal."

"Aww... Meester!"

To my surprise, my classroom was unlocked, and somebody was in there, waiting for me. Fatima's mother.

"Good morning, Miss Vicky," she said, her gimlet eyes boring holes into me. "The Hall Monitor let me in. I want to talk to you about the work you are planning this semester. I know that Mr. Wayne..."

CONFRONTATIONS

I cut her short. It takes a lot for me to see red, but I was furious. Did she not know that I planned most of Mr. Wayne's lessons? Or that Mr. Wayne took days off at will, leaving me to set his lessons and instruct the substitute teachers? And why should I have to explain all my lesson preparations to her?

"I'm sorry," I said grimly. "I don't have time for this. And I really don't appreciate all your emails, or being stalked. Fatima is a good girl, and she's doing very well. If you are not happy with her education, I suggest you move her to a different school. Right, the school bell will ring any minute now and I have a lot to do. So, if you'll excuse me..." I wrenched the door open and stood back.

Fatima's mother looked shocked, and her pale face reddened.

"Well!" she said. "If you will not cooperate with me, I must talk to your Principal again."

"Please do that," I said, and closed the door firmly behind her. I couldn't count on Mr. Brewster to back me, as he didn't relate easily to female staff, and thought that Wayne walked on water. But by now, I was beyond caring.

Something good came out of that encounter. Mr. Brewster's Deputy sided with me and a new school rule came into force. From now on, parents couldn't wander around ASS, accosting the teachers at will. The security guards at the entrance gates were ordered not to admit Fatima's mother during school hours. If she, or any parents wanted to speak to a teacher, they now had to make an appointment.

It didn't stop the emails, but now they were sent to Mr. Brewster, or his Deputy, and were no longer filling my inbox. In fact, this was the last one I saw, as Mr. Brewster finally agreed that the woman was a nutcase. He ignored all further messages from her. Hooray!

"dear Mr Brewster,
Mr. Wayne's class did a vocab quiz today and also questions from the yellow book chapter 12. I feel English is the biggest subject and it needs more concern and follow up. I hope you agree.
Fatima's mother"

There was also other good news. Dr. Cecily, one of the Three Fat Ladies, handed in her notice. She'd secured a job as some kind of advisor to the Crown Prince, and would be leaving ASS. This didn't affect me much, being in the Middle School, but I was pleased that one of Daryna's enemies would no longer be there to needle her.

Smokers' Corner was buzzing with the news and all the other ASS gossip. All the regulars were there, apart from Rashida, and much of the gossip centred around her in her absence.

Our contracts stated that we were not permitted to give paid private tuition to students without the school's permission. Rashida, ever money-conscious, had flouted that rule for years. Unfortunately, she'd taken it a step further. The story was that she'd deliberately given a bright student low grades, and then charged his parents for extra tuition. Mrs. Sherazi, the school owner, had found out and was justifiably furious.

And there was more gossip. Young Mohammed whispered that Dawn, another of the Three Fat Ladies, and crazy Brent had become an item. There must have been a big age difference, and it was hard to imagine the two together.

"Oh well, at least they won't spoil another couple," said Joe.

"It's t-t-t..." stammered Saeed.

"It's true?" suggested Joe.

"No, it's t-t-t..."

"It's Tuesday?" Colton tried.

"No, it's t-t-t...turning c-c-cold now, isn't it?"

Essam, from Egypt, who taught Arabic Studies in the High School, happened to be at Smokers' Corner, sitting next to Colton. Since the beginning he had always called Colton 'Mr. Kelton' but nobody had ever corrected him.

"Mr. Kelton," he asked, turning to Colton, "are you cold?"

"Yeh, I do feel a bit cold. The wind is quite chilly today."

"Hee hee!" wheezed Mr. Essam. "I will call you 'Mr. Colton', because you are cold! Mr. Colton! Hee hee!"

Back at the hotel there was more news concerning the Three Fat Ladies, although this snippet was told to me confidentially. Daryna invited me into her room.

"So," she began, "I was going to suggest to Rita that she might prefer to teach computer skills in future. She's brilliant at computers, a real natural. I thought she'd jump at the chance, but she didn't, at all. She must have heard about my plan through the ASS grapevine. She storms into my office and goes completely berserk! And you know how big and loud she is..."

"Wow, scary! Was anyone else in the office?"

"Yes, my secretary was there. Anyway, Rita is bawling at me, stamping her feet and slamming that huge fist of hers (it's the size of a ham!) onto my desk. She is *livid*, and I'm just glad she didn't explode - that would have been messy!"

I shuddered at the thought.

"Somebody told me ages ago that she's on medication for mood swings," said Daryna, "so I wasn't too surprised. But my secretary went ashen and just gaped."

"Gosh, you're brave!" I said. I'd heard Rita in full voice and it scared the chorizo out of me.

"Well, she finishes up by stomping round to my side of the desk, still shouting, and says, 'blah-blah-blah, you can kiss my ass', and bends over, pointing at her planet-sized derriere. My secretary is shaking by now. I can see her knuckles have gone white. Rita marches out, satisfied that she's made her point, and I just get on with my work."

"Well, I'd have been terrified! I hope that was the end of the story?"

Daryna laughed and took another sip of coffee. "Of course it wasn't! You know ASS! I'd already forgotten about it, but it seems that my secretary got straight on the phone to Mrs. Sherazi and told her all about it. Mrs. Sherazi was horrified and told my secretary that she would not be renewing Rita's contract for next year as behaviour like that was unpardonable. So I wrote a long begging letter to Mrs. Sherazi, explaining that Rita's on meds for mood swings, she was probably just having an 'episode', and that I'm sure she didn't mean it, etc."

I was impressed. The Three Fat Ladies had done nothing but make Daryna's life a misery, and here she was standing up for them.

"Well, I got a very terse reply from Mrs.

Sherazi. She said that my letter didn't sway her at all, and that her decision was final, and never to write her begging letters again. And, to make matters worse, she summoned Rita, and ordered her to apologise to me."

"Did she apologise?"

"Yes, she did, though I didn't really want the apology. I forgave her immediately, but after having got Mrs. Sherazi's reply to my letter, I knew she'd need to look for another job."

"Oh dear. Then she doesn't know about that?"

"Nope. She will soon, though. The Letters of Intent we have to sign if we want to come back next year are beginning to arrive in people's mailboxes now."

Were they indeed? Should we come back? Without Fatima's mother on my back, school life had settled down somewhat. I thought perhaps we should stay one more year, just to put money aside for our future. The thought wasn't attractive, as my heart was in Spain, but it would be the sensible thing to do. However, I knew Joe would fight me tooth and nail. I doubted I'd ever persuade him to stay in Bahrain another year.

January was an interesting month. Jake and his girlfriend, Emily, both had birthdays in January, so the rest of us hatched a plan. How about a stay at the luxury Gulf Hotel? Colton and I spent a hilarious half-day checking out the hotel, and working on a deal. We were given a guided tour of a typical guest room. The staff seemed to think that the not-very-good-unless-you-were-a-contortionist view from the window, of the King's palace, was the main selling feature. And they got very excited about offering a complimentary 'KG chocolate cake'. We didn't like to ask what exactly that was.

But the 16 fine-dining restaurants, and lagoon-style pool set in tropical gardens, were attractive. And, as the hotel blurb states:

"Platinum rooms offer contemporary furnishings, luxury bedding, 24-hour room service, evening turndown, attentive butler service, in-room safe, private lift, satellite TV and Internet access. In addition, individually controlled air conditioning and mini-bar ensure a perfect stay, whilst the luxury bathrooms offer shower, bath tube and an extra plasma TV."

A bath tube and plasma TV in the bathroom, plus the complimentary KG cake? We were also promised balloons, a Happy Hour, and breakfast with a 'live cooking egg'. How could we resist? Colton and I signed on the dotted line and booked a Platinum Room.

I confess, I'm still not sure what a bath tube is,

or a KG cake, or a live cooking egg. One day I must remember to ask Jake.

Now we had to wait for Emily's birthday later in the month to surprise both Jake and Emily with our gift.

The death of the young Tunisian who had set himself on fire, after having had his fruit stall confiscated, was announced on the 4th of January. Over 5000 people took to the streets of his home town, demanding better living conditions and a stop to police brutality and corruption in Tunisia. The Arab Spring, unnamed as yet, was born.

COUSIN ELIAS'S EASY PEASY CARROT CAKE

Ingredients (Makes a 20cm (8 inch) cake)

115g (4oz) butter, melted

3 eggs, beaten

5 heaped tbsp natural yoghurt

225g (8oz) carrots, peeled and grated

175g (6oz) ground almonds

115g (4oz) soft light-brown sugar

115g (4oz) shelled walnuts, chopped

55g (2oz) dessicated coconut

115g (4oz) stoned dates, chopped

1 tsp ground cinnamon

½ tsp freshly grated nutmeg

1 tsp baking powder

Method

Preheat the oven to 170°C/gas mark 3/340°F.

Grease a 20cm (8 inch) round cake tin and line with lightly oiled greaseproof paper.

Mix together the melted butter and beaten eggs.

Add the yoghurt, then the carrots and all the remaining dry ingredients. Mix well.

Pour the mixture into the prepared cake tin.

Bake for approximately 1 hour.

Leave to cool in the tin.

Turn out onto a wire rack to become completely cold.

Cut a slice (or two) and enjoy!

19

FIELD TRIPS AND TERRAPINS

Every chair in Smokers' Corner was occupied. Young Mohammed toyed nervously with his phone, lost in his own worries. The Egyptian teachers sat huddled together, faces serious, talking Arabic in undertones. We knew what they were discussing and the reason for their troubled expressions.

After weeks of demonstrations and ugly scenes, the Tunisian president had stepped down and fled to Saudi Arabia, but not before dozens of lives had been lost in fierce clashes between security forces and demonstrators.

The world was watching. With the departure of the Tunisian president, crowds surged onto the streets of Egypt, chanting, "Tell Mubarak there is a plane waiting for him, too!" Our Egyptian friends had all left family behind in Egypt, and were justifiably nervous.

Discontent was contagious, infecting other Arab countries. Speculation was growing amongst politicians, scholars and ordinary people, all wondering whether other countries, such as Algeria, Jordan, Libya and Syria would follow suit.

Unaware of the first uncertain trickles of the Arab Spring, Joe, Colton and I chatted away at the other end of Smokers' Corner.

"So when we're floatin' down the Boise River, we have this contest. It's called 'Wizard Staff'."

"What's that?" I asked, fascinated.

"Well, we use duct tape 'n' stick all our empty beer cans together to make a long staff. Then we prod other people as they float past."

"How do you win the contest?" asked Joe.

"Whoever has the longest staff is the winner," said Colton.

"And what do you win?"

"Oh, nuthin..." Colton's impish grin lit up his face.

The conversation was cut short by the arrival of Rashida, who shoved her way past the Arab teachers. Colton, always the gentleman, sprang up and gave her his seat, but received no thanks. Rashida was already rummaging in her bag, and we all knew what was coming next.

"Colton, give me cigarette. Today I leave mine in the classroom."

Colton obliged.

"Vicky," she said, inhaling deeply and blowing smoke straight at me. "How are your chickens?"

I sighed. "I don't know, Rashida. We didn't go home for the Winter Break and our neighbour isn't the letter-writing sort."

"You remember I tell you we give our chicken husband to man at shop?"

"Yes, I remember, he put it on his farm. Did your husband get those chicks he promised your grandson?"

"No, and now we have no chickens."

"Why not?"

"Before, we have two chickens, now we have not any chickens." Her fingernail scratched thoughtfully at a stain on her sleeve. "The chickens, they love the chicken husband very much. When chicken husband go, they are very sad. They do not give eggs, and they stand, very quiet, all the day."

"They missed him?"

"Yes. Even when my grandson talk to them and give them tomato, they sad. One day, my husband went in the balcony, and the chickens not in the balcony."

"Where were they?"

"I do not know. I think they, how you say it, commit sui-dice?"

"Oh, what a shame. Or perhaps they flew away to find him?"

"No." Rashida shook her head sadly. "I think they jump off balcony and commit sui-dice."

I could see Joe and Colton struggling to keep straight faces.

Rashida brightened suddenly and dug in her bag.

"I have this for all of you!" she said, pulling out a paper bag.

Rashida giving something away? Now that was unusual.

"It is Arabic bread," she said, and passed the bag around.

We each broke off a piece and tried it. It was very tasty, fresh, and fragrant.

"And now I must go to my class," said Rashida, beaming broadly. "Colton, you will give me more cigarettes for later."

Colton placed a couple of cigarettes into her grimy outstretched hand and Rashida departed.

"I've never seen her give anything away before," I remarked, somewhat uncharitably.

"Hey, she got the money off me this morning," said Colton. "She said she'd forgotten her purse and didn't have money for lunch."

That figured. Rashida's penny-pinching was

legendary. She was famous for going to the canteen, buying a sandwich, eating most of it, then demanding her money back claiming it didn't have enough meat in it.

My classes were particularly unruly that day. Cheeky Mohammed and Ahmed had set up sports kit, shoes, borrowed spectacles and a hat to create a 'new student' in an empty chair. For some unknown reason, they introduced the student as Gorg Washingtun, writing his name at the top of the quiz paper I was giving the class that day. I went along with it, although the lesson became more and more rowdy. Fatima rolled her eyes but little Huda, the mute, actually smiled.

Eventually, I had had enough, the class had become almost uncontrollable. The door opened, and Hawa slipped in, dressed from head to toe in aquamarine.

"How you spell 'quotient'?" she asked, whispering into my ear, unaware of Gorg Washingtun sitting in the front row.

I spelled the word, and she darted back to her class.

"What did Miss Hawa want?" asked cheeky Mohammed.

"I was just going to tell you," I answered, my face poker-straight. "The Ministry of Education is giving the school a surprise visit. Expect that door to open any minute. Straighten your desks, make sure you have your books open in front of you, and no more talking! The Ministry may ask you questions about today's lesson."

Gorg Washingtun was hastily dismantled, the kids quietened down and I had no more trouble. The trick worked so well that I used it on all my classes that day.

Hawa had been ordered to organise a Grade 6 field trip, which I was looking forward to, but with some trepidation. I had heard that field trips were difficult, owing to a lack of places of interest in Bahrain, as well as the students' rowdy behaviour.

A classic example was a High School field trip that took place about a month later. A European group was visiting the Bahrain Fort at the same time as our ASS students. A well-dressed lady smiled at the students and said, "Hello", whereupon our students rudely mimicked her. The lady was visibly affronted and was swiftly ushered away by her party. The lady was none other than Queen Margrethe II of Denmark.

"We are going to the City Center mall for our Grade 6 field trip," announced Hawa, adjusting her lilac beaded *hijab*. "We go to Magic Planet."

I raised my eyebrows in question. I knew that Magic Planet was an amusement arcade.

"This is how we do it in ASS," said Hawa. "You see! We will tell the kids to bring money to

FIELD TRIPS AND TERRAPINS

spen', then they mus' write what they spen', and how much is left over."

It seemed a rather elaborate way of making the kids do a sum, but I figured a day out of the classroom would be nice.

The day of the field trip arrived, and the kids all climbed aboard Jasim's bus, as well as other buses hired for the occasion. The boys were shrill with excitement, and it was hard work just getting them to remain seated. Jasim stood up and barked an order in Arabic, and the kids immediately subsided. Then he poked the door closed with his long stick, started the engine. We were off.

Each child clutched a 10BD note (£16.50 or $26USD) for spending, although many had 50BD or more. Even Fatima's eyes were shining, and little Huda's downcast face held a tiny smile.

At City Center, we all piled out and the teachers issued last-minute instructions. I joined forces with Hawa and young Mohammed and together we marched our charges through the mall, up the moving staircases and to Magic Planet, trying not to lose any kids on the way. Unfortunately, Magic Planet refused to accept a lump sum and demanded 2BD per child. Nobody had any change. All 120 ASS kids stood in the line, impatient to experience the rides and amusements, but were forced to wait and be processed separately. Young Mohammed and I, intent on finding change, shot away into the mall leaving Hawa in charge. Half an hour later it was sorted and the students entered amidst whoops of excitement.

I enjoyed that day. I enjoyed watching the kids on the hair-raising rides, and little Huda laughing when her shoe flew off. I enjoyed seeing young Mohammed shooting foam balls at the kids, his crazy room-mate, Brent, forgotten. But most of all, I enjoyed watching Hawa on the caterpillar ride, her face set in a scream of terror as it whipped her around, until she climbed off, pale and laughing.

"Oh, oh, oh! I thought thi' ride only go slowly!"

The Grade 6 field trip was a success.

The four of us were at Bennigan's, relaxing and laughing, enjoying each other's company. The bar was rowdy that evening, filled with off-duty Naval personnel from the American Fifth Fleet.

"Hey," said Colton, "when your friends, the Gin Twins, come over next month, how's about I pick them up from the airport wearing my Green Man suit?"

What a brilliant idea! I was so looking forward to the Gin Twins coming over to visit us, and they

FIELD TRIPS AND TERRAPINS

would wet themselves laughing when they saw their chauffeur.

"Well," said Jake. "I finally sorted out Emily's birthday present. Good lord, what a performance!"

"Sir Jake, Sir Joe, Sir Colton, Miss Vicky? You wan' another drink?" interrupted a smiling Filipino barmaid.

We all accepted, and settled down to hear Jake's story. As always, he acted out the scene, waving his arms and changing his voice to suit the speakers.

"So," he began, "I've been thinking of getting Emily some kinda pet for her birthday."

"A camel?" suggested Joe.

"Oh yeah! That'd look good tied up outside the hotel, or our new apartments if we ever get there... Nah, a couple of terrapins maybe. You know that pet shop in the mall, the one with the aquariums outside?"

We all nodded.

"Well, I went in about a week ago and there's this Indian guy in there. So, no kidding, this is how the conversation went..." Jake stood up to demonstrate.

"Indian guy: Good morning, sir! How are you?

Me: I'm very well, thanks! Do you have terrapins?

Indian guy: (nodding away) Oh yes, we are having terrapins, sir.

Me: Do you have small ones?

Indian guy: Oh yes, we are having small ones, sir.

Me: Right! Good, do they grow big?

Indian guy: No, sir, they are not growing big.

Me: Excellent! Could you show me the tanks, and food and stuff, please? I'll pick a tank and then I'll come back next week and buy the tank and two terrapins.

Indian guy: Very good, sir."

The Filipino barmaid arrived with our drinks, and Jake stood aside, waiting while she served. We thanked her and turned back to Jake.

"So, did you go back?" I asked.

"Yep! I went back to the shop today. Good lord! This is how the conversation went:

Indian guy: Good morning, sir! How are you?

Me: I'm very well, thanks! I've come back, like I said.

Indian guy: Excuse me?

Me: I'll take that tank we decided on last week.

Indian guy: Excuse me? What tank is the sir wanting?

Me: (I'm a bit annoyed now, I spent ages with this guy.) You remember, that tank and two terrapins that don't grow big. For my girlfriend's birthday present.

Indian guy: You are wanting to buy a tank and two terrapins that are not growing big for your girlfriend's birthday present?

Me: Yes! Yes!" Jake paused, remembering his exasperation.

"He'd forgotten you?" I asked.

"That's what I thought! I spent a long time looking at tanks and terrapins with this guy, how could he forget? Then this door opens at the back of the shop, and...the Indian guy's identical twin brother walks out." Jake smacked his own forehead at the memory. "Then it all made sense!"

"I have the terrapins hidden in my room 'til Emily's birthday," said Colton.

Joe, Colton and I exchanged furtive glances. We couldn't wait to give Jake and Emily their birthday surprise.

HARISSA
SPICY CHILI SAUCE

It's recommended that you wear washing-up gloves when chopping the chilies or you could be subjected to some very unpleasant experiences! A jar of this may be kept in the fridge, but do cover it with more olive oil to preserve it.

Ingredients (Makes about 225g (8oz))

175g (6oz) fresh red chilies

2 tsp tomato purée

4 tbsp canned pimento, chopped.

4 garlic cloves, peeled

2 tsp each of ground coriander and ground caraway seeds

1 tsp ground cumin

Salt

2 tsp red wine vinegar

Olive oil

Method

Remove the seeds from the chilies if you don't want it too hot!

Chop the chilies and place in a blender (or pestle and mortar).

Add all the rest of the ingredients and a couple of glugs of olive oil.

Blend until you have a smooth paste and check the seasoning.

20
BIRTHDAYS AND VALENTINE'S DAY

The BWMDC
cordially invite
Emily and Jake
to
Bennigan's
on
Thursday 20th January
at
6.00pm
for a Birthday Presentation
RSVP

Thursday evenings were invariably celebrated at Bennigan's. It was the beginning of the weekend, so we could let our hair down a little.

That night, Jake, Emily, Allison, Colton, Kent,

BIRTHDAYS AND VALENTINE'S DAY

Joe and I were seated round a table. Emily said she was delighted with her birthday present, the terrapins, which she had named Stella and Art(ois). Sadly, Art died a few days later. Apparently he'd never been too lively.

We'd already enjoyed a few drinks before the Bennigan's staff birthday ritual began. The staff at Bennigan's were very good at celebrating their clients' birthdays, if a little unorthodox. We'd tipped them off, and Amlet, the manager, gave us a theatrical wink. He lowered the music volume, switched off the TVs, and dimmed the lights. A conga of Filipino bar and kitchen staff suddenly crashed through the kitchen doors, dancing, banging tambourines and singing Happy Birthday, although not to the familiar tune. The Filipino 'Happy Birthday' rendition involved lots of 'happy-happy-happies', tambourine beating and hand-clapping. The last in line bore the birthday cake, complete with burning candles.

The ritual didn't stop there. Whoever's birthday it was, in our case, Emily and Jake, was expected to stand on his or her bar-stool, with an over-sized salt and pepper pot in each hand, and dance along to the singing. It was always bizarre and unfailingly hilarious. Of course everybody else in the bar, whether Naval personnel, Arabs, or family gatherings, stopped to gape, adding to the embarrassment of the birthday people. I know, because I had to do it on my birthday.

Jake and Emily fulfilled their obligations without falling off their bar-stools, blew out the candles on their cake, and the bar staff retreated, leaving us in peace.

"From all of us," I said, placing two small wrapped gifts and an envelope on the table.

They opened the first gift. It was a book of matches Colton and I had taken from the Gulf Hotel.

They opened the second, a pen with 'Gulf Hotel' stamped on the side.

Jake and Emily exchanged puzzled glances.

"C'mon, open the envelope," urged Colton.

So they did, and drew out the hotel booking together with our suggested itinerary. Judging by their reactions, I think they were surprised and delighted, although Emily eyed the itinerary somewhat dubiously.

SUGGESTED ITINERARY AND ACTIVITIES
Friday 2.00 - 6.30pm
Check in. Ride in private elevator. Try out bed. Order butler to unpack suitcase, press clothes, and polish shoes. Eat fruit. Try on bathrobes. Try out bed. Play with balloons. Take a bath while watching plasma TV and using Bvlgari toiletry. Try out bed. Conduct meeting in private meeting

room. Eat KG chocolate cake. Admire view. Try out bed. Send the BWMDC an email (with photos) using hotel computers with high-speed Wi-Fi, in Platinum Lounge. Write on personalised stationery. Try out bed.

Friday 6.30 - 9.30pm
Happy Hour with complimentary alcoholic beverages.

Friday/Saturday 9.30pm - 2.00am
Dine at Zahle Lebanese restaurant with musicians and floor show. Mr. Wissam, the manager, is expecting you and looking forward to giving you personal service.

Saturday 9.00am (approx)
Read newspapers and magazines. Breakfast in Platinum Lounge with live cooking egg.

Saturday 12.00am - 2.00pm
Checkout.

Typically thorough, Jake and Emily chronicled their birthday adventures at the Gulf Hotel. Not only did they take photographs, but created a hilarious presentation so that we could share their mini-holiday experiences. Joe and Colton set up the school projector in our hotel apartment and we awaited their arrival.

Then Joe and Colton decided to commemorate the event by dressing up. I have no idea why, except that when you put those two together, nothing good comes of it. Colton donned his Green Man outfit, but with the addition of a jacket and necktie. But I was mortified by Joe's outfit. He appeared in nothing but a black necktie and black underpants, with a black whiskey-bottle bag strung, sporran-like, from his waist, and a white tea-cloth folded over his arm.

"I'm going to stand behind Emily's chair," he said, "like a butler."

"I've never seen a butler dressed like that!" I protested.

Jake and Emily arrived, full of their stories, and more than a little alarmed at Colton's and Joe's attire. Poor Emily was most uncomfortable as Joe stood at her elbow, straight-faced.

"Would Madam care to spank the butler?" he asked, dead-pan.

We all fell about laughing, except for poor Emily who looked justifiably horrified.

Allison was the next to celebrate her birthday. We clubbed together and provided a slap-up surprise breakfast and gave her money for an

BIRTHDAYS AND VALENTINE'S DAY

extravagant shopping spree in the malls. Jake and Emily were in charge of finding a birthday cake.

"We were looking at all the different cakes at the bakery counter," Jake told us. "You can choose one that's pre-written, or order one with your own message. I complimented the Indian guy behind the counter on the beautiful writing, and he says, 'Thank you, sir. I will bring to you the writer of the messages'. Before we can stop him, he shoots away, and comes back with the chef. Good lord. The chef is covered in icing sugar and stuff, and he's holding up his hands like a surgeon. I couldn't shake hands with him, so I just shook his elbow."

That January, ugly protests erupted in Yemen, Algeria, Jordan and Lebanon. On the 25th January, later called the 'Day of Rage', thousands of Egyptians marched in the streets, demanding that President Mubarak step down. The protesters made their way to Tahrir Square in Cairo and set up camp, claiming the Square as a symbolic stronghold. The government blocked Twitter, the Internet and mobile telephone services.

Our Egyptian friends at the school became frantic. Yussef couldn't reach his wife in Cairo to find out if she and their newborn triplets were safe. I watched him in Smokers' Corner, stabbing the digits of his mobile phone, again and again, making no connection. Essam lost his permanent grin and our Deputy Principal looked pale and anxious. The school gave all Egyptian teachers permission to go home early.

The Arab Spring was gathering apace.

I suppose we were naive, but Joe and I adopted the typical British stiff-upper-lip approach. We failed to recognise that these world events could have an impact on us. Of course we were horrified, watching the protests on TV, but never believed they would affect us in Bahrain. After all, Bahrain was a contented, peaceful, tolerant, wealthy island. Wasn't it?

I remember 11th February clearly as we watched the event on TV at Bennigan's. A huge announcement. After eight weeks of protests, and numerous deaths, the Egyptian President, Mubarak, stepped down from office.

His Deputy read a speech. "In the name of Allah the most gracious, the most merciful. My fellow citizens, in the difficult circumstances our country is experiencing, President Muhammad Hosni Mubarak has decided to give up the office of the President of the Republic and instructed the Supreme Council of the Armed Forces to manage the affairs of the country. May Allah guide our steps."

BIRTHDAYS AND VALENTINE'S DAY

Coincidentally, (or not) the King of Bahrain suddenly announced that he was giving 1,000BD (£1,600 or $2,600) to every Bahraini family. The money was coming out of his personal coffers, and all families, whether Shi'a or Sunni, would benefit.

"That's generous," I said to Joe. "I wonder why he's doing that?"

"Well, it just shows how rich he must be," said Joe, "to be able to give away so much without flinching."

"Nobody would protest here in Bahrain, would they?" I asked. "Bahrain seems to look after its people. They were saying at Smokers' Corner how education is free for the islanders, and their health service is free. And there's no income tax. So what have they got to complain about?"

How naive could I be? So we forgot about it, but not for long.

Two days later, on Sunday, the first day of the week, we returned to a very different school. In stark contrast to the week before, our Egyptian friends were besides themselves with joy. Yussef had contacted his wife and triplets and confirmed they were all fine. The Deputy Principal was handing out silver-and-gold wrapped chocolates in the corridor. Smokers' Corner was loud with backslapping and laughter.

To everyone's relief, the troubles in Egypt appeared to be over.

Egyptian parties were taking place in the Arabic staffrooms. Rashida, although Lebanese, visited each party, sampling the wares, and surreptitiously slipping food into her bag to take home.

However, a large number of pupils were absent that day. Bahraini staff were seen talking in whispers, their faces grave.

"Hey, all the other schools are closed!" said Jake.

"Why?" Joe asked. "What's going on?"

"The kids in my class, they told me that there's a big protest planned for tomorrow. It's all over Facebook and Twitter."

"What? A protest? Here on the island? Why?"

"Yeah, here in Manama. Looks like they've been inspired by the goings-on in Egypt."

"I don't understand," I said. "Who is protesting? And about what?"

I'm ashamed to admit that I don't enjoy or follow politics much, but gradually, I grasped the situation. The Shi'a were protesting against the Sunni government. The Shi'a, who made up seventy percent of Bahrain's population, were resentful. All the top governmental posts, the best contracts and most lucrative business deals, they claimed, were awarded to Royal Family members

BIRTHDAYS AND VALENTINE'S DAY

or Sunnis. The unelected Prime Minister of Bahrain, the King's uncle, was the longest-serving Prime Minister in the world. He had been appointed in 1971, forty years ago.

Followers were being whipped up by Twitter and Facebook, urging them to congregate for a 'Day of Rage'. It was obvious that Egypt's uprising had sent powerful shockwaves across the Middle East, which now lapped the shores of Bahrain.

That night, I checked out Twitter and was disturbed. Tweets were coming through, so thick and fast, I scarcely had time to read them:

"Join us! Shi'a should not be 2nd class citizens! #Bahrain"
"March to Pearl Roundabout, 14th Feb #Bahrain"
"Day of Rage. Be there! 14th Feb #Bahrain #Lulu #Pearl"

This was serious. As the crow flies, our hotel was roughly a mile and a half (2.5km) from the Pearl Roundabout, the centre of many intersecting highways. The Lulu mall was also situated there, hence the hashtag Lulu. Was this protest really going to take place in peaceful Bahrain? Was something terrible about to happen? We awaited the next day with trepidation, and my thoughts turned to our peaceful Spanish village where the only conflict was about football.

Valentine's Day, the 14th February 2011, dawned as a beautiful day, warm and cloudless. A Valentine's card and wrapped chocolates from Colton were left outside our door. Emily had sneaked out early, to fill their car with pink, heart-shaped balloons, as a surprise for Jake.

Jasim and the bus arrived on time and I spared a thought for Daryna. She now travelled in a separate school minibus, which picked her up at a ridiculously early time. She was the only passenger, and each day her driver arrived earlier and earlier.

The reason for this was Arab etiquette. Daryna was the High School Principal, an important person, and her driver didn't want to keep her waiting. Daryna, naturally polite, didn't want to keep her driver waiting. So each would arrive earlier every day, intent on not offending the other.

"If this carries on, I'll be catching the bus the night before," she said ruefully.

The journey to school seemed pretty normal. Jasim poked the door closed with his stick and ignored two sets of red traffic lights. The only unusual sight was the police presence on the road, much more than we'd ever seen before.

Less than half of the kids in my class attended

school that day. One of my pupils, Ameena, surprised me with a Valentine's card, and I began to take the register. There was a knock on the classroom door, and to my astonishment, Joe marched in. He presented me with a single, long-stemmed, red rose. As he is definitely not the romantic type, I was quite taken aback.

Of course this event set off whoops and whistles from my class.

"Mees! Give him a kiss, Mees!"

So I did, amidst much cheering.

"This is my husband," I informed them severely.

Later, I spoke to Hawa, who had watched the scene through her open classroom door.

"My husban', he never give me no rose!" she said.

"Well, it's a first for Joe..."

"So I phone my husban' and I say, 'Why you never buy me no rose?' and he say, 'You no' worry! If I buy you rose it mean I done something bad!'"

In my classroom, I did not launch into my planned lesson, much to the kids' delight. There seemed little point with so few kids there. And as the day wore on, we heard helicopter activity above us and police and ambulance sirens screaming past.

ROSEWATER AND PISTACHIO ICE-CREAM

Nadia won the MasterChef final with this delicious recipe and both judges literally swooned. (In fact, the judge said he wanted to live next door to her!)

Ingredients (Serves 4-6)

150ml (5 fl oz) full-fat cream

150ml (5 fl oz) double cream

55g (2oz) shelled ground pistachio nuts

½ tsp very finely ground cardamom seeds (use a pestle and mortar)

2 egg yolks

85g (3oz) caster sugar

2 tbsp rosewater

A drop of red food colouring

Rose petals to decorate (optional)

Method

Pour the cream, nuts and cardamom into a saucepan. Bring to the boil then set aside.

Beat the egg yolks and sugar in a bowl until they are pale, then beat in the boiled cream and milk.

Put it all back into the saucepan and stir constantly over a very low heat. Continue stirring until the consistency is that of custard but never allow it to boil!

Add the rosewater and food colouring.

Place all in an ice-cream maker and churn until thick and creamy. (If you don't have one, put the mixture in a plastic container and put in the freezer, stirring every now and then to break up the ice crystals.)

Scatter the rose petals on top to serve.

21

FUNERALS AND AN ATTACK

The school sent everybody home early that Valentine's Day. Back in our hotel room, I opened Twitter and watched the tweets (and photos) fly past. Many tweets were in Arabic, but there were enough in English to see what was happening.

There was no doubt about it, the protest was massive.

People were marching from all corners of the city and congregating at the Pearl Roundabout. Just like Tahrir Square, in Cairo, the Pearl Roundabout had become the symbolic stronghold of the protesters.

The demonstration made the BBC news, which reported that thousands had joined the march. Chillingly, tweets were claiming that the authorities had arrived and that police were firing tear-gas and rubber bullets, even though the protest was peaceful. One protester was reported killed and instantly proclaimed 'The Martyr'.

To celebrate the Prophet Muhammed's Birthday, the 15th February was a holiday. I was determined to ignore the buzzing helicopters and constant sirens and use the time to catch up with my grading. As usual, the sentences the boys had written made me wince. Fatima's, though, were perfect.

Fatima: My mother gives me <u>sympathy</u> if I hurt myself.
Cheeky Mohammed: The music was play by a <u>sympathy</u>.

Fatima: Animals will <u>perish</u> if you don't feed them.
Mustafa Kamel: I <u>perish</u> my shoos wen they are dirty.

Joe was snoozing, and my heart wasn't in grading. I turned back to Twitter, then wished I hadn't.

Muslims usually bury their dead within 24 hours. First the family wash the corpse, then wrap it in cloths. The body is then carried on a funeral march to its place of burial. It will be laid in the ground, usually without a coffin, on its right side, facing Mecca. I knew the funeral of yesterday's 'Martyr' was taking place, and was dismayed to read the tweets on my computer screen:

"Started walking w body of young man killed y'day police fired at us #Bahrain"
"#Bahrain Stop!Stop!Stop! We r all brothers and sisters! #Lulu"
"#Bahrain Footage appears to show police shooting into crowd. Can anyone verify?"
"Riot police charging, firing birdshot on peaceful protest #Bahrain"
"Teargas. Some people scared shitless incl myself. Gunfire made us all run back #Bahrain"

News of the protest and heavy-handed riot policing hit the world news that day. The BBC, CNN, and all the major news networks reported that there had been numerous injuries, and at least one more death at the funeral procession of 'The Martyr'.

My email box filled up with messages from friends and family, all basically asking the same thing: *"We've just seen the news, are you okay?"*

Hurriedly, I reassured everybody, *"We're fine, don't worry."*

And it was true. Although we weren't far from the clashes, our area of Manama was like an isolated and separate little world. If one blocked

FUNERALS AND AN ATTACK

one's ears to the helicopters overheard, and the sirens, one could imagine it was just another typical day.

"Do you think the Gin Twins will still come over?" I asked Joe, when he woke up.

"Oh, all this'll have blown over by the time they come," he said.

I hoped he was right, but the TV and Twitter were telling me otherwise. Now the demonstrators were pitching tents on the Pearl Roundabout, under the shadow of the giant monument. And, all the time, more people were arriving.

The next day, the 16th February, very few students came to school. Roadblocks had been set up on all the major highways to prevent movement and people reaching the Pearl Roundabout.

Hawa, young Mohammed and I combined classes, but school work was the last thing on our minds. Everybody had a story to tell, and many of the children had witnessed scenes from their own homes. Some had even joined yesterday's march.

"Mees, I went on the march yesterday!" whispered chubby Zainab, her eyes shining with excitement. She'd come to chat with me at my desk.

"Did you, Zainab? Wasn't that dangerous?"

"Yes, Mees. I went with my Mom and Auntie."

She adjusted her *hijab* and took a breath. "Mees, the police were firing and there was tear-gas, but we still walked. Mees, it's not fair that the Shi'a people can't get good jobs. My Mom says we have to tell everybody."

"But this is not a protest of Shi'a against Sunni, is it?" I asked.

"No, Mees! The Shi'a and Sunni people are together all the time, no problem. We are friends. But the government, they only give all the good things to the Sunni."

"What about the 1,000BD the King gave everybody last week?"

"Mees, my Mom says that was to keep us quiet! My Mom says that the King was worried after what happened in Egypt! That's why he give everybody money! Some Shi'a families won't take the money."

"Well, it worries me that you went on that march, Zainab."

"Mees, I'm going again tonight! I'm going with my Mom and Auntie, and my two little sisters. We are taking a tent, and we are going to stay at the Pearl!"

Cold shivers ran down my spine. "Zainab, I wish you weren't going," I said, because I couldn't think of anything else I could say.

All pupils and staff were sent home at lunchtime. There was a terrible atmosphere of

FUNERALS AND AN ATTACK

foreboding amongst us all, belied by the clear skies and warm weather. But the sirens and helicopters reminded us that something totally out of the ordinary was taking place.

"Are you sure it's still OK to come out to Bahrain?" wrote the Gin Twins.

"So far, yes," I answered, but for the first time, I didn't feel quite so confident.

I tried thinking of lighter subjects. Some weeks ago, knowing that the Gin Twins were coming over, I'd had an idea. I asked the Gin Twins if the children in their Year 6 class might like to write to my Grade 6 kids. I thought it would be nice if they became pen-pals, and find out a little about each others' lives.

Using the projector connected to my computer, I showed my classes a map of the world and asked them to point out Great Britain. They made many attempts, but the closest they got was Iceland.

So I asked them to point out Bahrain.

"Mees! I know!" said Ahmed, and pointed to China.

Only Fatima could find Bahrain. However, I forgave them. Bahrain is such a tiny island, a mere pin-prick, dwarfed by surrounding countries like Saudi Arabia.

I displayed pictures of the school the Gin

Twins taught at, and West Sussex, to all my classes.

"Mees!" said Mustafa Kamel. "The houses are all stuck together!"

"Yes, Mustafa, they're called 'terraced' houses. They're very common in Britain."

Mustafa Kamel wasn't impressed. I suspected he lived in one of those white, pillared mansions I'd often seen. A far cry from a terraced house in a seaside town in West Sussex.

The Gin Twins started the ball rolling and the letters from England arrived. I distributed them to my classes. I wish I could show more but the following are typical of the rest:

"Dear Friend,

My name is Molly. I like annoying my brother Paul. I hate sprouts. I never had a party. I am 10 years old and I hope you write back.

Molly"

"Dear friend,

In my house we have 4 dogs, 8 goldfish, 2 rabbits and 1 cat but the cat died before I was born. The things I would like to know are you a boy or a girl. I'm not sure how you live your life in Bahrain

so please tell me. My teacher says you have lots of sand. We have a beach but its horrible stones and seaweed smells. Our school is called st marys after jesus's mum. My mums mum and dad live near me so I can have a cup of tea and they have choclate they hide in the frig. Do you have secret choclate.
bye friend
from Ross"

"Dear Friend,
My favourite game is british bulldog. I have freckles. When do you break up from school? Its not very hot here its always raining except for today. My mum works as a cleaner and my dad is a chef and waiter.
yours sincerely,
Liam"

"Dear Friend,
My fevered subjects are English, Maths and PE. On weekends I love to sit on the settee and wach TV. My mum works over night and my dad is a plasterer but he dose not work becase he has a broken leg but he is fine. My sister is cald chalet and my brother is smelly. I used to have a hamstter cald honey but she died but I'm over it.

What is your family like? What is Bahrain like? I hope thats not to many questions.
Ben"

The noise of the helicopters and sirens grew deafening and I couldn't keep my mind off what was happening just a few miles away. Back at the hotel, I switched on the TV and saw thousands more were flocking to the Pearl. By evening, reports claimed that there were 15,000 people there.

A tented town had sprung up under the towering statue. The cameras rolled, revealing pitched tents with people seated in and amongst them, chatting, eating, and making tea. It looked like a vast Arabic picnic.

On Twitter, the tweets were coming thick and fast. *"No Sunnis, no Shiites. We are all Bahrainis!"* was echoed again and again. People were posting up photos of the crowds, and the tents beneath the monument. The atmosphere was joyous, like a huge carnival.

I thought of Zainab, her mother, her aunt and little sisters, and hoped that the authorities would leave them all alone. Zainab was on my mind as I went to sleep that night.

I woke early the next day, mentally running

FUNERALS AND AN ATTACK

through my planned lessons. Perhaps get the children to finish their replies to the letters from England? But there would be no lessons that day.

Just before dawn, on 17th February, just as the middle eastern sun rose in an apricot sky, something appalling happened. Something so shocking that the world was stunned into disbelief.

In a vicious surprise attack, riot police opened fire on the sleeping, unarmed, peaceful protesters camped under the Pearl monument.

Live ammunition was used. The stunned demonstrators fled their tents into a barrage of tear-gas grenades and were beaten with police batons. Terrible injuries were sustained and lives lost, although reports differ as to exactly how many.

Riot police also targeted doctors and medics and prevented ambulances from reaching the Pearl Roundabout to collect the wounded.

Zainab! Did she and her family camp under the Pearl monument that night?

The school closed its gates. The island was reeling from the news. CNN and the BBC reported the story all day to a shocked world. I reassured my family, Twitter, and Facebook friends as best as I could, but Internet access was patchy. Some blamed the government for the loss of communication, as had happened in Egypt, but

I don't know if that was true. I do know that I saw horrific photos on Twitter, photos that mysteriously vanished, marked 'unavailable' when I tried to retrieve them to show Joe.

Joe didn't want to know or talk about it, he was too upset. Jake and I sat side by side, not saying a word, mouths open, watching the live tweets fly past on the computer screen.

"I pray for all #Bahrainis"
"I am tired, shattered and broken. I saw ppls brain's splattered & men in uniform shooting boys Why? #Bahrain"
"Panicked crowds running thru hospital after police attack. Drs rushing to ER. Tear gas grenades outside, wafting in #Bahrain"
"Blood on the street now #Bahrain"

Some Tweets were directed at me:

"@VictoriaTwead take care of yourselves ♡"
"@VictoriaTwead reading tweets from others in #Bahrain please be careful and take care"
"@VictoriaTwead my goodness, the lengths to which you will go for book and story fodder! #wishyouthebest"

Messages popped up for me from Facebook friends, this one echoing most of them:

FUNERALS AND AN ATTACK

"Good to hear from you Vicky and glad that you are safe. Just been watching the most terrible scenes on the news, protesters walking along and having live shots fired at them, killing many. We will be watching closely. Stay safe and we will keep watching, lots of love xxx"

Then came an email from the British Embassy, and I knew that we wouldn't be welcoming the Gin Twins to Bahrain after all.

22

UPHEAVALS

The message from the British Embassy read as follows:

"BAHRAIN PROTESTS - ADVICE FOR BRITISH NATIONALS.
In light of recent developments, the Foreign and Commonwealth Office has changed its travel advice to advise against all but essential travel to the Kingdom of Bahrain.
We have also advised British nationals currently in Bahrain to monitor the media, to limit travel around the island to essential journeys only, and not to go out when demonstrations are taking place. If travelling, they should maintain a high level of security awareness, particularly in public places and on major

highways, and avoid large gatherings, crowds, and demonstrations.

The airport remains open and transiting through the airport is unaffected by this advice.

We have taken this decision in response to reports of live fire in the capital Manama today. The United Kingdom is alarmed by reports of soldiers firing on protesters in Bahrain. This is an extremely worrying development.

We welcome the proposal of the King of Bahrain that the Crown Prince should initiate a dialogue between the different communities. Bahrain should take further steps on reforms that meet legitimate aspirations for greater social and political freedoms.

The British Embassy Bahrain is located in central Manama, an area close to where violence has occurred, and is closed temporarily."

So, the Embassy was advising against travel to Bahrain? Understandable, but deeply disappointing. I knew the Gin Twins would not be visiting after all, and they confirmed it.

I worried about Zainab, but it was now the weekend, and I wouldn't hear anything about my students until school opened again on Sunday.

A massive march took place, ending at the magnificent Grand Mosque, or *Al-Fateh*, just a stone's throw from our hotel. This time, it was a pro-government march, chiefly Sunni. As in the anti-government demonstrations, red and white Bahraini flags were everywhere, waved by hand, attached to cars, worn and held aloft. But this time, huge pictures of the King and Prime Minster were being handed out and displayed.

"C'mon," said Colton, "let's join 'em!"

And so, still not really appreciating recent events, we were drawn into the chanting, happy throng. These people were not anti-Shi'a, but demonstrating their love for Bahrain. It was infectious.

The weekend was rife with rumours. Military people-carriers were photographed moving in to surround the Pearl Roundabout. Or were they moving out? Hundreds more police were said to have been recruited, all from foreign countries, promised permanent citizenship by the government, provided they do their job. Reports circulated of large numbers of Shi'a arrests, of hospitals being blocked, the injured and dying prevented from being treated. It was said that doctors were being punished for administering to wounded protesters. I wasn't sure how much of this was true, but I suspect a large proportion was.

Another rumour, that the unpopular Prime Minister, the King's uncle, was poised to resign, was certainly not true.

In spite of the horror at the Pearl Roundabout,

the anti-government protesters regrouped. They swarmed over newly erected barbed wire to reach the Pearl monument again, their symbolic stronghold. Many were women, bearing flowers. This time, the police held back.

Colton and Kent went to give blood at the hospital, but were turned away.

Although a general strike had been called, we boarded Jasim's bus on Sunday as usual, and were delivered to the school without mishap. Poor Daryna was not so lucky.

The day was cooler than normal, around 20°C (68°F), which is not really very cold for us British. But, for Canadian Daryna, it was positively balmy. Her usual minibus arrived but, to her horror, it was driven by a masked man. A sinister, woollen ski mask covered his head, leaving just slits for his eyes. Daryna refused to get into the minibus and backed away, terrified.

The driver jumped out and marched towards her. Daryna, eyes huge, prepared to bolt back into the hotel.

"Mees!" called the driver, "please go in the bus!"

"Who are you?" asked Daryna, one hand on the hotel door, convinced he was a terrorist.

"It is I, your driver!"

"How do I know that?"

"Mees, you know my voice!"

"Take off your mask and show me!"

The driver's voice sounded familiar, but she was still unsure, and not prepared to take any chances. Obediently, the driver tugged off his mask to reveal his familiar features.

"Mees," said the driver reproachfully. "Today it is *freezing*. I am cold, so I wear my hat!"

They both had a good laugh about it. The driver clearly thought the Principal was nuts, and Daryna thought the driver was a wimp for needing a balaclava in such mild temperatures.

Only four children turned up in my class that day, and Joe had none. Hawa, young Mohammed and I combined classes again. Wayne didn't show up. We were ordered to carry on as normal, presumably to demonstrate the school's solidarity with the government by not participating in the strike, but it was difficult. Zainab wasn't there, and we had strict orders not to discuss the protests, either with the students, or with each other.

In the privacy of Smokers' Corner, however, discussion was rife, and the jokes were, too. We wondered if our photocopying man was responsible for reproducing all the posters of the King and Prime Minister that suddenly appeared everywhere.

When a low-flying helicopter hovered above the school, Colton said, "That'll be Miss Daryna, calling another meeting." Daryna had become notorious (and unpopular) for her numerous High School meetings.

The Arab teachers thought this so funny, they nearly fell off their chairs laughing. Essam high-fived Colton and sat wheezing with laughter for a full five minutes.

And so, during the next days, life on the island continued, but the atmosphere was uneasy. Gradually, more students returned to school, including Zainab, much to my huge relief.

The protesters had successfully reclaimed The Pearl Roundabout. Marches were taking place every day, but it was said that Saudi tanks were poised to enter Bahrain via the causeway. The Royal Families of Saudi Arabia and Bahrain have strong ties, having intermarried. Everybody knew that the Bahraini government had a powerful ally, should it need to call upon it.

Then, on the 24th February, my class was interrupted by a messenger. Joe and I were summoned to report to Administration. Were we in trouble? What had we done? We were both nervous, but reported as requested.

"Your keys to your new apartment," said a smiling Miss Naima, handing us a bunch of shiny new keys and a form to sign. "You can move out of the hotel this weekend."

At last! We thought it would never happen! Joe

won the bet. His predicted day, 1st April, was the closest, just 34 days adrift.

That night, we had a crazy time at Bennigan's and Jake and Colton had the devil in them. Kent went to the Gents, and was scared half to death when Jake and Colton suddenly burst in, shouting. Unfortunately, an Arab who had his robes hitched up, relieving himself alongside Kent, was equally terrified, and Jake and Colton had to apologise profusely.

Then, they stormed into the Ladies, knowing I was in there. I was in a cubicle and nearly did a vertical take-off in fright. Luckily, nobody else was in there at the time.

When it was time for Colton to go to the Gents, the rest of us left, taking all our possessions. The Filipino staff played along, quickly clearing the table. We hid out of sight and watched. Colton returned to find a clean, empty table and no sign of his companions. He was totally bewildered.

"Hey," he said to the bar-staff. "What happened to my friends?"

"What friends?" they answered.

Colton scratched his head, whereupon we jumped out at him. All very childish, I know, but exquisitely funny at the time.

Jake didn't get away with it either. By now I was famous for the barking that had earned me the name of Dogsbody. When Jake visited the

Gents, I crouched down on all-fours behind a pillar in the bar. When he came out and passed by, I darted out and bit him on the ankle. Jake was so astonished, he kicked out, leaving me with stars spinning round my head. Serves me right, but Jake has never stopped apologising even to this day.

All weekend Jasim operated a shuttle service with the school bus, bringing our stuff from the hotel to our new homes. He rattled across the sand at such a pace that we had to hold onto the rails until our knuckles went white. At last we shook hands with the hotel staff and Toothy, and left the hotel for the last time.

Our new apartment was gorgeous. Everything in it, cooker, fridge, microwave, washing-machine, furniture and fitments, was brand new. The kitchen, fully fitted, was roomy enough to include a table and chairs. Two en-suite bedrooms and a separate bathroom, interconnected by a long passageway, led to a vast living and dining room. Comfortable chairs and sofas surrounded a large coffee table and faced a huge flatscreen TV. These, and a big dining table with six chairs, seemed inadequate for the space.

The view, from our apartment on the 8th floor, was breath-taking. The beautiful *Al-Fateh* mosque, the sea, and the distant towers of the Financial District, all were visible through floor-to-ceiling windows that seemed to overlook all of Manama. Acres of smooth marble and wood floors left an impression of sparkling spaciousness. The colours may not have been our choice, but I loved it all. How I wished the Gin Twins hadn't needed to cancel their visit!

It was like Christmas as we unpacked all the cardboard boxes revealing brand new rugs, bedding, bedside lamps, cutlery sets, pots, a kettle and much more. We would be living in luxury.

I needed to buy a few things from the mall, and my journey by taxi took me past the Pearl Roundabout. I was astonished to see, with my own eyes, the tented town. Tents so numerous that little streets had been created, with generators, bathroom facilities, and food for sale. Police and armoured vehicles hung back, merely observing.

Jake and Colton helped us set up the Internet in our new apartment. Twitter was still busy with pro- and anti-government tweets, and the belief that it was unlikely that the Bahrain Grand Prix would take place. I tweeted rarely, very aware that all tweets were being monitored and identified by the government. We were in a potentially dangerous situation.

Messages from the British Embassy arrived daily, warning us which areas to avoid, what protests were planned, and recommending that we leave the island. The Saudi troops, tanks and armoured vehicles waiting at the other end of the causeway, were no secret.

Curiously, we didn't feel unsafe. We lived close to the school, and our area of the city seemed far removed from the troubles, despite being little more than a few miles from the Pearl Roundabout. Joe and I longed for the normality of our Spanish life, but also felt we were in no immediate danger. And the novelty of the new apartment was wonderful.

The move saw a shake-up in the rooming arrangements. Young Mohammed no longer had to share with crazy Brent and was a much happier bunny. It was strange but, apart from young Mohammed and crazy Brent, we were unaware of any other conflicts between room-mates. But now other stories were emerging.

THE FNJ (FIGGY-NUTTY-JAMMY) BRIOCHE

Nadia says, "This really is one of the most fabulously Arabic answers to the North American classic, the peanut butter and jello sandwich. The fig jam is just divine, whilst the presence of lightly toasted almonds makes it sparkle."

Ingredients (Serves 1)

Fig jam

2 slices brioche, lightly toasted

Flaked almonds, toasted

Method

Simply spread the jam over the toasted brioche and sprinkle with the toasted almonds.

Mmm, naughty!

23

CRAZY TEACHERS AND A PARROT

Joe and I, already so well accustomed to each other's foibles, felt very lucky sharing an apartment. Unmarried teachers had been allocated roommates, and exactly who shared with whom was a lottery.

Of course, not every pair would live together harmoniously. A case in point was young Mohammed and crazy Brent.

But now we heard the story of Ibekwe, the Biology teacher from Ghana, and a devout Muslim, and his roommate, Jeremy. Apparently Jeremy enjoyed one girlfriend after another, each of whom he moved into their hotel apartment. When Ibekwe returned from school and opened the door, he never knew who would be sitting on the sofa watching TV.

Jeremy drank alcohol, stole Ibekwe's food from the fridge, and borrowed money from him that he never repaid. He held wild parties and the guests often vomited in Ibekwe's bathroom. Jeremy had his car washed by Indians but never paid them, and Ibekwe was asked countless times to pay the debts. Jeremy ran up a huge bill at the hotel, the staff assuming it was also Ibekwe's responsibility, as they shared the suite. This was clearly not a match made in heaven.

Following the move to the new apartments, Ibekwe was allocated crazy Brent as his new roommate. Everyone wondered how the pair would get on.

Although we were delighted with the new apartment, the only fly in the ointment was the caretaker. He was a creepy Egyptian individual who we named 'No-Problem' as that was his stock response to everything. We avoided asking him for anything, as he would outstay his welcome, bowing obsequiously and refusing to leave, even after being tipped.

Neither did we like the way he entered our apartment at will, while we were at school. Like a detective, I set up traps to find out if he'd been snooping around. He had. He even left audacious notes for us on our kitchen table, suggesting we were using the wrong kind of washing-powder, or such like. I don't think he did any harm, but it was an invasion of our privacy.

"If the troubles here on the island were sorted out," I asked Joe, "do you think we should stay another year?"

As yet we hadn't committed ourselves or signed the Letters of Intent that the school had issued. However, and in spite of the fact that we were very happy in our new accommodation, I already knew Joe's answer.

"Not on your life!" he said. "What? Another year here, when we could be in El Hoyo, pleasing ourselves, eating our own eggs and grapes, and drinking Paco's wine? Getting up when we want? Doing whatever we like? No, I *don't* want to come back here for another year."

I agreed whole-heartedly with him, but I also felt another year in Bahrain would make our financial future more secure.

As usual, I made myself a list, to weigh up all the pros and cons.

REASONS FOR STAYING IN BAHRAIN:
Money
Fantastic friends
Fantastic apartment
No house maintenance
School work will be easier next year because we know how it all works

Hot all year round
Everyone speaks English
Free medical care
Everything convenient, shopping, etc.

REASONS FOR STAYING IN SPAIN:
No teaching
No political flare-ups
Our own house, no intruders
Our garden
Get up when we like, please ourselves
Village life
Wildlife and birds
Chickens, our own eggs and grapes
Paco's wine
Peace and quiet, no traffic

I sighed. My list hadn't really helped. But my heart was in El Hoyo, however strong the reasons for staying in Bahrain might be.

But things in Bahrain weren't getting any easier. One evening, at Bennigan's, we chatted with a Gulf Air pilot. He told us that flights between London and Bahrain had been reduced from five to just two per week, and that the crew often outnumbered the passengers.

And, much to Joe's disappointment, it seemed that the Bahrain Grand Prix would be cancelled. It was estimated that the loss to Bahrain would be in the region of four billion dollars.

On the 5th March, demonstrators formed a human chain from the Pearl Roundabout to the Grand Mosque, Al-Fateh. They waved 1BD notes as a protest that the King had allegedly sold prime land to his uncle, the Prime Minister, for a paltry 1BD per square foot. Demonstrations took place every day and didn't seem to lessen.

Daryna had the apartment next to ours but we were all so busy, we hardly saw one another. One day Joe and I returned from school to find a note pushed under our door. I unfolded it and read:

"Oops! He's done it again! Wanna know more? Call next door! He was assaulted by a violent desk! D."

I put my school bags down, and shot next door. Who was she talking about? I was pretty certain I knew.

Daryna made coffee and settled herself to tell the story. As usual she wore her pink fluffy robe with matching slippers. If her staff could see her leisurewear, they wouldn't believe it, such a contrast it was to the designer outfits she wore at school.

"Have a cake," she said, indicating a huge box of cream cakes on the table, ready to pass out to staff at a meeting scheduled for the next morning. "Those things are winking at me, and I have to spend the whole night with them in the apartment!"

"Who's done what again?" I asked with my mouth full.

"Brent!" she said, shaking her head in despair, spilling coffee into her saucer. "He's had another of his 'turns'."

I raised my eyebrows.

"You know how I've taken most of Brent's classes away from him, because he can't teach, loses the kids' work, and they all hate him?"

"Yes..."

"And how I have to use him to cover classes when teachers are absent? And how he treats the kids, refusing to shake hands?"

I nodded again. We knew Brent never shook hands. Colton and Jake had told us how he accepted work from the students. He would take the corner of the paper, between finger and thumb, screw up his face and say, 'Dirty, dirty...'.

As Colton had often said, 'the man's crazy and dumber than a box of rocks'.

"Saja was absent today," said Daryna. "She'd left all of her lesson plans written on the board, but some bright spark had rubbed them off. I usually get the Hall Monitor to pop in at the beginning of Brent's lessons, but he didn't do that today.

Anyway, Brent talked about the Theory of

Knowledge for a while and none of the kids knew what he was talking about. Four of the boys, who'd obviously heard about Brent's, er... peculiarities, all got up and approached him at the front. They smiled at him and leaned on his desk, all holding out their hands for shaking."

I nodded again. I could picture the scene. The High School boys obviously thought it was a big joke, trying to force Brent to shake hands.

"Well, Brent leans back to avoid them, and they must have nudged the desk forward. Brent goes berserk! 'Don't you dare threaten me and push desks at me!' he shouts and jumps up and grabs one of the boys by the throat."

"Oh no..."

"Well, the Hall Monitor rushes in and rescues the boy, who is really shaken. He's got a red mark on his neck, and I'm expecting huge complaints from his parents."

"So what happens now? Brent is totally unstable. Who knows what he'll do next!"

"I know! For some reason the Three Fat Ladies and Miss Naima love him. I can't fire him, only Mrs Sherazi can, and I doubt she will. All I can do is issue a third formal letter of warning, which I've done."

Quiet, young Mohammed had blossomed since he'd stopped rooming with Brent. In Smokers' Corner he'd often join in conversations and had even been known to tell jokes, although none of us understood them.

Sometimes he told us about his life in Lebanon, where his parents owned a Turkish coffee shop. One day, as Rashida snored her way through a free period beside us, young Mohammed told us about his uncle's parrot.

Apparently this parrot was smarter than the average bird. His uncle had even trained it to use the family toilet, and taught it never to fly away even with the window open. The parrot would eye the open window and his owner would say 'No!'

The parrot would feign nonchalance, whilst gradually edging its way around the room towards the open window, until it was scolded again. The parrot would shrug, give up the battle, and toddle back to its cage.

The parrot also had a fine speaking voice. As soon as it heard a key in the lock, or a knock on the door, it would shout, *"As-salaam alaykum"*, the Arabic greeting for 'hello'.

One particular day, the uncle was asleep on the couch when somebody knocked on the door.

"As-salaam alaykum!" called the parrot, but the uncle didn't wake up.

The visitor waited politely, and when nobody came to the door, he knocked again.

"As-salaam alaykum!" shouted the bird again.

"*As*-salaam *alaykum!*" answered the visitor, but still nobody came to open the door. The visitor was becoming impatient. "It's me!" he shouted, "your friend Ibrahim."

"*As-salaam alaykum,*" shouted the parrot, then made a whistle that sounded very much like the Arabic word for 'Who?'

Ibrahim, outside, was getting annoyed. "I told you, it's me, Ibrahim! Now are you going to open this door or not?"

"Who?" whistled the parrot.

"Oh, I've had enough of this!" said Ibrahim, thumping the door once more with his clenched fist, and stomped away in fury.

The bang woke Mohammed's uncle. He ran to the door and opened it in time to see the furious retreating figure of his friend Ibrahim.

"Ibrahim! My friend!" he shouted, but Ibrahim refused to turn back. It took many apologetic phone-calls and explanations before Ibrahim would speak to the uncle again.

Tears of mirth poured from young Mohammed's eyes as he relived the story, and his spectacles misted. "That parrot!" he said, catching his breath. "Do you know, it even bowed whenever it heard the call to prayer?"

"Does your uncle still have it?" I asked.

"No," said Mohammed, shaking his head sadly. "We gave it some cucumber and it died."

Rashida woke up with a violent snort and looked at her watch. She yawned and stretched, revealing damp stains under her arms.

"Is that the time?" she said. "Colton, give me cigarette!"

Colton obeyed and Rashida left, tucking the cigarette into the groove in the wall for later.

"Hey, animals are clever," remarked Colton. "Back in Boise, I had a friend who had this little three-legged dog. We called it Min Min Pin. It managed perfectly okay all the time, but when girls came into the house, it would go all pathetic and wobbly. And they'd say, 'Awww...' 'n' pick it up, 'n' it would bury its head in their boobs..."

I laughed all the way back to my classroom.

Bahrain faded into the background in the news, when a devastating Japanese earthquake took centre stage, but terrible things were still happening on the island. Through the grapevine we heard again of doctors being beaten for attending to protesters, of people hounded and arrested for taking part in the protests, and of police night-raids in outlying Shi'a villages.

Then, on the 13th March, the school day started normally for us, but would collapse into chaos.

24

GET OUT!

Something was happening. During my first two lessons I was regularly interrupted by the Deputy Principal tapping on my door.

"Is Noor here? Her father's come to take her home."

"Omar's mother has come to collect him."

"Can you send Khaled out, please? His mother's here."

At first, just one or two parents arrived, demanding their children, but by 11 o'clock, they were arriving in droves. So many parents turned up at once that Jasim and the security staff were forced to shut the gates. Parents were asked to name their children, one by one, through the bars. We all stood in the courtyard as parents shouted and tried to push the gates open. Saeed took charge and grabbed a megaphone.

"M-M-Mohammed Y-Y-Y..." he stuttered, but by the time he got to the end of the name, Mohammed Yasr had already been united with his anxious mother. It would have been funny if it hadn't been so frightening.

"What's going on?" I whispered to Hawa.

"I don' know," she said. "More problem. How I buy my chicken for dinner tonigh'?"

The school was cleared and Jasim drove us home. As we pulled away, I looked out of the bus window to see fresh graffiti scrawled on the outside walls. 'Freedom' and 'Down Khalifa' was painted in huge letters.

We were unaware that ugly clashes were taking place at several locations. Protesters had managed to blockade the main roads into the Financial District using anything, including bricks laid out to spell political messages. They burned car tyres on the tarmac which explained the doughnut-shaped marks we had seen when we first arrived in Bahrain.

The protesters were fought by security forces who used tear-gas and rubber bullets. More clashes were being reported from Bahrain University.

Then police attempted to clear protesters from the Pearl Roundabout, which by now had been occupied for a month, again with tear-gas and rubber bullets. Witnesses reported that thousands of demonstrators converged onto the Roundabout and that the security forces were overwhelmed and had been forced to retreat.

Another worrying factor was that anti-government protesters were now erecting makeshift checkpoints, particularly at the entrance to Shi'a areas. These were manned by masked men, armed with makeshift weapons, such as ceremonial swords and lumps of wood. It was no secret that many anti-government protesters distrusted Westerners. Britain had handed over Bahrain to Sunni rule decades ago, and the US Fifth Fleet, with the King's approval, was based in Manama. Therefore, Joe and I, as Britons, and our American friends, were not the flavour of the month.

Emails from the British Embassy were crystal clear:

"Following an increase in protests over recent days, confrontations between protesters and police today (Sunday 13th March), and reports of protesters establishing roadblocks, we advise British nationals currently in Bahrain to remain at home until further notice."

Don't leave home? We heeded that advice. The

school was located in a fiercely Shi'a area, so, as far as we were concerned, a no-go zone. From our apartment window we could see crude, but unmanned, roadblocks created by overturned dumpsters and bricks. We remained in our apartment that day.

And at the back of everyone's mind was the army of UAE and Saudi troops, and tanks, poised at the end of the causeway.

On the 14th March, our fears were realised. The Saudi army began to roll across the causeway into Bahrain in a slow, sinister, never-ending line. I watched the comments on Twitter and saw the photographs as the armoured vehicles, nose to tail, approached Manama.

"The Times is reporting that more than 1,000 #Saudi troops have entered #Bahrain"

"Tanks! Watching #Saudi military arriving. More than I can count. There will be blood. #Bahrain"

But amidst the terrifying comments, somebody with a sense of humour, tweeted:

"The beginning of the end? Troops from Saudi arrive. But.. But.. wait, we are used to being invaded by the Saudis EVERY weekend!"

GET OUT!

The message from the British Embassy, although it had closed its gates until further notice, was brief, but chilling:

"The British Embassy is aware of the arrival of Peninsula Shield coalition forces in Bahrain. We continue to advise British Nationals to remain at home until further notice."

Daryna knocked on our door. She was in her pink robe, with rollers in her hair.

"Joe! Vicky! Don't go into school tomorrow! There are road blocks everywhere! Tell everybody, no school."

She needn't have bothered, none of us had the slightest intention of going into school.

On the 15th March, the King announced that, until further notice, Bahrain was under Martial Law. The Ministry of Defence issued a threatening statement, warning that action against demonstrators camped on the Pearl Roundabout would be swift. Martial Law meant curfews, more raids, and no gatherings of any kind.

The United States Embassy advised expats to make arrangements to get out of Bahrain. Teachers began returning their hire cars, and making preparations to leave.

The school called a meeting, held at our apartments, as we couldn't go into school. They said that they had seen the US Embassy notices, and that if anyone wanted to leave the island, they had the school's blessing until the end of the Spring Break. The school would remain closed for now, but would open as soon as possible. For our own safety, anybody who stayed was under house arrest.

They also added that, in their opinion, we were safe, and that the owners, and their grandchildren, would be staying on the island. It reminded me of the British politician who insisted that eating beef was safe, during the Mad Cow epidemic, his little daughter munching a fat beefburger beside him as he spoke.

Dr. Cecily, one of the Three Fat Ladies, spoke at length at the meeting.

"Hi, y'all," she said, addressing the ceiling. "It's good to see everybody from ASS."

"WHERE ALL STUDENTS SUCCEED," we chanted without enthusiasm.

Dr. Cecily was no longer employed by ASS, but worked for the Crown Prince. She offered advice on how to behave should we be stopped at a checkpoint. It was the same information provided to its personnel by the US Fifth Fleet Naval Base:

Before entering, lock all car doors and close windows

GET OUT!

Don't panic, be polite
Don't run through the checkpoint
Don't disobey the sentries
Don't hand out passports, or any ID, to anyone not in uniform
If you must pass out ID, open your window the barest crack
If asked, state you are an American (or Brit, in our case)
At an unofficial checkpoint, never open car doors or windows

The next big event to hit world news came soon after. The storming of the Pearl Roundabout by security forces and the burning of the tent city came as little surprise. From our apartments' rooftop we could see and photograph the black smoke rising, drifting over the city.

Pro-government supporters claimed that protesters had burned their own tents, which seemed highly unlikely.

The ASS teachers began to evacuate. One by one they said goodbye and caught planes back to the States or wherever they came from. Our crowd had a 'last night' at Bennigan's, (disobeying the house-arrest rules), which was a sombre affair, even though it was St Patrick's day. Bennigan's served green-coloured beer, my wine was green, and more cardboard shamrocks adorned the walls, but it wasn't a happy evening.

Would everybody return after the Spring Break? Or would the troubles worsen? Would we ever see each other again? Everybody seemed to be leaving, apart from Joe and myself.

The strongest reason for *not* evacuating was a simple one. My daughter was getting married in Australia. When we arrived at the school in August, we applied for a short leave of absence to attend the wedding. The wedding was during school time but only I, not Joe, was permitted to go. Although disappointed, Karly understood perfectly. Of course, back then we didn't know that an uprising was about to take place.

I'd booked and paid for my flight to Australia months ago. It made very little sense to leave Bahrain, travel back to Spain, then fly out to Australia, all in the space of a few days. The flight from Bahrain to Australia, approximately 14 hours, and the return flight to Spain, would have added double the excruciating hours.

So we decided I would travel to Australia, as planned.

"What do you want to do?" I asked Joe. "You could come to Australia, after all, now that the school's closed. Or do you want go back to Spain?"

"Absolutely not! I won't go back to Spain

without you. I'll be perfectly alright here, don't worry. You just have a good time in Oz, you won't be away for long."

I wasn't happy about leaving him, but Joe can be a terrible stick-in-the-mud. I couldn't persuade him to come with me to Oz, or to go back to Spain.

I also knew that he was refusing for another reason. The school had been good to us. They paid us well, provided fantastic accommodation, and looked after us. Nearly all the teachers had evacuated, so when the school opened, we would be sorely needed.

"Karly would so love you to be there at her wedding," I said.

"No, I'm needed here, and you'll only be gone a few days. Her mother being there is the most important thing. You'll have a wonderful time, and so will she. Don't worry about me."

I knew nothing was going to change his mind so, for now, I dropped the subject. I had a little longer to convince him to come with me. I'd choose my moment.

My other worry was my wedding outfit. I didn't have it sorted, and Daryna, who I was going to ask to be my fashion advisor, had left the country. Worse still, the souk, where I intended to have my outfit made, was out of bounds. It wasn't far from the Pearl Roundabout and the troubled areas, and, being under house arrest, I wasn't supposed to venture out.

Then, in total disbelief, I watched the TV on the 18th March. No, surely there must be some mistake? The videoclip I saw on CNN was only seconds long, but unmistakable.

In the early hours of the morning, the authorities moved in and tore down the iconic Pearl monument. The massive proud statue, that had stretched high into the sky, had been reduced to a pile of concrete rubble. It had been the most familiar landmark on the island, and now it was dust. One of its legs had fallen across a demolition vehicle, killing the driver. Another lost life to add to the many already claimed since February.

The government insisted that the Pearl monument had been knocked down to make room for a new traffic system. We knew the real reason was that it had become a symbol of the uprising.

Everybody, including the British Embassy, urged us to leave.

"Don't you think we should go?" I asked Joe again. "What's next? What if the rumours are true, and Iran intervenes? They could supply the protesters with weapons. Why don't you come to Australia, see Karly get married?"

Joe shook his head. "No, I'm staying. It'll be okay."

GET OUT!

The British government laid on a charter flight to evacuate Brits from Bahrain. It went home empty. What people in Britain didn't know was that tickets for the specially laid on flight cost far more than the regular flights that were leaving all the time, or so we were told. As we didn't want to return to the UK, it didn't concern us anyway.

Parked in all the strategic places were armoured vehicles and tanks, their guns pointing up the highways. Manama was a chilling place to be. I wouldn't be sorry to go to Australia, I only wished that Joe would agree to come too, but he was determined to stay. My flight was scheduled for the 29th March so I still had time to persuade him.

On the 20th, in an effort to regain normality, ASS again opened its gates. No students appeared. Also there were very few teachers. Hawa was there, and so was young Mohammed, but most of the others had left the island. The wonderful, colourful Wayne, so admired by Mr. Brewster and Fatima's mother, left, never to be seen again, and an expensive school projector disappeared at exactly the same time.

By the 23rd, only twenty out of 120 Grade 6 pupils attended school. As usual, Hawa, young Mohammed and I combined classes, but we taught no lessons. With numbers so low, we decided to show our charges movies.

"Mees, I brought a movie on my memory stick, can we watch it?" asked Mustafa Kamel.

"I don't see why not, I can easily set up the projector," I said. "What is the movie?"

"Mees, it's called Eeet."

"Oh, ET? I love that movie! ET-go-home..." I growled, waving my finger like ET does in the film.

Mustafa Kamel gave me a strange look but didn't say anything. I connected the computer and projector, then spoke to the class.

"Now, I'm going to leave you watching the movie. I'll be just outside in the corridor, doing some grading. Behave yourselves, or I'll be back in to give you a verb test or something."

"Aw...Mees!" they protested and settled down to watch the movie.

The movie was obviously a big success because I hardly heard a squeak out of them. Mr. Brewster came along the corridor, with Mrs. Sherazi, the school owner, Miss Naima, and the Deputy Principal.

"Ah, Miss Vicky," said Mr. Brewster, "How many pupils do you have in your room?"

"The whole of Grade 6," I said. "Twenty, I think, They're watching a movie. If we get more pupils in tomorrow, we'll try to hold proper lessons."

Mr. Brewster nodded in approval.

"What movie are they watching?" asked Mrs. Sherazi.

"ET. They seem to be thoroughly enjoying it!"

Mr. Brewster opened the door a crack, and peered into the dark room. The class was so rapt in the movie, they didn't even notice him.

"Good," he said to me, quietly closing the door again. "That'll keep their minds off things. Then to Mrs. Sherazi, "Shall I take you upstairs to see Grade 7 and 8?"

The party walked off, and I continued grading and preparing until the bell rang. Then the door opened, and the class filed out, white-faced and silent. It wasn't until the next day that I discovered why.

25

PICTURES

The next morning, a few more pupils came to school, and I was summoned to the Deputy Principal's office. She looked worried.

"Miss Vicky, I'm sorry to say that I've had three complaints from parents. They say their children had nightmares because of the movie you showed them yesterday."

"Really?" I asked, astonished. "I don't understand..."

"What movie did you show them?"

"ET, you know, the cute little alien that gets left behind and wants to go home?"

"Are you sure? Fatima's mother says it was IT by Stephen King, and that Fatima was up all night, terrified by it. And Khaled's mother said he wet the bed."

PICTURES

I gaped at her. No wonder they were so quiet!

The Deputy, a lovely lady, understood that I'd made a genuine mistake. Somehow she smoothed things over and it was never mentioned again. I only hope I haven't permanently damaged any young minds, and I deeply regret my carelessness.

Hawa, young Mohammed and I struggled on, day after day, as most of the kids returned to school. We were the only available teachers, so our days were heavy. Then, on the 29th March, I was due to fly to Australia. I'd left lots of work for the substitute teacher, but I knew this was a very difficult time to be leaving.

"It's not too late," I said to Joe, as I kissed him goodbye. "If you change your mind, you can always catch a plane and join me."

But I knew he wouldn't. There were very few teachers left in the High School, and even their Principal had gone. He was badly needed.

Mahmoud, my favourite taxi driver, took me to the airport. We passed the Pearl Roundabout, now just a giant circle of churned soil and sand. Shaking his head, he waved a hand at the tanks and armoured vehicles.

He was Shi'a and eager to tell me of the latest events on the island. He told me that journalists were being gagged and deported, preventing them from telling the world what was really going on. He repeated another story, which we'd often heard, about people being arrested and disappearing without a trace. He told me that there were underground jails in the desert, packed full of prisoners. Also of raids on villages, doctors and nurses being beaten, Shi'a mosques destroyed, torture, and dumped bodies.

On the airport road, we were stopped at a checkpoint. A tank stood by, gun-barrel trained up the highway, soldiers manning the post, cradling rifles. Two armed policemen rattled questions at Mahmoud, who replied politely, and they peered at me in the back seat. Their eyes raked me up and down. I tried to look friendly and courteous but my mind was on the contents of my suitcase.

I always keep a journal and I'd kept notes as the uprising progressed. My notes included details of demonstrations, news reports of police brutality, copies of tweets, links to websites with articles and pictures of anti-government activity. Journalists had been beaten, imprisoned and deported for much less. And my camera was crammed with photos of graffiti, illegal checkpoints and the tented city under the (now fallen) Pearl monument. How could I be so stupid?

One policeman stood over us as the other walked to the back and opened the trunk. I feared my heart would explode in my chest. However, they didn't open my suitcase or ask me any questions. Hopefully they just saw an elderly, harmless-looking Western female. They waved us through. It took a long time for my heart to stop pounding.

I travelled light as my trip was only for a few days. I hadn't been able to get to the souk, but the Indian tailor had kindly come out to our apartment. Unfortunately, I hated the finished outfit he'd made, but it was the bride that was important, not the bride's mother.

The flight to Sydney was wonderful. The plane was practically empty, and after taking an American sleeping pill given to me by Colton, I stretched out over five seats, and slept the whole way there.

Karly and her husband-to-be, Cam, had rented a lovely house in Narrabeen, in the suburbs of Sydney, for the wedding. I shared a bedroom with Karly's bridesman, (no, that's not a typo) Luciano, and my 40 year old niece, Becky. Becky and I shared a single bunk, and Luciano slept in the bunk above. We called the room the 'dorm'. It was a trifle cramped, but great fun, reminding me of my student days. And it was lovely seeing Becky again. I hadn't seen her since she'd come to visit us in Spain, when we had the Siamese cat family and Chox.

I loved Luciano on sight, he was so gentle and thoughtful. I understood why Karly had kept in touch with him since university, and why she'd asked him to be her bridesman, along with her bridesmaids. Luciano put us to shame. Becky and I soon had our stuff strewn around, but Luciano's clothes were always neatly folded and tidy.

My son, Shealan, was there, with Hannah, his lovely new wife. And I got to meet Cam's parents, Di and Barry, who were absolutely delightful, as were the rest of his family.

The outdoor wedding was glorious, overlooking Sydney Harbour. Karly, Cam and his parents had worked hard, and everything went perfectly. The reception in a nearby hotel was lovely too, even though Karly set light to her veil when cutting the cake. But that's another story…

Joe kept in constant touch via email, and I was shocked to read the following:

"Young Mohammed has been sent back to Lebanon," he wrote. *"The authorities are clearing out young men who may be Shi'a terrorists. Honestly! Mohammed a terrorist? Ridiculous!"*

I was sorry to hear of young Mohammed's fate. Nobody could be less politically active, and I knew his family depended on his income.

Too soon I had to return to Bahrain, although it was good to see Joe again and show him all the

PICTURES

wedding photos. Daryna and most of the teachers had returned.

However, there were some exceptions. Young Mohammed was still banished. The wonderful Wayne and the Athletics Director, Jane, who'd been involved in the basketball fiasco at the beginning of the year, and her hen-pecked husband, were never seen again.

The Spring Break was over and the new term began. Before, there had been many pictures of the King and Prime Minister plastered all over the school walls, but now they seemed to have multiplied. Wherever one looked, the King was watching, smiling benevolently. Occasionally the pictures would be defaced or the eyes gouged out, but these were quickly replaced. There seemed to be a never-ending supply.

I quickly caught up with all the ASS gossip. Daryna was a rich source, and she often popped in with the latest snippets.

One day, Colton was in our apartment.

"...me and my buddy Tucker, we always planned to make a raft like Huck Finn, y'know, 'n' take it down the Boise River, but we never did. Folks would use all sorts, noodles, kids' paddlin' pools, inflatable killer whales..."

He stopped as somebody knocked on our door.

"Hey, that'll be Jake," said Colton, chuckling.

"I'm gonna hide behind the curtain 'n' give him a fright."

He slipped behind the full-length curtain as I answered the door. It wasn't Jake, but Daryna, full of the latest stories about Brent.

"Do you know? He's lost all his class's assignments for the entire third quarter? He's making them do it all over again. His class came to see me today, en masse. They're furious, and I don't blame them!"

Daryna chattered on, but I was only half listening, acutely aware of Colton hidden behind the curtain, just a few feet away.

After five minutes, Colton had had enough. Casually, he stepped out from behind the curtain as though it was the most natural thing in the world.

"Hi, Miss Daryna, how are you?" he said to his Principal, and walked past her and into the kitchen to join Joe.

"Hi, Colton," said Daryna, not batting an eyelid.

She turned back to me and carried on chatting. She was a cool lady and very little ruffled her.

Two other things happened that week that I remember clearly. On the 14th April, the normally silent Nepalese caretaker staff at school, were wreathed in smiles.

"Happy New Year!" they said as they passed us in Smokers' Corner.

Joe and I were both bewildered until we discovered that the Nepalese calendar is different, and that they were celebrating the birth of the year 2068.

The other event occurred over the weekend. The weather was getting warmer but, as yet, we didn't need to turn on the air-conditioning. At night, I would open the curtains and huge windows to allow the cool air to flow through the apartment while we slept.

Joe woke up one night to hear the wind howling, but promptly went back to sleep. The next morning I was first out of bed and instantly knew something was amiss. Instead of my bare feet making contact with smooth polished floors, I felt grit. To our horror, we'd had a sandstorm overnight, and our apartment was so full of sand that we left footprints. There was sand everywhere, and in everything, including our computers and the kitchen. It took us four hours to clean up, and we swept up enough sand to create a small beach. All our food tasted of sand for days to come.

At school, posters of the King were still multiplying. Every available space had been taken, and, in many cases, the students' display work had been taken down, to be replaced by the

King's image. A vast picture of the King hung down the front of the school building.

To celebrate the visit of King Abdullah of Saudi Arabia to the island, all ASS students were allowed a 'free dress' day, meaning they could wear whatever they liked to school. The Sunni kids dressed in green, as a mark of respect for Saudi Arabia, and carried Saudi or Bahraini flags. Of course my classes were excitable that day, as children always are on non-uniform days.

During the morning my class was interrupted by Mr. Brewster.

"Could you send your students out into the courtyard?" he asked.

I went with them and was surprised at the scene. The entire Middle School was outside and a television camera crew was setting up. Joe had a free period, and he, Hawa, other teachers, and I stood behind the camera team, watching.

First, the children were ordered to sing the Bahraini National Anthem, as the cameras rolled. Then the director ordered them to back away, and at his signal, come rushing forward, waving their flags and cheering. The cameras captured the scene. This was repeated several times until the director was satisfied.

I believe the resulting film was shown on TV that night, probably as proof of the nation's love for their country and ruler. We knew the whole event had been orchestrated and I have lost confidence in TV reporting ever since.

That week, something extraordinary happened. One of the young American teachers in the High School crossed the line. In front of his class, he ripped down a picture of the King, crumpled it up and dropped it on the floor. It was a stupid, dangerous thing to do. We were not permitted to discuss the situation in Bahrain with the students, or even amongst ourselves. To destroy a picture of the King, in front of the students, was a major insult.

The students were shocked. Within minutes some used their smartphones to report the incident to their parents, some of whom were high-ranking ministers. The teacher was summoned by the school owner, and fired. For his own protection, he was removed from the island within 24 hours.

Through the ASS grapevine, we heard that another young American teacher from the High School had also publicly destroyed a picture of the King, tearing it in half. His job hung in the balance, and we waited with bated breath. Everyone knew that it would take just one phone call from a parent to have him removed. Luckily for him he wasn't reported. The school, already so short of teachers, allowed him to get away with it.

Back in the UK, the Royal Wedding between Prince William and Kate Middleton was being screened. Worldwide coverage meant that we could watch it, too. King Hamad and his son were invited, but did not attend, following an outcry from the Human Rights movement in Britain. Too many reports of Bahraini killings, torture and mysterious disappearances had filtered through into the media and their attendance would have been very controversial.

Daryna was glued to her television screen, watching the ceremony and commenting on the fashions.

But the Royal Wedding wasn't the only reason I remember that day so clearly.

LENTIL DREAM

In Nadia's words, "This dish is a dream, not only because of its gorgeous flavours but also because it's a dream come true for any host who has both veggie and non-veggie guests. It's a fantastic accompaniment for lamb, chicken or fish, but also works well with just rice and salad."

Ingredients (Serves 6-8 as a side dish)

170g (6oz) brown lentils

4 tbsp olive oil

4 onions peeled and sliced

1 whole garlic bulb, peeled and crushed

A very large bunch of fresh coriander, chopped

1 tsp fine salt

1 heaped tsp each of ground cumin and ground allspice

1tbs lemon juice, or to taste

1 tsp pomegranate syrup (from Middle Eastern/Turkish

shops, large supermarkets or online)

Method

In a heavy-based saucepan, simmer the lentils in 750ml (1¼ pints) water for 20 minutes.

Remove from the heat, drain, and set aside.

Heat 2tbsp of the oil in a frying pan and fry the onions until they are brown.

Remove the onions with a slotted spoon and set aside.

In the same pan, heat the remaining 2 tbsp of oil, then add the garlic. Cook for 1-2 minutes stirring continuously.

Add the coriander and stir until it softens.

Add half this mixture and half the onions to the lentils. To this lentil mixture, add salt, spices, lemon juice and pomegranate syrup and simmer for 20 minutes.

Before serving, sprinkle the remaining coriander and onions over the top.

26

LETTERS

It was Friday, the first day of the weekend, and Joe and I had our usual afternoon siesta. This time was sacred to us, especially after a day at school when we would fall exhausted into bed.

By now, all our friends knew never to disturb us between the hours of three and five, even at weekends. We hadn't been in bed for more than an hour, when somebody knocked on our door. A disgruntled Joe answered it.

"Just stay where you are," he said to me. "I'll chase whoever it is away. It's probably Jake or Colton. They should know we're not to be disturbed during our siesta."

Joe knew how hard I worked and was very protective of my free time, especially when I napped.

In fact it was our lovely young friend, Saja.

"Hi, Saja! How are you?" he asked.

"Is Vicky there?" she said, ignoring his question. "I need to speak to her."

"Saja, she's asleep and I don't want her disturbed. Please come back later."

Joe was very fond of Saja, but even she wasn't getting past. Had Joe known the real reason for her visit he would immediately have let her in. Alarm bells should have rung had Joe been a little more perceptive. He would have noticed that Saja was unlike her polite, cheery self and seemed edgy. Alarm bells would have rung had he checked his phone, containing frantic text messages from her, calling for help. He hadn't, and assumed this was simply a social call. He firmly, but politely, closed the door on her.

"It was Saja," he explained, climbing back into bed. "I told her to come back later."

At 5 o'clock there was another knock on our door. Joe answered it and it was Saja again. Without a word she walked straight past him and fell into my arms, sobbing.

Eventually we extracted the story. Saja was an American, but fluent in Arabic, as her family originated from Iraq. She'd always been friendly with No-Problem, the caretaker of the apartments. She treated him like a father, as there was a large age difference, and they chatted in Arabic. When she cooked, she'd sometimes take him a plate.

That day she'd been shopping in the mall, and No-Problem had helped her carry her groceries up to her apartment. Instead of leaving them at the door, he had entered, and then made a pass at her. Saja was distraught. How dare he? She pushed him away, but he persisted. She escaped, but was deeply shocked.

Joe was furious. "He can't be allowed to get away with that, the creep! We should call the police!"

"No," said Saja, a little more composed now. "Would you and Vicky go down to reception and talk to him?"

Of course we would!

No-Problem was behind the reception desk and greeted us, although he must have wondered at our stony faces. Saja trailed behind, and all four of us sat in the reception area.

No-Problem didn't speak much English, but I think Joe made it very clear that his behaviour to Saja had been disgraceful. He denied everything. Saja, braver now, verbally attacked him in Arabic. What right had he to show her such disrespect? No-Problem shook his head again, denying any wrong-doing.

Daryna was informed and, that Sunday, she and Saja reported No-Problem to the school administration. Daryna, Joe, and I were summoned to the owners' offices to give our side, through a translator. Had we ever heard of No-Problem molesting anyone before? Yes, we had. He'd tried it on with Andrea, but she was street-wise and had kicked him out. She'd never even bothered to report it. Could Saja have led No-Problem on? Absolutely not! Perhaps he got the wrong message? No! That didn't happen, we were positive. Did No-Problem ever enter our apartments? Yes, he did. He even left notes in our kitchen.

To our dismay, Saja's story wasn't believed. At the very least, No-Problem should have been dismissed. Instead, a few days later, he was transferred to the Elementary School as a security guard. Saja, a teacher in the High School, would not have to cross paths with him again.

We'd been warned that any Arab's story would be believed over a Westerner's. Personal experience now confirmed this to be the truth.

My students continued to try my patience and I sometimes wondered if I had managed to teach them anything at all during my time with them.

Fatima: The girl sewed a <u>frill</u> on her dress to make it look pretty.
Omar: I got a big <u>frill</u> wen arsenal scord a goal.

Fatima: I like to read <u>historical</u> books about people who lived long ago.
Mustafa Kamel: My sister goes <u>historical</u> when she see a spidder.

Fatima: If I am hungry between meals, I eat a <u>snack</u>.
Ahmed: A bo constrikter is a poisnus <u>snack</u>.

But they taught me many things, too. I was fascinated by their lives and culture, so different from ours. For example, I had noticed that the girls who wore *hijabs* seemed to have masses of hair piled up on top of their heads. I asked Zainab how long her hair was, under her *hijab*.

"Mees," she said, "it's not very long. We all wear very, very big hair clips on the top of our heads. We like that 'humpy' look. Very trendy, Mees! It's the style!"

That day my class was writing letters in response to those sent from England by the Gin Twins.

"Mees!" said Mustafa Kamel. "Mees, give me another! This one says his father is a fisherman! He is poor, Mees!"

I was shocked, but Mustafa Kamel wasn't the only one to complain.

"Mees! This one's father is a chef!"

"Mees! This one has no car!"

I reprimanded them severely. In fairness, it wasn't their fault. They'd been raised to consider themselves superior to poorer people. They were also blatantly racist, and the very mention of India had them scornfully wobbling their heads and laughing.

I resolved, some time in the future, to show them my favourite YouTube clip, 'Where the Hell is Matt?'[1] It shows a young man doing a silly dance around the world, joined by people from every race and creed, from Papua New Guineans to Buddhist monks. I can't watch it without shedding a tear, and I hoped that maybe it would teach them something.

At the end of term, I did find time to show them the clip. Some got it, most didn't.

"I can't believe how racist they are," I said to Hawa.

She shrugged.

"Tell me abou' it," she said. "See your skin, is darker than mine." She compared her pale arm with my tanned one. "But I lower in their eyes because I Malaysian. Now I have their respec' because they now forgot my race. But nex' year new kids and I start again."

Sometimes life seemed very unfair.

My classes completed their letters to be sent to England. They'd been warned not to mention the troubles as I suspected the authorities would censor any outgoing mail. I didn't want to be responsible for getting the school into any trouble. The following are a few examples:

"Dear Molly,
My name is Fatima and I am a straight A student. My favorite subjects are Math with Miss Hawa and Art. My Art teacher takes my canvases to galleries and stuff.
I have really curly hair and the boys sometimes call me chicken noodles. It is brown and so are my eyes. My favorite color is cyan. I don't have a brother or a sister but I don't really want one.
I live next to the seashore too! I'm really good at swimming but we never swim in the ocean, only our pool which is very big. When I was 7 I had a swimming test but the light was bad so I didn't win, but I cried for a long time. I have experienced a lot of sports such as tennis, basketball, karate and ping-pong. My house has a gym and tennis court.
I speak Arabic, French and English fluently. What languages do you speak?
Your friend,
Fatima"

"hey ross
I read your letter it was good. You have alot of animals in yore house. Why you have alot of animals in yore house? My uncle has a falcone that bites me. I'm unpleased about what is going on in Bahrain. I am muslim not catholic. I love watching tv i watch it so much i have to wear glasses. I like to go on holiday and we are going to syria this year. I like machester united liverpool arsenal barcelona. I like choclate and keep it in my closet. I have amazing friends but one is mysteerious.
Plese write back,
Mustafa
PS I am a boy
PPs ive seen pictures of your beach and peer. I live on an island in a very big house."

"Hello Liam,
I don't now how to play british bulldog. i love watching tv and football but i can't play good beceus i am fat. i have a bother called Yssef and he is ANOYING. i have a bother called Ahmed and sometimes we wrestle in bed. i like to play drums. do you play a insterment? my favorit subject is english except when Ms vicky is in a bad mood. our teachers are nice but some are not. my best friends are mohammed r, mohammed Y,

mohamed A and Mustafa but hes not speaking to me now.
ok bye
Mohammed"

"Dere Ben,
I got your leter and i am going to answer it now. bahrain is really peasfull but there are some people who wants bahrain to be for another country and they make roadbolocks. my favorite food is piza i like it alot. i like to play with my playstayshun and i am very adicted to it. my made makes nice hottdogs.
Hassan"

Oh dear, my English teaching, and my careful focus on spelling and vocabulary, hadn't seemed to have made much of an impression. Sighing, I slipped the letters into an envelope and posted them to the Gin Twins in England.

The 12th May was another 'Bahrain Day'. All the students were dressed in red and white, the colours of the Bahraini flag. A table was set up in the courtyard, manned by some older High School boys. They were inviting the Middle School children to write comments in a big, open book.

"What is that book?" I asked one of my students.

"Mees, you write your name in the book, and your phone number, Mees, if you love the King."

I turned away. The book made me feel uncomfortable.

At the High School, tempers were becoming frayed. Already short of teachers, some of the younger ones frequently took days off, leaving others to cover for them. Exams were looming, and both students and teachers alike were irritable.

"I know all my students are going to fail," Joe said gloomily. "They refuse to do any homework, and they never study in class. And that Talal! Honestly, I despair..."

"What's he done this time?"

"I asked him for his homework, and he told me to wait a minute. Then (he thought I hadn't noticed), he tears off a corner of his exercise book and scribbles something in pencil. So I ask him again for his homework, and he brings up this note."

"What did it say?"

Joe shook his head. "Word for word, it said, 'Talal is sick today. Signed Talals mother.' It was so ridiculous I just laughed."

"Hey, I nearly got into trouble today," said Colton. "I was eating sunflower seeds with my students, 'n' you know they're banned because of the mess. Anyway, Miss Daryna comes in. She stands in the doorway, glaring round at 'em all, 'n' sees a coupla students eatin' seeds, 'n' she bawls 'em out. She looks at me, but I've got a mouthful, so I just nod, 'n' use my eyes for expression. Got away with it, I think."

We were in Smokers' Corner, escaping from the school building. Our chairs were ones that had been thrown out, tatty-looking, but useable. The chairs stayed out at night, as it never rained, but this morning, one of them was damp and smelled strongly of cat. We assumed that feral cats slept on the chairs at night, and that particular chair had been watered by an especially pungent tom.

Rashida's familiar footsteps clopped around the corner. She paused to pry out her half cigarette from the wall, and squinting, held her lighter to its ragged end. Then she spotted Colton, and quickly replaced the stub in its hiding place.

"Ah! Colton! Give me cigarette! I leave mine in the classroom."

Colton rolled his eyes at us, but handed her one. She lit it, and looked for a chair to sit down.

"Here you go," said Colton, eyes large with innocence. "Come and sit here."

He gestured to the stinky chair.

Rashida plonked herself down, wriggling her voluminous backside, making herself comfy. It was hard to keep a straight face.

She inhaled deeply. "Look! I have new trouser!

I queue at City Center, they were making a very nice bargain, two trouser for just 6BD!"

We admired them, but it was difficult not to laugh.

"Have you sign your Letter of Intent yet?" she asked, looking around at us all. "Today I sign my contract. I am coming back."

So, yet again, the school had forgiven her for her misdemeanors. I wasn't surprised, as they were desperately short of teachers. I suspected, too, they'd keep Rita, the Fat Lady who'd been so rude to Daryna. Daryna had confided in me, straight after the Spring Break, that she wasn't coming back. She'd had enough. ASS would be looking for a new High School Principal, although they didn't know it yet.

"I'm coming back," said Colton. "Unless I find another job, but that's not likely." Apparently teaching posts all across the United States were hard to come by.

They both looked at Joe and me. We'd discussed it many times, but still hadn't decided definitely whether to leave, or not. I knew that Joe was desperate to go, but he was handing the final decision to me.

I was in an agony of indecision. To make matters more difficult, we knew that Colton and Jake would be returning to Bahrain after the summer, and would be very disappointed if we

LETTERS

did not. Our friendship with them had grown very strong. Breaking the bonds would be difficult.

Joe shrugged. "We're not sure," he said. "We haven't made our minds up yet. It depends..."

A low-flying helicopter's blades whipped his words away.

"What did you say?" shouted Colton, and Rashida leaned in, cupping an ear.

That helicopter decided me. I suddenly knew what to do, and took a deep breath.

"We're not coming back," I said clearly, as the helicopter swung away. I caught Joe's look of astonishment and relief. "We're going to hand in our letter of resignation and go back to Spain."

That night we wrote the letter.

"Dear Ms. Naima,
Please accept this as our formal notification that we are resigning from ASS as High School Math/Physics teacher, and Grade 6 English teacher and will not be returning in August 2011.
This decision was not an easy one, but we have decided that we would like to return to our home in Spain and retire. We very much appreciate the opportunities we have been given here, and the welcome and support the school has given us.
We wish ASS every success in the future,
Yours sincerely,

Joseph and Victoria Twead"

We pinned up a calendar in the kitchen so that we could cross off the days until we would be back in Spain. All we had to do now was stay in one piece. But first we had to make it through exam time, and with students like ours, this was not going to be easy.

---

1. http://youtu.be/zlfKdbWwruY

PARSLEY TAHINI DIP

"This is such a fabulously versatile summer dip that I beg you to try it," says Nadia. "It is the perfect partner for barbecued or grilled fish, lamb or chicken. And, for all vegans, it's ideal when poured over steamed vegetables or dipped into with a hunk of hot pita bread."

Ingredients (Serves 6)

1 tsp salt (exercise your taste buds!)

1-2 garlic cloves, peeled and roughly chopped

300ml (½ pint) white tahini (the wholefood one won't do!)

Juice of 2 lemons (taste and decide!)

Warm water to thin

A very large handful of fresh, finely chopped parsley

Method

Pound the garlic and salt with a pestle and mortar until really smooth.

Add the tahini and mix with a whisk.

Add the lemon juice and keep whisking.

When it looks really strange and sticky, add the warm water, whisking all the time. Finally, stir in the green parsley.

27

EXAMS AND CHEATING

There was no doubt about it, Talal was Joe's most troublesome student. Both his parents were doctors and very supportive, and Talal was bright, but he was lazier than a comatose camel.

"Talal," said Joe in the classroom one day. "Have you done those study questions I set you?"

"Yes, Meester Joe, honestly!"

"Then where are they?"

"At home, Meester, I swear to God! You can ask my mother!"

"Okay, Talal. I'll phone her and just check."

"Yes, Meester, she'll tell you."

"What is your mother's telephone number, Talal?"

"No problem, Meester, I'll just look." Talal starts fiddling with his Blackberry. "Oh! I just remembered! My mother, she changed her number."

"You're getting an 'F' for that assignment, Talal," said Joe, and firmly updated his gradebook.

Talal's parents despaired of their son's lack of achievement. In an effort to improve his grades, Talal's father suggested that Joe should teach *him* the topics covered, and then he could help his son at home. This worked quite well. The pair of them could be seen in the school library on many a day, Joe's bald head almost touching the father's headdress as they pored over pages of calculations together.

Did Talal's grades improve? They did not. When the troubles in Bahrain escalated and doctors and hospitals were targeted, Talal's family made the decision to move to Canada. Daily, the problems in Bahrain intensified, and the hospitals were the scene of much violence. Talal's family decided to bring their moving date forward, and needed Talal to sit the exams early. To enter a good college in Canada, Talal first had to pass his exams at ASS. A special paper had to be prepared for him.

"I've already written my exam papers," Joe growled, scratching his nethers in annoyance. "And now I have to write another one, just for Talal! As if I don't have enough to do!"

EXAMS AND CHEATING

He wrote another paper, however, and administered it himself. Talal sat in front of him in an empty room, nervously waiting to start.

"Talal, are you ready?" asked Joe.

"Yes, Meester Joe. Meester Joe, did I tell you that you are the best teacher ever?"

"Here's the paper, Talal. You can start now."

Talal finished his two-hour paper in barely 35 minutes.

"Are you sure you're finished?" asked Joe. "Have you attempted all the questions and checked through your answers?"

"Yes, Meester. I've finished." He handed his paper to Joe. "Meester Joe?"

"Yes, Talal?"

"Tell my mother that I love her."

"Behave yourself, Talal. It's just an exam, not worth committing suicide over."

"Okay, Meester." Talal pulled a long face, sighed and left the room.

That evening, Joe marked the paper, which didn't take long. At the top of the first page, Talal had written, *"Mr. Joe, I love you so much. Please give me a good mark. I am sorry I was bad in your class."*

Joe flicked on, and there were messages on almost every page of the script. *"Mr. Joe, I know this answer is wrong but you can see I tried."* And, *"Mr. Joe, please be kind."* On the last page, Talal had written, *"Mr. Joe, I am begging you. I must get 60%*

or my dad will kill me. I know you can't live with that on your mind because you are a wonderful person."

Talal's paper scored 23%, and Joe was being generous. Talal came to collect his grades and say goodbye, as he and his family were leaving the next day.

"Meester Joe! Look! You have made a very terrible mistake! You have given me only 23%!"

"Yes, Talal."

"But I tried my hardest!"

"Talal, your paper was dreadful. You know you didn't work for it. I gave you 23%, and you hardly deserved that."

"But Meester! That's an 'F'!"

"Yes, Talal."

Talal begged and pleaded, until finally, knowing that he was starting a new life in Canada, Joe generously raised it to a 'D'.

"I'm changing it because I know you *can* do much better," he said. "And you make me laugh. Now, go away, and good luck in Canada."

Two days later, while Joe was teaching, his phone rang. It was Talal, phoning from the plane heading toward Canada.

"Meester Joe, why you give me a 'D'?"

"Because that's all you deserve, Talal. In fact, you should have been given an 'F'."

Deep sigh.

"Okay, Meester. Have a nice life."

EXAMS AND CHEATING

And he hung up. We never heard any more from Talal. No doubt he is now tormenting his Canadian teachers.

Cheating amongst the students was legendary, as we discovered very early on at ASS. My Middle School pupils cheated as a matter of course and didn't consider it a great crime. They routinely copied from each other, wrote answers on their hands or ankles, and the girls expertly slipped cheat-sheets inside their *hijabs*.

Often, older brothers and sisters, or parents, would do their homework. I once had a note from a mother complaining that the homework I set was too hard, and that it had kept the maid up all night.

Even marks entered into grade-books weren't immune. One day, Joe momentarily turned his back to write on the board, leaving his grade book open on his desk. A little mouse of a girl swiftly erased her own grades, substituting them with much better ones. He only discovered the forgery when he noticed the sevens were not crossed, which he always did.

Cheating in the High School was sophisticated and intensified as the exams approached. Daryna discovered that the photocopier man was making a tidy profit, printing off extra copies of the questions, then selling them to the students.

Teachers were warned never to leave papers in

unlocked desks, or in unattended bags. Students used their smartphones to snap pictures of the exam questions. One teacher was careless and his department's exam paper soon circulated round the school. He denied it and poor Andrea was blamed. We knew the truth, but the teacher never confessed. Few people knew that he was responsible, not Andrea. As a result, the questions were scrapped and Andrea had to rewrite the paper, much to her annoyance.

Many of the teachers were also guilty. They freely handed out questions to their classes or created study guides with questions identical to those in the final exam. Hali-Barry included exam questions in emails he sent to his students. He thought he'd got away with it, until a few honest students reported him. Hali-Barry accused another member of his department of hijacking his computer. All nonsense, of course, and he was issued with yet another formal warning letter. Daryna was forced to create new exams, not allowing teachers to see the questions until the day of the exam.

During exams, cheating was easy. In multi-choice question exams, the students developed a code of foot-tapping, or coughs, so that everybody knew which answer to circle.

Even with two invigilators (or proctors, as the Americans call them) per room, it was impossible

EXAMS AND CHEATING

to watch every student all the time, the exams being held in small and often overcrowded classrooms. It was a simple matter for students see their neighbours' answers even while seemingly looking at their own.

One teacher had a brainwave. He set up a (dummy) TV camera at the front of the room and warned the students they were being filmed.

The students were forbidden the use of mobile phones. However, they couldn't be searched, particularly the girls, and many cellphones slipped through. That meant they could text each other.

Daryna devised a system that seated students alphabetically, with each exam room allocated a letter of the alphabet. Students of different ages, and sitting different subjects, were mixed together in the same classroom. It did cure the problem of students seeing each other's work but not that of smuggled-in mobile phones. It was also a nightmare for the invigilators. One student, sitting Algebra, would complain that graph paper was needed and another that a map was missing from his World History exam.

"How was your day?" I asked Joe as Jasim drove us home after the first day of exams.

"Terrible," he groaned. "I got 'M' and had a whole roomful of Mohammeds."

Jasim was driving particularly erratically that

afternoon. A Range Rover pulled out in front of us and Jasim screeched to a halt. Spitting Arabic, he thumped the dashboard with his outsize fist and jumped out of the cab. We watched as he and the other driver bawled at each other, waving their arms.

"What is he saying?" I asked.

"Oh," said Saja, fluent in Arabic. "The other driver questioned Jasim's parentage, and Jasim told him he drove like a castrated camel."

The next morning, the bus was early, rare for Jasim, but the figure in the driver's seat looked unfamiliar. We climbed on, curious to know where Jasim was. This driver was polite, but spoke no English. When we were all seated, he pushed the button and the door didn't close. Joe jumped up and showed him how to operate the stick and poke the door closed.

Saja chatted with the driver, then turned to speak to us.

"Jasim's getting married today," she smiled.

Ah, that explained Jasim's absence today and his testiness yesterday.

Once the exams were over, the time for the High School trips began. The destinations of these trips were usually European. Accompanying teachers travelled for free, so places were much sought after. In our group, only Colton was lucky enough to be selected.

EXAMS AND CHEATING

"Colton, how did your trip go?" I asked.

Colton and Essam had accompanied a school trip to Italy, via a stop in Cairo.

"Huh," he said, with a chilled Bennigan's Coors in his hand. "I'm tellin' you, it didn't start good. At Cairo airport, I had to queue in a different lane 'cos I'm American. The kids were standing in a separate line, parallel to me, laughing their heads off 'cos I was with the Indians and everybody else. My line was three times the size of theirs. I got the last laugh though."

"Why?"

"'Cos one of our student's names was Ali Khalil, 'n' that's the name of a wanted terrorist."

"Ali Khalil?" interrupted Joe. "The same Ali you and I teach?"

"Yep."

"That's ridiculous!" he said, spluttering beer. "For goodness sake! Ali? He's by far my best student, as well as the best behaved!"

"Tell me about it," Colton continued. "And our Ali's only 15. Our lot were delayed for hours. Except for one of our girls who had a different-coloured passport. She's the daughter of some minister here, 'n' she got waved straight through."

"How about you, Jake?" asked Joe. "How on earth did you get picked for a trip? One minute you were here, and the next we heard you were in Spain."

As always, Jake took his time, and demonstrated his talent for storytelling.

"Y'know, when I was at High School myself, our teacher took twelve of us on an amazing tour of Spain and France. I can remember thinking at the time how incredible it would be if, someday, I, too, had the opportunity to take young people on trips abroad, you know, to appreciate other cultures."

The rest of us were grinning already.

"Good grief." Jake rolled his eyes.

"So, how did you suddenly get picked for this Spanish trip?" Joe asked again.

"Well, good grief. When the Hall Monitor whispered to me in an ominous tone that Mrs. Sherazi wanted to see me in her office, I thought I was in trouble."

We all nodded.

"So I was summoned, and I go up in the elevator to the third floor. Rawan, my head of department, is already there, and we're made to wait with that secretary with purple hair, for 15 minutes, until Mrs. Sherazi is ready to see us. Have you ever seen Mrs. Sherazi's office?"

We all shook our heads.

"No kidding, you could easily put Colton's, Dogsbody's and my classroom into it, plus a few more, and it's still bigger than that. We teach the future of Bahrain in classrooms one-tenth of the size of that office. Good grief. Rawan has already told me that the Arabic teacher, who was supposed to be going on the trip, didn't have his visa sorted. So, Mrs. Sherazi was asking yours truly, no, *telling* yours truly to take his place. She leans forward, and says, 'Jacob, you are leaving tomorrow for Spain. You will be at the airport at 8:45pm, sharp. You will keep me informed of our students.' I didn't have a chance to respond before she rattled off in Arabic for ten more minutes to Rawan. So that was that. I'm off to Spain. No questions asked."

"You didn't mind, though, did you?" I asked.

"What, an historical trip for 10th Graders? I teach World History, so I was excited. I had my reservations about a trip with Rawan, though. Rawan is, as we all know…well…bat-shit crazy. She's terrifying and everyone stays out of her way, but she likes me, or she did, so that helped."

"How was Spain? Did your kids behave?"

Jake guffawed and set down his glass in readiness for the tale. Secretly, I was very jealous of his trip to Spain, while Joe and I were stuck in Bahrain, but I knew the story would be good.

"Behave? Good lord! You must be joking…"

COURGETTE MUTTABAL

"This is an easy but deliciously summery dip," says Nadia. It goes beautifully alongside any plain meat or fish. Serve with warmed pita bread.

Ingredients (Serves 6 as part of a meze)

450g (1lb) courgettes (pale green ones if possible)

Olive oil

2 large garlic cloves, peeled

Salt

Juice of 1 or 2 lemons

4-6 tbsp tahini, loosened with a little warm water

Method

Peel the courgettes and cut them into thick slices.

Heat a generous tbsp of oil with a few tbsp water in a pan and steam-fry the courgettes in the covered pan until soft.

With a pestle and mortar, pound the garlic and courgettes with 2 tsp of salt until smooth.

When ready to serve, stir in most of the lemon juice, then gradually add the tahini.

Beat well and adjust the flavour with more lemon juice, salt and a good slosh of oil.

Garnish with spices/herbs of your own choice. Mint, pomegranate seeds, etc.

28

BAD BEHAVIOUR

Jake took a sip of beer, ever the showman, timing perfect. Colton, Joe and I waited.

"Good grief. When we arrive in Spain it's late, and both the kids and teachers are tired. We go out for a brief dinner and then everyone heads to bed. All good so far. The next morning I am jolted out of bed by a knock at my door. It's one of the boys and he tells me, ever so politely, that Miss Rawan needs me right away. So, I shower, and then head to the lobby.

"In the lobby, there's hysteria, mass confusion, and three crying and pale teenage girls to greet me. Of course, I am overwhelmed with horrific thoughts as to what could've happened. Did someone die overnight? Did someone go missing? Did someone's parents pass away? Who is sick?

Who got raped? What did our boys do now? Being a teacher, you always try to prepare yourself for every outcome. My head slipped into teacher mode for about five seconds, that is until Rawan informed me of the problem."

Jake halts his tale to lubricate his throat. The rest of us are smiling, we know this is going to be good.

"Good grief. Anyway, Rawan is looking at me, all bug-eyed. 'Ghosts! Ghosts!' she says. 'Jacob, we have ghosts in this hotel!'

"Let's take a moment to review what's happened. The one day we're free to have a sleep-in, I am jolted from a deep slumber. Not only do three of our girls believe they have had a visitation from malicious spirits, but my leader, my friend, my partner in calmness, also believes this to be true.

"As politely as I can, I ask, 'Um, say again, ghosts?' I am told that while the girls showered, they heard banging on the windows, the floor, the ceiling, and the walls. I am also informed that as one came out of the shower, she caught sight of a foggy handprint on the mirror. This evidence has lead three teenage girls, *and* a 'responsible' adult, to construe that the hotel is haunted, and Spanish ghosts are having some fun. Good grief.

"Rawan demands that I immediately arrange for a hotel transfer because we can't endanger the lives of our precious students by succumbing them to the freewill of supernatural beings. I'm at a loss for words and can't process all that is being thrown at me. I calmly tell her that we can't transfer, because we have already paid in full and that this hotel is part of our scheduled program.

"Rawan is now staring at me. She's convinced I'm a ghost-loving traitor, probably with evil powers, who knows? Whatever, I don't side with her, so I am the enemy. She rings our tour guide, Fabio I think his name is. He tells her the exact same news. She turns a peculiar shade of purple and is beside herself with anger, but quietly fades away, back to her room until lunch time. By lunch all is forgotten and Rawan and my students find hundreds of other things to complain about. The food is gross (paella). There is far too much walking (3-5 miles). They're still hungry and want a McDonald's."

We were all laughing, but Jake held his hand up.

"Wait, wait! I haven't told you about the Mystery of the Disappearing Students yet! Now, this one, you won't believe. Good grief."

"More ghosts?" asked Joe.

"Nope. We took the kids to this really nice restaurant in Malaga to experience a delicious, authentic Spanish meal. 'Course they wanted burgers, but that's not the point. I was sitting with the teachers, and every time I look up, there are kids going to the bathrooms at the back of the restaurant. And the strange thing is, they weren't coming back! Every time I looked, there were less kids sitting at the tables." His eyes grew large at the memory of it.

"Did you check it out?" asked Colton.

"Did I check it out? Of course I did. First, I watched. Two boys got up from their table and walked, very nonchalant, to the back of the restaurant. Then they looked around, and instead of opening the door to the boys' bathroom, they slipped through this other door."

We were really interested now.

"So I said, 'Excuse me', to the other teachers, and headed for that door. (Dramatic pause.) Well, good grief." Jake leaned back, clasping his hands behind his head, eyes wide with disbelief.

"What was it?"

"Where were the kids?"

"Did you find them?"

"Yep, I found them. That door, that blue door, that innocent-looking door at the back of the restaurant, that door led straight out to a nudist beach!"

We shouted with laughter as Jake grinned, shaking his head.

"I'm telling you, it was like another world! Like walking through the back of the wardrobe in

'The Lion, the Witch and the Wardrobe'. Busy Spanish restaurant one side, then this beach on the other side! You know, sand, ocean, people sitting and lying around. And the women are all topless!"

"Oh my..." I held my hand over my mouth.

"Well, I look around, and our party is just standing there, eyes on ten-foot stalks. I mean, when does an Arab boy ever get to see a woman, apart from her face? They were in a state of shock! They just didn't know where to look next, and their cameras were snapping everything. The girls were giggling hysterically, peeping out from behind their hands, and the boys, well, they just couldn't get enough."

"What did you do?"

"Well, first I had a good look myself. No, only joking! I thought I'd better get them back in, before Rawan sussed what was going on. All I could think about were the complaints we were going to get from Mrs. Sherazi and the parents. So I rounded them all up and, made them pop back through that door into the restaurant in ones and twos so as not to arouse any suspicions."

That summer term was filled with the students' silliness, and Daryna grew very anxious about Graduation Day. We were told that in past years, the students' behaviour had been appalling. They'd been known to heckle the speakers, throw things, and stampede. It was rumoured that the Gulf Hotel, which hosted the event, had refused to accept this year's booking because of the students' riotous behaviour the year before. I don't know how true that was, but it did again eventually take place at the Gulf Hotel.

Daryna was in a state of nerves. She spent hours writing her speech, then rehearsing it. With help from an Arabic teacher, she even included a few sentences in Arabic. When she was happy with it, she sent it to Mrs. Sherazi for approval. Mrs. Sherazi summoned her to her office.

"You should see that office, Vicky! It's the size of a tennis court, stuffed with antiques, a table that could seat an army, Persian rugs as thick as duvets, and a forest of potted palms."

"I know, Jake told us about it."

Mrs. Sherazi handed Daryna back her speech and Daryna glanced down at it. Red lines had been struck through most of it, including the Arabic sentences she had so carefully rehearsed.

"Short," said Mrs. Sherazi. "Keep it short."

"That's probably because she knows how badly the kids will behave." I said to Daryna.

"If I were you," said Joe, "I'd just say a couple of sentences, and keep walking as you talk. That way you'll be a moving target when they throw stuff."

Daryna smiled thinly. I don't think Joe's comment helped.

"As I was walking out of Mrs. Sherazi's office, across those Persian rugs, she suddenly calls me back. 'Your blouse,' she says, 'Change it.' I said, 'Sorry? What's wrong with my blouse?' She points with her pen, and I suddenly understand what she's saying. You know that black and white top I have with the geometric design?"

I nodded. I remembered it, and it was very nice. The back had a tiny slash that briefly revealed a minute glimpse of bra-strap when she moved.

"Well, that slash at the back must have offended her. She said, 'Jasim will drive you,' and waved me out of the office. She must have phoned him straight away because he was waiting for me when I left the building."

"With the bus?"

"Yes, he opened the door and we drove off, even though I was late for a meeting. Anyway, as I'm getting in, Jasim asks if I'm thirsty. I thought that was nice of him, but I said, 'No' politely. 'Are you sure, Ma'am?' he says again, and I say, 'No, thank you'. Well, he looks really disappointed, but carries on driving. Then, instead of going back to the apartments the usual way, he swings off to this area I've never seen before. It looks really run down with little poky shops, you know what I mean?"

I nodded.

"I'm looking at my watch and wondering where on earth we are going, when Jasim pulls up outside this little old shop. He jumps out, and I see him buy a brown bottle and slip it into his pocket."

"What was it?"

"I have no idea! So we drive home and I run inside, up to my apartment, and quickly change. Then I come out again, and see him in the bus, taking crafty swigs from that bottle."

"I'd love to know what it was," said Joe.

"So would I! But I'm guessing it's something frowned upon by Muslims. He drove even faster than usual, that's why I've got this bump on my forehead. I banged my head on the window when he was driving across the sand. I think he was trying to break some speed record."

When the time came, Jasim drove us to the Gulf Hotel. Attending the Graduation Ceremony was compulsory for teachers. Joe and I were allocated seats amongst the students, in the vain hope that we could keep order, should it be necessary.

Last year, the students had been permitted four invitations each, but had manufactured forgeries to invite their friends along too. This time Daryna had the tickets numbered. Colton was asked to check off each invitation as the guests arrived in their Aston Martins and Porsches. Jake, ever confident and a fine public speaker, officiated as master of ceremonies, a task he performed flawlessly.

Thanks to Daryna's preparation and organisation, the ceremony went fairly smoothly, with very little heckling and no missiles thrown. When it was over, most of us retired to the bar in relief.

Colton and Jake had told us that 'Skip Days' were common in the US, but I'd never heard of them before. Students took a day off, en masse, the idea being that the sheer numbers of absentees would prevent them from getting into trouble for playing truant.

The younger ASS High School students decided to hold a Junior Skip Day. Jasim and the security guards were alerted, expecting trouble, and it came.

Taking advantage of a moment when only one guard stood at the school gate, the truants, wearing hats, masks and fancy-dress costumes, stormed in. They stampeded into the school shouting, blowing horns and letting off industrial-sized party-poppers that fired countless bits of glittery paper into the air. In the courtyard, the wind lifted the shimmering paper squares in clouds, glinting in the sunlight, higher than Joe's classroom window on the second floor.

In ran the students, through the High School building, up one flight of stairs and down the other, the security guards, teachers and Saeed in hot pursuit. Mrs. Sherazi appeared and could do nothing but watch, hands on hips, her face set in a severe frown.

"I c-c-c..." said Saeed later, in Smokers' Corner.

"Couldn't believe it?" suggested Colton.

"No, I c-c-c..."

"Called the police?" helped Joe.

"No, I c-c-c...caught one on the stairs and locked him in the stationery cupboard," said Saeed.

The Junior stampede ended as soon as it began, leaving the poor Nepalese staff to sweep up the swirling pieces of metallic paper and remove the silly-string from the walls.

Removing unwanted stuff was also a problem in my classroom. I was sick of my fingers making contact with revolting globs of chewing gum that my little darlings had stuck under their desks. I decided to do something about it.

BAKLAVA
SENT DIRECTLY FROM HEAVEN

"I must warn you that these delightful delicacies are an expensive indulgence that should probably be allowed out once a year," says Nadia. Feel free to experiment with the flower waters.

Ingredients (makes 20-25 pastries)

FOR THE FILLING:

350g (12oz) shelled pistachio nuts, finely chopped

2 tbsp caster sugar

1 tbsp rosewater

1tsp ground cardamom (optional)

FOR THE SYRUP:

300ml (½ pint) water.

450g (1lb) granulated sugar

1 tbsp lemon juice

1 tbsp each of rosewater and orange-flower water

FOR THE PASTRY:

450g (1lb) packet fresh filo pastry.

250g (9oz) unsalted butter, melted.

Method

In a bowl, mix the filling ingredients, cover and set aside.

Preheat the oven 180°C/gas mark 4/350°F. Butter a 30x28cm (12x11 inch) baking tray.

Bring the water, sugar and lemon juice to the boil in a medium saucepan. Don't stir but keep it bubbling for about 4-5 minutes.

Add the flower waters and set aside to cool.

Unwrap the pastry and keep under a damp towel or it will very quickly dry out. (Be warned!)

Lay one sheet in the baking tray and brush it with butter. Repeat, without pressing too hard, until you've used half the pastry packet.

Now scatter the sugared pistachio mixture all over the pastry.

Repeat the buttering and layering of the remaining pastry.

With a sharp knife, cut diamond or square patterns all the way through.

Bake for 20 minutes, then increase to 220°C/gas mark

7/425°F and cook for 10-15 minutes until puffed and golden.

Pour the syrup on slowly (you may not need it all).

Serve cold if you can wait that long!

29

BRENT AND CAMELS

Chewing gum was banned in school, but some kids always flouted the rules. They tried keeping their jaws motionless if they thought I was looking in their direction, but soon forgot, and the chewing action would attract my attention.

"Mohammed, are you chewing gum?"

"No, Mees!"

"Mohammed, are you sure?"

"No, Mees! I swear to God!"

Of course, within minutes, I'd catch him again and order him to spit the gum into the bin. The girls were even more guilty than the boys.

Worse still, the little urchins stuck the plugs of gum under the desks and chairs, which infuriated me. Kids from my next class sat down and found it sticking to their clothes.

"Do wha' I do!" said Hawa, her eyebrows shooting up into her mauve embroidered *hijab*. "If I see them chewing, I make them stay in lunch time. I say to them, 'You have a lunch date wi' Miss Hawa today,' and I tell them bring rulers."

"Do you make them do extra Maths?"

"No! Not do Math! They clean off gum from under desk! They scrape i' off with ruler. If they don' bring ruler, they mus' use hand!"

What a good idea! I warned my classes and started a chewing gum punishment-list. At the end of the week I held my first chewing gum detention.

Reluctantly, the kids arrived, clutching their rulers. First I made them turn over all the desks and chairs, revealing the nasty blobs of gum.

"Mees!" Ameena complained. "That's disgusting, Mees!"

"Yes, it is. Perhaps it'll teach you not to chew gum in my class in future."

It wasn't easy to supervise. Protesting loudly, they began to scrape the gum, but not for long. Soon Cheeky Mohammed and Mustafa Kamel were chasing screaming girls around the classroom with revolting globs of pink gum stuck to the end of their rulers.

Eventually, I was satisfied. We put the room back to rights and the kids ran out into the courtyard to enjoy the rest of their break.

BRENT AND CAMELS

But it wasn't only the students who were badly behaved. In fact they were saints compared with some of the High School teachers. A group of younger teachers frequently played truant, nursing hangovers, or simply deciding to take days off. Some of them even flew to Dubai to a rock concert, much to the fury of Jake, Colton and Joe, who had to cover their classes.

Always short of teachers, Daryna was forced to use crazy Brent, but soon regretted her decision.

As usual Brent insisted on spelling each name out and the students were losing patience. He did a head count, compared it with his list, and discovered there were more students in the room than there should have been. Some of the students, although not supposed to be there, had come to sit with their friends.

More students tried to come in, and Brent lost the plot. He sprang to the door and slammed it shut, preventing anybody else from entering. Legitimate students, arriving late, tried to open the door, but Brent was having none of it.

"Meester Brent! Let us in!" they called. "We're supposed to be having a lesson in there now!"

"Go away! No more students!"

The students knocked on the door. "Meester Brent! Open the door! Let us in!"

"Go away! No more students!"

Brent jammed the door closed with his foot. The students already in the room were becoming uneasy, and the illegal ones decided it was time to get out.

Brent refused to move. The students outside were now banging on the door, shouting to be let in, and the ones inside were shouting to be let out. Brent just kept his foot in place and blocked the door. The students inside began to panic.

The commotion in the corridor attracted Daryna's attention and she demanded an explanation.

"We've got a lesson in there, and we can't get in," the students complained. "The door is blocked!"

"Stand aside," she ordered, and rapped on the door. "Open this door now!" At that point she believed students were preventing entry, and that they were unattended. It never occurred to her that it was the teacher.

But Brent's foot stayed in place.

"Meester! It's the Principal! You've got to open the door!" the shocked kids said from inside.

"Meester! It's the Principal, open the door!" yelled the kids outside.

Whether Brent didn't hear, or didn't understand, we'll never know, but his foot remained in place. Daryna shoved the door as hard as she could, assisted by a couple of burly students. A gap revealed enough of Brent's shoe for her to realise he was blocking the door, not the students.

Reluctantly, he opened the door and allowed her in. She sent him to her office to calm down, and found someone else to cover the lesson.

Brent was one of our favourite topics at Bennigan's. He was always doing something for us to marvel at. And on the bus, Saja made us laugh with yet another crazy Brent story.

"Brent was in the next classroom," she began, "and the noise was just awful! I could hardly hear myself speak. He's got no control, you know."

"That man is dreadful," Joe grumbled. "I don't know what he's doing in teaching."

Saja nodded. "Ralph, the Geography teacher, is opposite and the noise is disturbing him, too. So, Ralph walks across, and politely asks Brent if he'd mind keeping the noise down as his kids are sitting an exam. Brent just ignores him, and the noise continues, worse if anything! So Ralph goes over again and complains. Brent looks at him and says, 'I'm perfectly aware that you don't like me, but there's no call to take that tone!' Well, Ralph gets annoyed and it soon breaks into a slanging match between the two of them. Ralph is swearing, and Brent is shouting. Both of their classroom doors are open, and their kids can hear it all."

Joe and I listened, agog.

"So I thought I'd better get out there to try and intervene, calm them down, if I could. I go over and say, 'Guys, guys, there's no need for this, you know.'"

Joe and I smiled at each other. We imagined the scene. Ralph and Brent, two huge angry men, dwarfing the gentle and softly-spoken Saja.

"Now my class are listening too," she continued. "Well, it takes awhile, they're shouting and insulting each other, and I'm trying to stop them. Eventually they calm down a bit and walk off into their own classrooms."

"I'm glad it didn't come to blows," I said.

"I think it nearly did," said Saja. "Anyway, I went back into my classroom, and my class are all big-eyed, because they've been listening, and ask, 'Miss, which students were fighting?' and I have to say, 'Er, it wasn't the students, it was the teachers.'"

Strangely, Brent and his new roommate, Ibekwe, managed to co-exist quite well in their apartment. Daryna guessed that was because Ibekwe was a bit of a bully, and left rules and labels pasted everywhere. Perhaps Brent had met his match.

BRENT AND CAMELS

The weather grew hotter as we hurtled into summer. We'd be gone before the real heat set in, the heat that could melt the glue holding one's shoes together. The days in Bahrain were slipping through our fingers like desert sand.

"Joe, we still haven't been to see the King's camels," I said as we sat with Colton and Jake in Bennigan's.

"Hey, why don't we go this weekend?" Jake suggested. "An outing with the grandparents."

They often referred to us as 'the grandparents' because of the huge age difference between us.

"I'd love that!" I said, and looked forward to it. "Perhaps we could ride on one!"

It worried me that I'd told my readers, jokingly at first, that my book about our stay in Bahrain would be called 'Two Old Fools on a Camel'. The title had stuck, but we hadn't ridden, or even seen, a single camel. I felt as if I'd been fraudulent, or transgressed the Trades Description Act. Perhaps here was an opportunity to set that to rights with a ride on one of the King's camels.

Colton and Jake drove us there and we sang songs, including 'Afternoon Delight', which still made me squirm. Was it really almost a year ago since that joke began? How much had happened since then!

The King keeps 450 camels on a farm that is open to the public every day. Perhaps 'farm' is not the best description, as the place is just dry sand, and the 'farmhouse' is the King's palace, hidden by trees, behind extremely high walls.

However, astonishingly green plants grow in fields alongside the camel compound, fodder, I assume, for the camels. How water is provided for the trees, crops and camels, I do not know, but when money is no object, I guess anything is possible.

The heat hammered us as we left the cool of the air-conditioned car and walked through the entrance gates and past a sign that read:

NOTICE
1) PLEASE KEEP SAFE DISTANCE FROM THE CAME S.
2) THROWING UNWANTED MATERIAL OR HITTING CAMELS ARE STRICTLY PROHIBITED
3) PHOTO RAPHY TO BE TAKEN BY KEEPING SAFE DISTANCE.
4) FEEDING OF CAMELS ARE NOT ALLOWED UNDER ANY CIRCUMSTANCES.
5) FREE ADMISSION.
BY ORDER SECURITY

BRENT AND CAMELS

. . .

Camels, the colour of desert sand, were everywhere. Some were tethered, others hobbled, their front legs loosely tied together. Small herds milled about in separate enclosures, and the sound of camel grunts and flatulence filled the air. I expected the place to smell, and the flies to be a pest, but that wasn't the case.

"Why would the King want so many camels?" Joe wondered. "Do they race them, or eat camel meat?"

"I don't think so," I said, having researched a little. "Camel meat is very strong, I don't think it tastes nice at all. I think he keeps them because they are a symbol of wealth and position from bygone days."

We walked close, but not too close, to big tethered males in the centre of the compound. They reared their heads as we passed, looking down at us from hooded eyes. Indian staff in mule carts forked out piles of green vegetation for the camels to graze on.

We visited various enclosures and saw lady camels, teenage camels, young camels, old camels and pregnant camels. Colton slipped a worker 2BD to allow us into a pen with mother and baby camels. The babies stared at us with liquid eyes then turned to drink from their haughty, loose-lipped mothers.

I'm very fond of camels. I like their snooty attitude and beautiful eyes, fringed with thick lashes. I fell in love with one particularly gorgeous camel I named Camilla, who seemed to have a permanent smile.

"Can't we take her back to Spain?" I asked Joe. "I'm sure the King wouldn't notice just one missing. We could tether her with Uncle Felix's mule in the village."

Camels chewing, camels drinking, camels standing, sitting, kicking, dozing, dreaming, playing. Noisy camels, silent camels, foaming camels, defecating camels, flatulent camels. I wanted to walk around the entire compound and see them all.

"Come on," said Joe, sweat pouring down his face. "Let's go. Once you've seen one camel, you've seen the lot."

But I had my way, and we strolled around under the beating sun, and I happily snapped camel photo after camel photo.

So, did we ride a camel? I'm afraid not, although we would have, given the opportunity. So, I apologise if this book's title is misleading. I suppose it should have been titled 'Two Old Fools in Bahrain'.

But it isn't.

Suddenly, it was the last week of term. We packed all our possessions into large cardboard boxes and shipped them back to Spain. It surprised me how much stuff we'd acquired during the year.

The Middle School students were supposed to sit an external exam, but the question papers were held up in Customs, much to their delight. The last day was a 'Fun Day', which was great fun for the students, not so much for the teachers.

On the last school day, I took a deep breath and gazed round my classroom. I was astonished at how fond I'd grown of my students. Cheeky Mohammed, Mustafa Kamel, Ahmed, silent Huda, Fatima, Khaled, Zainab, Ameena. I'd miss them all. Many had given me gifts that day. Little camels, chocolates and pretty candles. Somehow I'd have to squeeze them into my suitcase.

The final bell rang, and the class exploded out into the corridor, whooping with excitement. Escape! The school holidays had begun.

One child trailed behind. It was Huda. She raised her face to meet my eyes, the first time she'd ever looked at me directly. I'd never noticed what huge, beautiful brown eyes she had.

"Goodbye, Mees Vicky," she whispered. "I'll miss you."

I opened my mouth, but it was my turn to be tongue-tied. By the time I'd collected myself, she'd run out of the classroom, and my life, for ever.

TEPSI
AUBERGINE, ONION AND POTATO BAKE

Nadia says, "This dish fills the house with such a delicious aroma that guests are instantly soothed the moment you open your front door."

Top Tips: Sprinkling salt over the aubergines draws out the bitterness that sometimes can be found in them. It also means they absorb less oil during the frying stage. Also, remember if your oil is not sufficiently hot, you may end with very greasy aubergines.

Ingredients (Serves 4)

2 aubergines, thickly sliced

Salt and black pepper

2 large potatoes, peeled

2 large tomatoes

2 large onions, peeled

4 garlic cloves, peeled

Olive oil

Vegetable oil

2-3 tsp ground mixed spice (or pumpkin pie spice if in the US)

200ml (7 fl oz) lamb or vegetable stock

Juice of ½ a lemon

1 tbsp tomato purée

Method

Preheat the oven to 180°C/gas mark 4.

Place the sliced aubergines in a colander. Sprinkle salt all over them and leave aside for an hour.

Slice the potatoes, tomatoes and onions, to the same thickness as the aubergines.

Thinly slice the garlic.

Pour 2-3 glugs (maybe more) olive oil into a frying pan. Gently fry the onions and garlic until they just begin to brown. Remove the onions and garlic with a slotted spoon and set aside.

Add a splash of vegetable oil to the olive oil and bring slowly up to heat.

Fry the potatoes slowly until they are golden brown and almost cooked through. Remove the potatoes and set aside.

Rinse the salt off the aubergines and thoroughly dry them with kitchen paper.

Add a bit more vegetable oil and bring slowly up to heat. Gently fry the aubergines until they are golden brown.

Place on kitchen paper to remove excess oil.

In a baking dish, alternately layer the aubergine, tomato, onion and garlic, and potato, sprinkling each layer with spice, salt and pepper.

Pour the stock, lemon juice and tomato purée into the dish, and bake uncovered for 50-60 minutes.

30

HOME

The students may have left but I still had work to do. I cleared my desk and threw away unclaimed assignments, broken pencils and all the other clutter that accumulates in teachers' desk drawers. Some other teacher would be sitting at this desk in future.

I came across Huda's homework exercise book and shook my head. Why had she handed in an empty exercise book every single week? I flicked through the pages, preparing to throw it into the rubbish bin.

To my astonishment, I found homework assignment after homework assignment. They were poorly written, and riddled with spelling mistakes, but they were all there, dating back from the beginning of the school year. Why hadn't

I seen them? I hadn't seen them because Huda had written in the book in the Arabic way, from the back to the front. I'd opened it normally, and it had appeared empty to me.

Saying goodbye to Hawa was very hard. We hugged and I felt the soft chiffon of her *hijab* against my face.

"Thank you for everything," I said tearfully. "You've been a wonderful friend."

"You keep in touch!" she said. "You know where I am. I be here at ASS fo' many year, you see!"

Mr. Brewster shook my hand. "Er..." he began, looking uncomfortable and staring over my shoulder at a point on the far wall. "I'm not very good at saying these things...but I've been very pleased with your work. I'm sorry to see you go."

One last visit to Smokers' Corner to see Joe and our friends and await Jasim with the bus. Yussef gave us an Egyptian key-chain, with tiny camels and pyramids hanging from it.

"Goodbye, my friends," he said. "Enjoy your retirement in Spain, and think of us here at ASS next year."

"And you enjoy your summer with your wife and triplets," I said.

Saeed stood up and clasped Joe's hand warmly with both of his.

"S-s-s..."

"Safe journey?" suggested Joe, smiling.

"No, s-s-s..."

"See you?" helped Colton.

"No, s-s-soccer s-s-season starts soon, Mr. Joe. I'll be w-w-watching Liverpool and thinking of you."

Essam was too upset to say anything. Joe kissed him, Arabic style, on each cheek and I shook his hand.

Rashida clopped round the corner. "Ah, good!" she said. "You still here! I want to catch you. I am going to mall now, to buy little dinner, but I have forget my purse. Please lend me 2BD."

Joe handed her a 5BD note, which she snatched with grubby fingers.

"Goodbye, everyone," we said, and walked away to punch our cards for the last time. "Colton, we'll see you later at Bennigan's."

Amongst the many goodbyes, I heard Rashida's voice cut through. "Colton, give me cigarette."

So many goodbyes. Goodbye to Jasim, who smiled and flashed his gold teeth, before leaving us at the apartments and speeding away in the bus. Goodbye to Saja, Emily, Allison and Andrea, and all the others at the apartments. Warm hugs with Daryna.

"Keep in touch," she said, and we have.

Then one last glorious, hilarious session at

Bennigan's with Jake and Colton. Of all the wonderful people we had met and would miss, those two friends were the hardest to leave.

Mahmoud, the taxi driver, took us to the airport. As usual, he told us sickening stories of what was still happening in Bahrain, stories that never reached the media. We listened silently, watching the familiar Bahraini scenery through the car windows.

We drove past the Pearl Roundabout, that stage of such violence, vast and naked without its monument. We passed soldiers, armoured vehicles, and checkpoints, although this time we were not stopped. Neither of us said a word to each other. Our thoughts were crowded with memories of the surreal year we had spent on this Middle Eastern island. This time tomorrow, we would be back in Spain.

The plane began to descend. It was a cloudless day and I saw whitewashed villages, nestling in the mountains, loom larger. We reached the coastline, and the sea, dotted with ferries and boats. Then the runway opened in front of us and the plane landed with a bump at Almería airport.

Joe squeezed my hand and our eyes met. I

read relief and excitement in his, and I'm sure mine expressed the same.

Home!

Our Spanish taxi driver loaded our suitcases into the trunk.

"Where are you going?" he asked.

"El Hoyo, please," we said happily.

"*¿Perdón?* Where is that?"

It was no surprise that he didn't know it. El Hoyo is tiny, and we were accustomed to having to give directions. The taxi driver looked dubious, but we set off along the motorway, then turned up into the mountains. Everything looked exactly as we'd left it, one year ago. I opened the window a crack, just to sniff the scented, familiar, mountain air.

Higher and higher we drove, into the mountains, passing pine woods and carpets of wildflowers. And then we crested a mountain and our familiar valley stretched below us, the cluster of houses that was El Hoyo, huddled at the bottom.

"Turn down this track, please," said Joe.

The driver brought the taxi to a stop, and peered down the steep track.

"No," he said. "I will leave you here. I do not like to drive my taxi on bad roads."

Joe was annoyed, but we had no choice. We unloaded and paid the driver, who turned and sped away.

"It doesn't matter," I said. "Our cases aren't heavy, and it's all downhill. Thank goodness most of our stuff was sent on ahead. And we've got wheels on both our suitcases. We'll enjoy the walk. We've been travelling for such a long time."

Joe scratched himself, but reluctantly agreed. We set off down the track, avoiding potholes and fallen rocks as best as we could. Swallows swooped and swerved above us and bee-eaters crossed our path in a noisy chatter. A gentle breeze fluttered the almond and olive tree leaves.

All went well until one of Joe's suitcase wheels came off.

"Now what?" he grumbled, trying to fix it, without success.

It was a Friday afternoon and we knew that, until the evening, few people would be in the village. But, as luck would have it, our knight in shining armour was around the next twist in the track. A small, stooped figure, leathery face shaded by a flat cap, rounded the bend, followed by, not a white steed, but a mule. Uncle Felix!

"¡Buenos días, Tío Felix!" we called, broad grins on our faces.

Uncle Felix touched the peak of his cap in greeting. He was a man of few words. He stopped, and his mule lovingly nuzzled his shoulder. We patted her, but as always, she only had eyes for her master.

Uncle Felix was a retired shepherd and had never been outside El Hoyo, apart from a brief spell as a young man, conscripted into Franco's army. I'm sure he'd never heard of Bahrain, and we didn't bother to tell him we'd just arrived home after a year spent working there.

Uncle Felix squinted at our suitcases, then indicated with a gnarled hand for Joe to lift them onto the mule's broad back. He steadied the mule as Joe heaved the cases up.

The mule rattled her ears but didn't flinch. So we began our strange procession down the track and into the village. First came Uncle Felix, followed by the mule, with Joe and I walking either side of her, balancing the suitcases on her sturdy back.

I recalled that this was the second time she'd rescued us, the first being when the Gin Twins and I had driven home one night in a storm, many years ago. A huge tree had fallen across the road and the mule had dragged it away, clearing our path.

"Thank you!" we said when we reached the village square and lifted the cases down.

Uncle Felix touched his cap again, and shuffled away, his mule close behind.

"Well, it's not far n..." I started to say, but a shout stopped me in mid-sentence.

"You're back!" said Marcia, hobbling out of her shop doorway.

She hadn't changed a bit. Apart from a white apron, she was dressed in black, hairpins still dropping from her silvery hair. We hurried over, embraced, and exchanged kisses. She leaned on her stick, looking up at us.

"Are you back for good?" she asked. "How was Arabia?"

"Yes, we're here to stay," we answered, smiling. "Arabia was hard work. We're very glad to be home."

"I have many letters for you," she said. "Many bills, and a letter from your daughter in Australia, and some postcards from different friends."

Nothing went unnoticed in El Hoyo, and we were accustomed to having our mail scrutinised.

"Geronimo! Wake up!" she called. "The English are back!"

We turned. We hadn't noticed the figure slumped on one of the benches in the square, shaded by a tree. It straightened and got to its feet.

"Welcome back!" said Geronimo, slipping his omnipresent beer bottle back into his pocket and walking over, the breeze stirring his long, curly hair. His three moth-eaten dogs, who'd been snoozing under the bench, ambled over and sniffed our hands and luggage. Geronimo clapped Joe on the back, and kissed me politely.

"How did you like Arabia?"

"We *didn't* like it," said Joe, and pulled a face. "How's things with you?"

"*Mal*," he said, shaking his head, as he always did. "Real Madrid is not playing well at the moment. They need to make a change in their team. Here, I will help you with your luggage."

Within minutes, we were turning the key in the lock of our front door.

"Come in," I said to Geronimo. "I don't know what's in the cupboards, but I'm sure we can find something to drink." I wondered if we had any brandy, Geronimo's favourite tipple.

"Thank you, no," he said, turning on his heel and shooing the inquisitive dogs back out into the street. "I will see you later."

The houses on either side of us stood quiet and empty. I imagined our neighbours, Paco and Carmen-Bethina, and the Ufartes, would arrive in the village later, for the weekend.

Our house was dark and cool and smelled musty. We flung open the living-room windows and made a tour, beginning in the garden. Outside the kitchen door, the grapevine was a thick thatch, the young grapes already forming. Paco's horticultural interest, however, didn't stretch to flowers, so the raised beds and pots were filled

HOME

with dead plants. We ignored them, and went straight to the chicken-coop.

Only one poor, lonely, chicken remained.

"Oh dear," I said sadly. "I guess the other girls didn't make it. I think this one is Regalo. I recognise her beak." Regalo had been thrown over our wall, and she had been the youngest of the bunch. "I'll let her out into the garden, she can't do any damage."

"We'll get her some friends once we've settled in." said Joe.

Regalo marched out and started to scratch and peck at the weeds that had sprung up between the paving slabs. We left her to it, and explored the rest of the house.

Considering nobody had been there since the Gin Twins visited in October, the year before, the house wasn't too bad. We switched on the electricity and I swept and dusted while Joe walked down to the garage to check on the car. He turned the ignition but the battery was as flat as the Bahraini desert.

"That's a nuisance," he said, when he returned. "We'll have to wait for Paco. Can't go down and buy any food until we get the car started."

"I'm sure I can find something to eat. Tins, or whatever."

We busied ourselves making up the bed, and

sorting things out. The TV wouldn't give us a picture, the dishwasher refused to work and we had no telephone or Internet. But we didn't care. We knew we'd slowly regain normality. The main thing was, we were home!

A fist thumped on the front door.

"English!"

Paco and Carmen-Bethina had arrived. They'd heard from Marcia that we were back. Paco thrust two bottles of his homemade wine into our hands while Little Paco grinned shyly beside them. Little Paco's voice was breaking and he'd shot up during the year we'd been away. Now he was taller than his mother. We all hugged, and talked at once.

"Bianca had eight puppies," said Little Paco, proudly. "They all have new homes, except for one, which we are keeping."

Paco said ruefully, "I am sorry about the chickens. They died, one by one, but I think they were old?"

"Yes, they were. We're just grateful to you for looking after them while we were away. We still have Regalo and we'll soon get a few more to keep her company. How is Sofía?"

Carmen-Bethina's face dimpled into a broad smile. "She is still with her solicitor boyfriend." She leaned forward and whispered loudly, "I think she may have found 'The One!'"

"Pah!" yelled Paco, thumping his fist on the door frame. "That daughter of ours will never be satisfied! You wait, she'll find something wrong with this one, too!"

Carmen-Bethina ignored her husband and looked at me. She smiled and winked. Maybe this time her prayers in church had been answered.

"Have you tried your car?" asked Paco, more comfortable with practical matters.

"It's dead, I'm afraid," said Joe.

"We will soon have that running," said Paco, and marched Joe out of the door.

Carmen-Bethina and Little Paco departed and I carried on unpacking and loading the washing machine. Joe came back, a smile on his face.

"We got the car started. We can go shopping now."

I looked at my watch. "Oh dear, it's too late, the shops will be closed. Never mind, let's take a bottle of Paco's wine up onto the roof terrace, and sit up there for a while and watch the sunset. We can search for something for supper later."

Joe didn't need his arm twisting and we climbed the stairs, bottle and glasses in hand.

We watched the sky turn red and orange, and the Spanish sun sink slowly behind the mountain. An owl hooted, answered by another. The swallows faded away and were replaced by bats, swooping around the flickering street lights, snatching moths on the wing.

"I've been dreaming of this," said Joe.

"I know, I almost have to pinch myself."

"No more helicopters."

"Nope, just swallows and bats."

At last, hunger drove us back down to the kitchen. I found a tin of baked beans and a packet of crackers. That would have to do. As I reached for the tin-opener, somebody knocked on our door. Little Paco stood on our doorstep.

"Veeky, Papa and Mama sent me to fetch you and Joe. We have dinner on the table, and Mama says there is plenty for everybody."

I threw the beans back into the cupboard.

A few minutes later, we joined the family, including Uncle Felix and several cousins, round Paco's table. Questions were fired at us. Did we see the troubles? Had we liked the Arabs? What was the school like? What did we have to wear? Were the children well-behaved? What was the food like? Were we going back?

Two young girls slipped into the house, dressed as American cheerleaders, and clutching the hand of a toddler, helping him climb the steep doorstep. They'd grown, but I recognised them at once. The Ufarte twins. And was this the baby we'd left behind? The baby born on Christmas Eve, the star of the Christmas procession?

HOME

"*Hola, Tía Veeky, hola Tío Joe,*" they chanted.

"Can we come and do some baking at your house this weekend?"

"Mama and Papa said you wouldn't mind."

"Mama's having a baby soon."

They skipped out again, leaving us smiling. So all was well with the Ufarte family.

The food was delicious, and the wine plentiful. The conversation buzzed around me, and in the distance I could hear the twang of a Spanish guitar starting up. I pictured Papa Ufarte sitting on their doorstep, strumming his guitar, as Mama Ufarte and their friends and relations gyrated and clapped their hands, dancing in the street.

It had been a long day, and my eyes started closing.

We were home.

GARLIC PRAWNS WITH SMOKED PAPRIKA

GAMBAS AL AJILLO CON PIMENTÓN

This is one of our favourite tapas dishes that goes well with a cold beer, or as a supper snack. It combines some beautiful, authentic Spanish flavours, like prawns from the Mediterranean, Fino sherry from Jerez, and smoked paprika. A combination that can be enjoyed at any time and is particularly delicious eaten outdoors.

Ingredients (Serves 4)

1 kg (2.2lbs) prawns

4 garlic cloves, peeled and chopped

Olive oil

Black pepper

1 teaspoon hot smoked paprika

Splash of Fino sherry

Method

Thoroughly wash the prawns. Peel, leaving the tails on.

Heat a generous slug of olive oil in a large terracotta *cazuela* or pan.

Add garlic, paprika and sherry, and fry for 2 minutes to infuse the olive oil.

Add prawns, season with black pepper and fry, turning regularly for 4 minutes, or until cooked through.

Serve on a bed of salad accompanied by fresh, crusty bread.

31

EPILOGUE

We keep in contact with Daryna via email. Her year in Bahrain helped her decide that she'd had enough of the world of education. She is now happily retired, concentrating on her love of fine art, and enjoying the birth of her first grandchild.

Colton completed one more year in Bahrain, then moved back to Boise, Idaho, where he is, no doubt, enjoying the delights of floating down the Boise River in a tractor inner-tube. He shares a house with his buddy, Tucker. He no longer works as a teacher, but for a company registering domain names around the world. He is proud to be in charge of extensions for the Cook Islands, namely, co.ck. Bad Colton has kindly offered to register a domain for Joe, namely, joetweadhasalittle.

Jake also stayed another year at ASS, and then

EPILOGUE

returned to the US where he was soon offered a fabulous job at a university. He proposed to Emily on a South Carolina beach, and much to the delight of both their families, and us all, Emily accepted. It's Joe's belief that Jake will one day be the US President.

Neither Brent's nor Hali-Barry's contracts were renewed. Brent took up a teaching post in Russia, we believe, and is probably making a list of names in a classroom in Moscow. Hali-Barry disappeared entirely.

Allison, Saja and Andrea left ASS at the same time as we did, and are back in the US. Saja completed her Masters and Andrea is thinking of working in Dubai. We haven't heard from Allison since we last saw her in Bahrain. We wish them all every success in whatever they decide to do.

Young Mohammed was eventually allowed back into Bahrain and continues to teach at ASS.

We bequeathed Trollster to Jake and Colton. They, in turn, donated him to the teachers who replaced us. Trollster was not afforded the respect due a trolley of his status, became a toy, and was used for rides and other sporting purposes. Someone fell out of him and he suffered irreparable damage. RIP Trollster.

I'm told Bennigan's has changed both staff and premises. However, I'm sure wherever they are, they would extend you the same polite welcome, as they did us, night after night, back in 2010/11.

Human Rights organisations are still reporting abuses in Bahrain although at the time of writing these are overshadowed by events in Syria. A recent BBC report stated that, since the troubles began in Bahrain in 2010, "At least 60 people, including several police officers, have been killed. The opposition puts the death toll at 80, a figure the authorities dispute." If you are interested, I recommend a poignant but shocking award-winning documentary, produced while we were there, called, 'Bahrain: Shouting in the Dark'. It can be found on the following link:

https://youtu.be/xaTKDMYOBOU

Please be warned, it contains disturbing scenes.

If you'd like to see the photos from our year in Bahrain, please help yourself to the free *Two Old Fools on a Camel Photo Book 3* from:

www.victoriatwead.com/free-stuff

Life in El Hoyo changes very little. Joe and I are blissfully retired, apart from writing and editing, or publishing the occasional book. We rise when we please and no longer worry about the

EPILOGUE

arrival of the school bus, or curfews. The only helicopters overhead are on the lookout for wildfires, and they are very welcome.

And the only expanse of sand we see is our local beach.

So is that the end of the story? Perish that thought, of course it isn't.

A REQUEST...

We authors absolutely rely on our readers' reviews. We love them even more than a glass of chilled wine on a summer's night beneath the stars.

Even more than chocolate.

If you enjoyed this book, I'd be so grateful if you left a review, even if it's simply one sentence.

THANK YOU!

SO WHAT HAPPENED NEXT?
A PREVIEW OF THE NEXT BOOK IN THE SERIES

Two Old Fools in Spain Again

When Victoria and Joe return to their Spanish mountain village, they are still reeling from their year in the Middle East. Sighing with relief, they prepare to settle down to a peaceful life with the familiar characters of the village.

But life refuses to stand still, even in tiny El Hoyo. Lola Ufarte's behaviour surprises nobody, but when a millionaire becomes a neighbour, the village turns into a battleground.

Can Victoria and Joe help restore peace to the village?

Chapter 1
FAMILIES

There was mould on the walls. Green and white fluffy random blotches decorated the ceiling in most of the rooms. The mirror in the bathroom had begun to rust and the beds and curtains smelled musty, as did the clothes hanging in the wardrobes. Old Spanish houses need to be lived in, need to be aired, or the damp takes over.

Our home had missed us while we were away for a year working in the Middle East. When we flung open the shutters to let the fresh mountain air flow through, I could almost hear the house sigh with relief.

But living with mould and rust was far more attractive than living and working in Bahrain, a country in turmoil, rocked by the Arab revolution. Joe and I were home, back in El Hoyo and no clumps of mould or damp mattresses could spoil our joy at being in our own house and sleeping in our own bed again.

"Bleach," I said, more to myself than Joe.

"That's what we need, gallons of it. That'll put a stop to the mould."

If the house was bad, the garden was worse. Very few of my plants had survived the heat of the Spanish sun without water. The grapevine thrived, its ancient roots buried deep in the soil, but my flowerbeds and pots contained nothing but crisp, dry, brown sticks marking the places where shrubs and flowers had once bloomed.

"Don't you worry," I said to Regalo.

She was the only chicken to have survived, in spite of Paco's care, while we'd been away. Now she was relishing the freedom to wander freely about our overgrown garden. She didn't reply.

"I'll get this garden sorted out in no time. And we're going to get you some new sisters to keep you company. You'll be the oldest, so you'll be Top Hen."

Regalo had been the youngest of the flock, pecked and bullied by the others. It was ironic that she would now have a flock of her own to rule. Regalo looked up at me, head cocked to one side, then resumed her task of tugging out the weeds that flourished between the paving stones.

"I'm just popping round next door to see if Carmen has any bleach," I said to Joe.

He grunted and scratched himself, deep in concentration as he flicked through the manuals, trying to figure out how to reactivate the TV, dishwasher and Internet, all of which had refused to work since our return.

A curtain of chains to keep out the flies hung across the open door of our neighbours' house. Passersby couldn't see in, but anyone inside had a clear view out.

"*Pasa*, Veeky!" called Carmen, inviting me in.

I pushed the jangling metal curtain aside and entered their neat little house, already sniffing the wonderful aroma of something cooking.

Bianca, dozing under the kitchen table, raised her head briefly, opened one brown eye, wagged her stump of a tail and sank back to sleep. I remembered that she'd had eight puppies while we'd been away. It didn't seem two minutes since she'd been a puppy herself.

Carmen wiped her chubby hands on a tea cloth and kissed me soundly on both cheeks. She looked flushed and hot.

"I have made *churros* and there is fresh coffee. Sit down and I will pour you a glass."

I was always impressed by the delicious edibles that Carmen could conjure up on her one gas-ring stove and open fire. Being summer, the fire in the kitchen was not alight, but the kitchen was still very warm from her cooking session.

Carmen looked well. She was a few years older than I, but her face was still unlined and her round cheeks were rosy with health. Although she carried too much weight, she was never clumsy, but worked quickly and efficiently in her tiny kitchen.

She poured coffee into two glasses and sat down opposite me.

"You have lost weight," she said, looking me up and down.

I nodded. Bahrain had had that effect on both Joe and me.

She pushed a plate of *churros* across the table towards me and I selected one, still warm, dropping sugar as I bit into it. A few plates of these and I'd soon be back to my old plump self.

Churros are the Spanish equivalent of doughnuts, similar in shape to the horns of the *churro* sheep found in Spain. They are completely lacking in any nutritional value, extremely fattening and deliciously irresistible. The villagers often served them for breakfast with milky coffee or hot chocolate.

"How are you enjoying being back in Spain?" asked Carmen.

"Oh, it's great to be home," I said, after a sip of coffee. "It'll take a little while for us to sort everything out, but we don't mind. Our boxes haven't arrived from Bahrain yet."

We'd sent the boxes on to Spain a week before we'd left ourselves. As soon as we had the

Internet working, I meant to track them and find out where they were.

"Joe's trying to get the TV and other stuff working and I wondered if you have any bleach I could borrow? I'd like to attack the patches of mould that are all over the house."

"Ah, yes," she said, leaning sideways and pulling a yellow bottle from under the sink. The kitchen was so small, she didn't need to get up from the table.

"Thank you," I said. "Now, tell me about Sofía. Do you think this boyfriend is The One? How did they meet?"

"Yes," she nodded, beaming. "I think he might be The One. Paco, he does not believe it, because we all know how picky Sofía is. But me, I think Alejandro is The One." She paused, lost in thought, probably dreaming of future grandchildren.

"And how did they meet?"

"Sofía and young Alejandro have known each other since they were children. Can you believe it? He was right under her nose all the time. Paco went to school with Alejandro's father, who is also called Alejandro. Alejandro and Paco have known each other since they were boys. Of course Alejandro is a millionaire now, but we have always been friends."

"Sofía's boyfriend is a millionaire's son?" I asked, surprised.

"Yes, but he is also a solicitor. The family have machinery shops, a chain of them across Spain. Young Alejandro looks after the legal side of things. They have many houses, one in the city and some in the country. They have a house in El Hoyo."

"They do? Which one?"

"You know the house with high walls, below the square? The one with big gates?"

I knew the one. Most of the houses in the village were ancient cottages, like ours, but there were a few grand ones hidden behind walls, occupied only for a few brief weeks in summer. As one walked past, guard dogs barked a warning. I'd always thought it was unoccupied.

"They don't use the house much," said Carmen, reading my thoughts. "But they have workmen who feed the dogs and animals."

"Animals?"

"Yes, they breed rabbits for the pot and chickens. And the gardener grows vegetables. Now that young Alejandro and Sofía are together, we have a very good supply of rabbit, chicken and eggs."

"Sounds like Sofía has found an ideal husband!" I observed.

"You will meet Alejandro and his parents," she said. "They spend more time in El Hoyo now."

"And what about the Ufartes?" I asked. "Maribel is having another baby?"

Carmen nodded, then pursed her lips and lowered her voice. "Yes, she is… Between you and me, I do not think everything is going well with that family."

"Really? Why not? They were dancing in the street last night. And the twins seemed fine."

"Mark my words, I can see problems." She leaned forward and beckoned me closer, as though eavesdroppers might hear. I could feel her hot breath on my face. "Lola is back!" she hissed.

"Lola Ufarte?"

"Yes! Well, she isn't really a Ufarte, she's Maribel's sister. Did you know she has already been married twice?"

"Really? Has she?"

"Oh, yes. Mark my words, trouble follows that girl."

As I absorbed this information and opened my mouth to speak, the metal curtain swung aside, making me jump. Paco blustered in, a bunch of white rabbits dangling from one fist. He was not a large man, but he filled the room. A young dog bounded at his feet, rushed to sniff me then sat panting beside Bianca. Further discussion about the Ufartes was at an end.

"Veeky!" Paco roared, throwing the corpses on the table with a dull thud. "How are you? And Joe? Carmen, prepare the pot! I have been at the house of Alejandro and I have rabbits for you to cook. Veeky, would you like one? There is too much here for us."

I glanced at the limp, white bunnies and tried hard not to think of Snowy, my first pet at the age of seven.

"Thank you, no," I said. Then, fondling the spaniel's soft ears, "Is this Bianca's son?"

"Yes, I will teach him to fetch the birds when I shoot them next season. He is a good dog, like his mother."

"What's his name?"

"Yukky."

A curious name, I thought, then realised he was probably called 'Jacky', which would sound very much like 'Yukky' to my English ears.

"I just popped in to borrow some bleach," I said. "I must go. I have cleaning to do and Joe's trying to get all the appliances working again."

I grabbed the bottle, thanked Carmen, said my goodbyes and left.

Out in the street, the Ufarte twins were sitting on their doorstep like mirror images, heads together, brown legs stretched out. I remembered something.

"Girls!" I called. "Come with me, I believe I have something for you inside."

The twins jumped up and skipped over, following me into the house.

"What is it, *Tía* Veeky?"

"Is it something from Arabia?"

"TV's working," said Joe as we passed him in the living room.

In the kitchen I picked up a bag and handed it over to the girls. They wrestled it open and squeaked with delight at the set of five wooden camels, each one in a different pose, ending with a tiny baby camel. My mind briefly shot back to our visit to the King's camels in Bahrain and how we'd gazed with awe at 450 camels, all in one spot.

The twins scampered out and as I scoured at the mould with Carmen's bleach, I wondered again about Lola Ufarte. The last time we had seen Lola was just before we left for Bahrain. She'd been notorious for entertaining the males of the village and had finally run off with the foreman of a building gang. I guessed that hadn't worked out, but why did her return spell trouble for the Ufarte family?

That evening, we stood on our roof terrace watching the sun sink behind the mountain. The sky was stained pink, the distant sea shimmering with the sun's dying rays.

Poor, lonely Regalo had already put herself to bed. I'd watched her enter the coop and pace below the roosting perch, stopping at intervals to crane her head, eyeing the perch as though this was the first time she'd ever seen it.

She then returned to her feeder and ate some more, before standing below the perch again, trying to decide whether this was to be her roost tonight, or not. Still undecided, she checked out a few other places where she could sleep. Finally she climbed the ladder having decided the perch was best after all.

I never could understand this chicken ritual, because chickens are creatures of habit. They always sleep in exactly the same place every night. Why bother to check out alternative spots when they'll always end up in the same one? It would be like us trying out all the beds in the house before finally climbing into our own.

Because Regalo had been bullied, she always slept on the outside perch. Being the lowest in the pecking order, the others had never allowed her to roost inside. Even though she was the only remaining chicken, with the entire coop to herself, she still chose to sleep outside.

I sighed and shut the door of the coop. Next week we'd drive to the horrible chicken shop and get her some company. Following a last preening session, Regalo sank down, tucked her head under her wing and slept.

Joe and I leaned on the roof terrace wall. "Well, it's not been a bad day," Joe said. "At least I got the TV working and the dishwasher's fixed."

We watched the procession of villagers in the distance walking along the road, up the hill out of the village. This was a regular evening affair, a constitutional where neighbour would greet neighbour and dog would greet dog.

I squinted, trying to identify the individual villagers across the valley in the failing light.

Paco didn't normally bother with the evening constitutional, but I could see the round figure of Carmen and her daughter Sofía, walking arm in arm. I recognised Little Paco in a knot of teenagers.

"I can see the Ufartes," I said. "Carmen told me today that Lola Ufarte is back. She seemed to think that was a problem."

"Why?"

"I'm not sure. I didn't get the chance to ask."

The older Ufarte boys were growing tall. They kicked a ball ahead, while the twins walked with another little girl of their age. The adult Ufartes walked in a line across the road. Maribel waddled a little, weighed down by her unborn baby, one hand clutching the hand of the little boy we'd nicknamed Snap-On more than a year ago. Snap-

On had grown sturdy and was finally willing to walk by himself, which must have been a relief to his mother.

Maribel's husband and her sister, Lola, walked side by side, with the smallest Ufarte between them. Even from that distance, I could see that Lola's skirt was extremely short and her hips swayed as she walked. Every now and then, Papa Ufarte and Lola would swing the toddler into the air. It was an unremarkable family scene, but the shared act of swinging the baby between them was curiously intimate, and excluded Maribel, sending a little chill down my back.

I tore my eyes away and scanned the rest of the procession.

"Joe, can you see those two figures nearly at the top of the hill? One fat one and one thin one? With the two little dogs and a pram?"

Joe stared, screwing up his eyes.

"Yes... They look familiar, I recognise the big one's bald head. Isn't that Roberto and Federico?"

The Boys, as we called them, were a married couple, one of the first gay couples to marry after a law was passed in Spain legalising same-sex marriage. The Boys lived in the house slightly above us, on the land that used to be our orchard. They were a nice couple and none of the villagers seemed to object to them, which surprised me as our neighbours were staunchly Catholic.

I watched the two men crest the hill. I'd never seen them walking anywhere before. Their idea of exercising their dogs had always been to let them roam free in the village for half an hour in the evenings.

"I wonder what they're doing pushing a pram?" I wondered, swatting at a mosquito circling me hungrily. "Come on, let's go in, I'm being eaten alive."

Read more in Two Old Fools in Spain Again

THE OLD FOOLS SERIES
SEVEN OLD FOOLS BOOKS, PLUS TWO YOUNG FOOL PREQUELS, A COOKBOOK AND STILL COUNTING!

Book #1 **Chickens, Mules and Two Old Fools**
If Joe and Vicky had known what relocating to a tiny Spanish mountain village would REALLY be like, they might have hesitated...

Book #2 **Two Old Fools - Olé!**
Vicky and Joe have finished fixing up their house and look forward to peaceful days enjoying their retirement. Then the fish van arrives, and instead

of delivering fresh fish, disgorges the Ufarte family.

Book #3 **Two Old Fools on a Camel**
Reluctantly, Vicky and Joe leave Spain to work for a year in the Middle East. Incredibly, the Arab revolution erupted, throwing them into violent events that made world headlines.
New York Times bestseller three times

Book #4 **Two Old Fools in Spain Again**
Life refuses to stand still in tiny El Hoyo. Lola Ufarte's behaviour surprises nobody, but when a millionaire becomes a neighbour, the village turns into a battleground.

Book #5 **Two Old Fools in Turmoil**
When dark, sinister clouds loom, Victoria and Joe

find themselves facing life-changing decisions. Happily, silver linings also abound. A fresh new face joins the cast of well-known characters but the return of a bad penny may be more than some can handle.

Book #6 **Two Old Fools Down Under**
When Vicky and Joe wave goodbye to their beloved Spanish village, they face their future in Australia with some trepidation. Now they must build a new life amongst strangers, snakes and spiders the size of saucers. Accompanied by their enthusiastic new puppy, Lola, adventures abound, both heartwarming and terrifying.

Book #7 **Two Old Fools Fair Dinkum (coming)**
Subscribe to the Old Fools Updates for advance news, free books and recipes. https://www.victoriatwead.com/free-stuff/

Two Old Fools in the Kitchen, Part 1 (Cookbook)
The *Old Fools' Kitchen* cookbooks were created in response to frequent requests from readers of the *Old Fools series* asking to see all the recipes collected together in one place.

One Young Fool in Dorset (PREQUEL)
This light and charming story is the delightful prequel to Victoria Twead's Old Fools series. Her childhood memories are vividly portrayed, leaving the reader chuckling and enjoying a warm sense of comfortable nostalgia.

One Young Fool in South Africa (PREQUEL)
Who is Joe Twead? What happened before Joe met Victoria and they moved to a crazy Spanish mountain village? Joe vividly paints his childhood memories despite constant heckling from Victoria at his elbow.

THE SIXPENNY CROSS SERIES
SHORT FICTION, INSPIRED BY LIFE

A is for Abigail

Abigail Martin has everything: beauty, money, a loving husband, and a fabulous house in the village of Sixpenny Cross. But Abigail is denied the one thing she craves... A baby.

B is for Bella

When two babies are born within weeks of each other in the village of Sixpenny Cross, one would expect the pair to become friends as they grow up. But nothing could be further from the truth.

C is for the Captain

Everyone knows ageing bachelors, the Captain and Sixpence, are inseparable. But when new barmaid, Babs, begins work at the Dew Drop Inn, will she enhance their twilight years, or will the consequences be catastrophic?

D is for Dexter (coming soon)

Subscribe to the Old Fools Updates for advance news, free books and recipes. https://www.victoriatwead.com/free-stuff/

MORE BOOKS BY VICTORIA TWEAD...

Dear Fran, Love Dulcie (letters collated by Victoria Twead)

An unforgettable glimpse of life and death in the hills and hollows of bygone Australia through the letters of two newly-weds.

How to Write a Bestselling Memoir

How does one write, publish and promote a memoir? How does one become a bestselling author?

Morgan and the Martians - A COMEDY PLAY FOR KIDS

Morgan is a bad boy. A VERY bad boy. When a bunch of Martians gives him a Shimmer Suit that makes him invisible, he wastes no time in wearing it to school and creating havoc. Well, wouldn't you?

Two Old Fools in the Kitchen, Part 1 (Cookbook)

The *Old Fools' Kitchen* cookbooks were created in response to frequent requests from readers of the *Old Fools series* asking to see all the recipes collected together in one place.

ABOUT THE AUTHOR

Victoria Twead is the New York Times bestselling author of *Chickens, Mules and Two Old Fools* and the subsequent books in the Old Fools series.

After living in a remote mountain village in Spain for eleven years, and owning probably the most dangerous cockerel in Europe, Victoria and Joe retired to Australia.

Another joyous life-chapter has begun.

For photographs and additional unpublished material to accompany this book, download the **Free Photo Book** from
www.victoriatwead.com/free-stuff

CONTACTS AND LINKS
CONNECT WITH VICTORIA

Email: TopHen@VictoriaTwead.com (emails welcome)

Website: www.VictoriaTwead.com

Old Fools' Updates Signup: www.VictoriaTwead.com

This includes the latest Old Fools' news, free books, book recommendations, and recipe. Guaranteed spam-free and sent out every few months.

Free Stuff: http://www.victoriatwead.com/Free-Stuff/

Facebook: https://www.facebook.com/VictoriaTwead (friend requests welcome)

Instagram: @victoria.twead

Twitter: @VictoriaTwead

Publish with Ant Press: www.antpress.org

We Love Memoirs

Join me and other memoir authors and readers in the We Love Memoirs Facebook group, the friendliest group on Facebook.

www.facebook.com/groups/welovememoirs/

ACKNOWLEDGMENTS

I am eternally grateful to **Nadia Sawalha**, for her generous permission to use the Arabic recipes from her wonderful book, 'Stuffed Vine Leaves Saved my Life'. Big thanks to Nadia's lovely Uncle **Colin** who has supported me since 'Chickens' was launched, and shares our love of cats. And many thanks to Nadia's mum, **Bobbie**, for her patience and prompt answers to my silly questions.

Thank you **Daryna**, for helping refresh my memory about many of the crazy events described in 'Camel', and for being able to laugh at yourself.

Thank you, **Colton** and **Jake**, the brightest lights in our year in Bahrain. Where would I begin to describe how Joe and I feel about you both? I'll sum it up in a way only you two will understand. SWIO.

Thanks **Emily** (now Mrs Jake Cushing), for some superb photos which you can see in the free accompanying **Two Old Fools Photo Book 3, on my Free Stuff page**.

Many thanks **Mrs Sherazi**, for giving us the jobs at ASS in the first place.

Thank you **Mindy Sampson**, yet again, for your excellent proofreading services.

Thank you **Joe**, for editing the book, and typing (and sampling) the recipes. (If there are any mistakes, please don't blame Nadia, or me. Blame Joe.)

And finally, thanks to **Bennigan's**, our oasis in the desert.

This memoir reflects my recollections of experiences over a period of time. In order to preserve the anonymity of the wonderful people I write about, some names have been changed, including the name of the village and school. Dialogue and events have been recreated from memory and, in some cases, compressed to facilitate a natural narrative.

MORE ANT PRESS BOOKS
AWESOME AUTHORS ~ AWESOME BOOKS

If you enjoyed this book, you may also enjoy these other Ant Press memoir authors. All titles are available in ebook, paperback, hardback and large print editions from **Amazon**.

These two booksellers offer FREE delivery worldwide.
Blackwells.co.uk and **Wordery.com**

More Stores
Waterstones (Europe delivery), **Booktopia** (Australia), **Barnes & Noble** (USA), and all good bookstores.

VICTORIA TWEAD
New York Times bestselling author
The Old Fools series

1. Chickens, Mules and Two Old Fools
2. Two Old Fools ~ Olé!
3. Two Old Fools on a Camel

4. Two Old Fools in Spain Again
5. Two Old Fools in Turmoil
6. Two Old Fools Down Under
7. Two Old Fools Fair Dinkum
8. One Young Fool in Dorset (Prequel)
9. One Young Fool in South Africa (Prequel)

Dear Fran, Love Dulcie: Life and Death in the Hills and Hollows of Bygone Australia

PETER BARBER
**Award-winning bestselling author
The Parthenon series**

1. A Parthenon on our Roof
2. A Parthenon in Pefki
3. A Parthenon on our Roof Rack

Musings from a Greek Village

BETH HASLAM
The Fat Dogs series

Fat Dogs and French Estates ~ Part I
Fat Dogs and French Estates ~ Part II
Fat Dogs and French Estates ~ Part III
Fat Dogs and French Estates ~ Part IV
Fat Dogs and French Estates ~ Part V

Fat Dogs and Welsh Estates ~ The Prequel

DIANE ELLIOTT
Lady Goatherder series

Butting Heads in Spain: Lady Goatherder 1
El Maestro: Lady Goatherder 2 (to follow)

EJ BAUER
The Someday Travels series

1. From Moulin Rouge to Gaudi's City
2. From Gaudi's City to Granada's Red Palace
3. From an Umbrian Farmhouse to Como's Quiet Shores

NICK ALBERT
Fresh Eggs and Dog Beds series

Fresh Eggs and Dog Beds: Living the Dream in Rural Ireland
Fresh Eggs and Dog Beds 2: Still Living the Dream in Rural Ireland
Fresh Eggs and Dog Beds 3: More Living the Dream in Rural Ireland
Fresh Eggs and Dog Beds 4: More Living the Dream in Rural Ireland

For more information about stockists, Ant Press titles or how to publish with Ant Press, please visit our website or contact us by email.

WEBSITE: www.antpress.org

EMAIL: admin@antpress.org

FACEBOOK: https://www.facebook.com/AntPress/

INSTAGRAM: https://instagram.com/publishwithantpress

PUBLISH WITH ANT PRESS
AWESOME AUTHORS - AWESOME BOOKS

This book was formatted, produced and published by Ant Press.

Can we help you publish your book?

Website: www.antpress.org
Email: admin@antpress.com

Facebook: www.facebook.com/AntPress
Instagram: www.instagram.com/publishwithantpress
Twitter: www.twitter.com/Ant_Press

We publish beautiful, bestselling books.

www.ingramcontent.com/pod-product-compliance
Lightning Source LLC
Chambersburg PA
CBHW021137080526
44588CB00008B/97